YALE CLASSICAL STUDIES

YALE CLASSICAL STUDIES

EDITED FOR THE DEPARTMENT OF CLASSICS

by

G. S. KIRK

and

ADAM PARRY

VOLUME TWENTY
HOMERIC STUDIES

NEW HAVEN AND LONDON

YALE UNIVERSITY PRESS, 1966

*Set in Baskerville type and Printed in Great Britain
at the University Printing House, Cambridge
(Brooke Crutchley, University Printer).
Distributed in Canada by McGill University Press.*
Library of Congress catalog card number: 66–21522

Contents

The Gates of Horn and Ivory

ANNE AMORY

The Gates of Horn and Ivory

IN BOOK 19 of the *Odyssey*, Penelope speaks a few lines as famous as any in all Homer. These are usually rendered somewhat as follows:[1]

> Two gates there are for unsubstantial dreams, one made of horn and one of ivory. The dreams that pass through the carved ivory delude and bring us tales that turn to naught. Those that come forth through polished horn accomplish real things, whenever seen.   (19.562–7)

The lines are alluded to or imitated several times in antiquity, most notably by Vergil at the end of the sixth book of the *Aeneid* (VI.893–6), where he follows the whole passage closely, but not *verbatim*. The other instances are too brief to shed any light on the origin or meaning of the Homeric passage.[2] Modern allusions and imitations are generally drawn from Vergil's passage rather than Homer's.[3]

1. In order not to prejudice my argument, since it depends on a very close reading of these lines, I have not used my own translation here, but one of the standard ones, that of George Herbert Palmer (Homer, *The Odyssey*, translated by George Herbert Palmer, edited by Howard Porter, Bantam Books, New York 1962, p. 244). Future references to this edition will be made by "Palmer."

2. E.g. Plato, *Charmides*, 173A: ἄκουε δή, ἔφην, τὸ ἐμὸν ὄναρ, εἴτε διὰ κεράτων εἴτε δι᾿ ἐλέφαντος ἐλήλυθεν; Horace, *Odes*, III.27.40–2: "ludit imago | vana quae porta fugiens eburna | somnium ducit?"; Statius, *Silvae*, v.3.288–9: "Inde tamen venias melior qua porta malignum | cornea vincit ebur." Two other passages often cited as parallels for the Vergilian passage are Horace, *Satires*, I.10.31–3 and Ovid, *Heroides*, 19.195, but these two refer to the belief that dreams before midnight are false and those after true. This is a popular explanation even for the Homeric passage, but I see no indication that it has any connection with the gates of dreams; it seems an alternate belief, rather than the same one.

3. E.g. Spenser, *The Faerie Queene*, I.1.37 ff.; Tennyson, *Morte d'Arthur* 341 again refers to dreams after midnight. Harry Levin quotes from Robert

Even more numerous than imitations of the passage are attempts to explain or interpret the lines. That these began in antiquity is clear from Eustathius' commentary on the *Odyssey*. He prefaces his discussion of *vv.* 562 ff. by saying that many scholars have worn thin these doors of dreams by their attempts at interpretation—τὰς τῶν ὀνείρων ταύτας θύρας ἐξέτριψαν πολλοὶ τῶν σοφῶν.[4] He then presents a fine mixed bag of theories, most of which are entertaining, but as misleading as the dreams that come through the ivory gate. Three, however, are sufficiently relevant and durable to be worth examining.[5]

The first of these offers an interpretation based on the apparent etymological connection, or at least paronomasia, in the words which Penelope uses. As Eustathius puts it:

> The reason that the poet makes a horn gate the source of dreams which are true and accomplish true things is that there is a certain resemblance in sound between the words

Fitzgerald's translation of the *Odyssey*, 19.560–5, in elucidating the title of his recent book, *The Gates of Horn: A Study of Five French Realists* (New York 1963).

4. Eustathius, *Commentarii*, 1877.22–3 (713.30–1). That Eustathius is using ἐξέτριψαν metaphorically in the sense indicated is shown by the analogous statement which introduces the next batch of interpretations which he offers: καὶ οὕτω μέν τινες θυροκρουστοῦσι τὰς τῶν ὀνείρων πύλας 1877.31–2 (713.41–2).

5. Eustathius' discussion of 19.560–8 begins at 1877.8 (712.20) and runs through 1878.10 (714.45). The following paragraphs present my translations of the most relevant parts of his discussion, in which my additions or explanatory comments are enclosed in square brackets. Among the more fanciful explanations offered are these: "Still another group has compared to horns heavenly dreams, which they say are both sent from Zeus and true; for horns point upward. But to ivory they compare earthy dreams, for the horns [tusks] of elephants point downward" 1877.38–40 (713.3–5); though as a matter of fact Homer never mentions ivory as coming from elephants. Another is: "And there are some also who think as follows: whatever [dreams] any one sees when he is full of food, which the ivory-like teeth chew, these are deceptive. But whatever he dreams who is abstemious and who has soared aloft and inclines up along the horn, which is the part next to the authoritative head [the seat of guiding reason], these are true" 1877.43–5 (713.8–10).

κραίνειν [to accomplish] and κέρασι [horns], as if from the word κέρας were derived κεραίνω, that is, κραίνω. [Similarly the poet makes] an ivory gate the source of dreams which are false and deceptive, that is, which mislead, cheat, and only arouse expectations.[6]

Here the verb which Penelope uses for "deceive," ἐλεφαίρω, is supposed to be derived, via a hypothetical form ἐλπαίρω, from ἔλπω, and all are presumably to be connected with ἐλέφας (ivory), although Eustathius does not explicitly say so.

In modern times this kind of word play has often been assumed to be late and sophisticated, with the result that in the nineteenth century a number of eminent scholars, from August Fick to Wilamowitz, considered the lines a late interpolation. Others have taken the position that this kind of etymologizing is not the later learned, grammatical kind, but the sort which seeks truth and verification of reality in words and is frequent in early myth-building.[7] This is surely right, and enables one to keep the lines as genuine with a clear conscience, but it contributes nothing to the problem of the origin of the notion. Stanford speaks for many in his note on the lines:

> It is difficult to say whether the paronomasia on κέρας and κραίνω, and ἐλέφας and ἐλεφαίρομαι first suggested the notion of gates of horn and ivory, or whether a pre-existing legendary description prompted the word play.[8]

The second interpretation Eustathius reports as follows:

> Some, understanding the speech differently, more symbolically, interpret the horn gate as the eyes, taking the part for the whole, in that the outermost covering of the eye is horny. And they say that the mouth is the ivory [gate] because of the ivory-colored teeth, so that the wise

6. Eustathius, 1877.26–30 (713.34–8).

7. For both a survey of earlier opinion and a statement of the latter position, see Joachim Hundt, *Der Traumglaube bei Homer* (Greifswald 1935).

8. W. B. Stanford, *The Odyssey of Homer* (2 vols.), London 1947–8, *ad loc.* II, p. 338. Henceforward, this commentary will be identified by "Stanford."

Penelope is saying symbolically that the things which are seen as actual events are more trustworthy than things which are simply said to be so. Therefore, obviously [she means that] she will believe the things that are said about Odysseus as dream interpretations [only] when she sees them.[9]

This allegorical view of the gates of dreams is still current, especially in editions of Vergil, because it is the interpretation offered by Servius.[10]

The third interpretation from Eustathius has suffered a curious neglect, perhaps because it seems too simple:

Some say that the true [gate] is of horn, that is, transparent, whereas the false [gate] is of ivory, that is, blurred or opaque, because it is possible to see through horn... but not through ivory.[11]

This explanation, as we shall see eventually, comes the closest to what I think Homer intended in the speech he gave Penelope.

In this century, the most exhaustive inquiry into The Gates of Dreams appeared in a book of that title by E. L. Highbarger, published in 1940.[12] Since then, editors, teachers, and students have apparently felt that a reference to this work would absolve them of any responsibility for explaining, or even understanding, Homer's lines, though few readers of the book can find Highbarger's thesis entirely convincing.

9. Eustathius, 1877.34–9 (713.44–9).

10. Servius, *Commentarii in Verg. Aen.* vi.893: "Physiologia vero hoc habet; per portam corneam oculi significantur qui et cornei sunt coloris et duriores ceteris membris....per eburneam vero portam os significatur a dentibus; et scimus quia quae loquimur falsa esse possunt." Cf. the section on The Two Gates of Sleep in Brooks Otis, "Three Problems of *Aeneid* 6," *TAPA*, 90 (1959), 173–9.

11. Eustathius, 1877.33–5 (712.42–4).

12. Ernest Leslie Highbarger, *The Gates of Dreams: An Archaeological Examination of Vergil, Aeneid* vi.893–9 (Baltimore 1940). Quotations from and references to this work are cited by page numbers in parenthesis after the quotation or reference.

His argument runs as follows. First, noting that Homer says that the gate of true dreams is made from horns, in the plural, whereas Vergil uses the adjective *cornea* = of horn, Highbarger corrects the usual expression Gate of Horn to Gates of the Horns. He then identifies this gate with representations in Egyptian and Mesopotamian art of a Gate of Horns, which is also the western gate of the sky and an entrance to the nether world. He connects the whole idea with the cult of the sacred bull which was widespread in the Orient, in Egypt, in Crete, and in Mycenean cities, thus accounting for the transmission of the oriental conception to Greece (pp. 10–28). To explain the association with true dreams, he points to passages where Homer compares souls to a shadow or a dream; he recalls that ghosts wander before the gates of Hades; he equates this gate, and others, wherever convenient for him, to the Gates of Horn and Ivory; and he cites the appearance of Patroclus' soul in a dream to Achilles (pp. 35–8). This and all the souls whom Odysseus sees in the Nekuia, Highbarger asserts, "were 'genuine dreams' in Homer's meaning of that term. They could tell of that which they had seen or heard and their words could be believed" (p. 36).

The evidence for a horned gate, in the west and forming the entrance to the other world, is abundant, is found all over the Mediterranean, and goes back to prehistoric times.[13] So far, then, Highbarger's hypothesis may well be right. Difficulties begin when he identifies true dreams with ghosts (cf. p. 49). It is very unlikely that all the gates which Homer mentions are one and the same, identical with the Gate of Horns, as Highbarger would have it (p. 52). A more serious objection is that there is only one instance of a ghost coming as a dream in all of Homer, that of Patroclus' shade to Achilles; and this one scarcely fits the conditions in Penelope's speech, that a true dream come

13. See R. B. Onians, *The Origins of European Thought* (Cambridge 1951), pp. 236–7 and Gertrude Rachel Levy, *The Gate of Horn* (London 1948), pp. 67, 101, 129 and 131. (The Harper Torchbook paperback edition, 1963, is retitled *Religious Conceptions of the Stone Age*.)

through the gate of horns. For Patroclus comes to ask Achilles to bury him as quickly as possible precisely so that he may pass into the realm of Hades, for the other ghosts are keeping his unburied shade at a distance. Finally, Highbarger's interpretation rests first on a false attribution to Homer of the term "true dreams" or "genuine dreams," and then on a misleading equation between this term and "genuine ghosts" (p. 47). Neither Homer nor Penelope ever uses the term "true dreams," as we shall see (pp. 21–7 below). Highbarger's statement quoted above, that souls are "'genuine dreams' in Homer's meaning of that term" is thus nonsense, since Homer never uses the "term" of anything.

The discussion of the Gate of Ivory in Highbarger is even less satisfactory. He attributes to it also an oriental origin (pp. 19–21), identifying it with the Eastern Gate of the rising sun, "shown on Mesopotamian seals" as broad, adorned with shining rays, and attended by porters. He is forced to admit that this gate has no connection with ivory, but consoles himself by claiming that the Gate of Ivory, though it "is wholly a poetic concept" (p. 21), is "ultimately derived from what was once considered a reality" (p. 22; see also pp. 38 and 41). He quotes a number of irrelevant literary parallels from antiquity, adds some from Shakespeare and Milton, which can have no possible bearing on Homer, and then asserts, without any evidence to support his statement:

> From the earliest times a considerable degree of poetry grew up about this latter Gate [of the rising sun], and from its lyric associations the Greeks finally developed the Gate of Ivory, which likewise suggested the east and the realm of life.   (p. 22)

Highbarger goes on to identify the Mesopotamian gate of the rising sun with the Gates of Olympus, because Homer describes the latter as ponderous, as having the Horae as porters, and as made of cloud. "The white appearance of the clouds," says Highbarger, "gives rise to the notion of ivory, which also has associations with the gods" (p. 40). This might be so, if Homer described the gates of Olympus as made of white cloud, but in fact clouds in Homer are regularly pictured not as white, but as black, dark blue, purple, or shadowy.[14] Furthermore, Homer himself never associates ivory with the gods; the chryselephantine statues and the legend of Pelops' ivory shoulder which Highbarger adduces as support (p. 39) are both post-Homeric as far as we can tell.[15] Finally, it may be objected that the gates of the rising sun must be in the east, whereas Greek tradition usually located Mount Olympus in the north, in so far as it identified the abode of the gods with the actual mountain at all. Highbarger here offers only feeble and unsupported assertions that there was some "confusion or uncertainty in Homer" which led to "attempts" to locate Olympus in the east or northeast under the influence of "Oriental eschatology" (pp. 32–3 and 47).

To complete his interpretation of Penelope's speech, Highbarger argues that since dreams were believed to come from the gods, and since the gods clearly live on Olympus, the dreams they send to men must issue from the Gate of Olympus. This is true enough, but even if we accept Highbarger's dubious identification of the Gate of Olympus with the Gate of Ivory, there remains the problem of why only "false dreams" and not all dreams issue through the Ivory Gate. Highbarger says that the dreams sent by the gods were "*often* [italics mine] false in the sense that they were the likenesses of living men, or even the forms of the gods themselves. They were frequently deceitful and often their meaning was misleading or not clear, hence the

14. A glance at Benedetto Marzullo, *A Complete Concordance to the Iliad of Homer* (Guy Lushington Prendergast), and *A Complete Concordance to the Odyssey of Homer* (Henry Dunbar), both Hildesheim 1962, under νέφος and νεφέλη will confirm the truth of this statement. The only exception is the golden cloud in which Zeus and Hera sleep (xiv.343, 350). Later references to these concordances will be made by "Marzullo."

15. See H. L. Lorimer, "Gold and Ivory in Greek Mythology," *Greek Poetry and Life* (Essays Presented to Gilbert Murray on his Seventieth Birthday) (Oxford 1936), pp. 32–3.

interpreter of dreams (ὀνειροπόλος) must be consulted" (p. 42).
After citing four instances, only one of them relevant, Highbarger concludes: "A false dream, then, *regularly* [italics mine]
came from the gods who dwelt on Olympus" (p. 42). I do not
dispute that the gods in Homer sometimes, perhaps even
"often," deceive men, but of the ten dreams described or
mentioned in Homer, six are said by the poet or the dreamer to
have some connection with the gods, and only one of these is
deceptive, the baneful dream (οὖλος ὄνειρος) sent by Zeus to
Agamemnon in book II of the *Iliad*. The others are not questioned
by the dreamers and in fact they predict or indicate events
which actually happen. Even the instance of Agamemnon's
dream really disproves Highbarger's thesis, for, although it is in
fact false and is sent by Zeus, it is accepted as true by Agamemnon. Although the dream announces "I am the messenger
of Zeus"—Διὸς δέ τοι ἄγγελός εἰμι (II.26)—it leaves Agamemnon "thinking things in his heart that were not going to
happen in fact"—τὰ φρονέοντ' ἀνὰ θυμὸν ἅ ῥ' οὐ τελέεσθαι
ἔμελλον (II.36). If Highbarger were right and it was generally
believed that false dreams came from Olympus, as opposed to
those which came from Hades, then Agamemnon, stupid as he
is in Homer, must surely have had more qualms about the
dream than he is shown as having.

The most critical instance of a dream in this context is, of
course, Penelope's dream about the eagle slaying her pet geese.
Highbarger, in an argument so confused and circular that it is
impossible even to summarize it, several times uses this dream to
support his theory, asserting each time that Penelope attributes
it to a god.[16] This statement is categorically false. Penelope

16. Highbarger, p. 33: "[Penelope] attributed such dreams to some god
(δαίμων) and declared her inability to know whether she could trust them."
P. 34: "Penelope's skepticism seems to be due to the fact that the appearance in her dream came from the realm of living things, and was neither a
god nor a ghost.... In each instance the appearance was sent by a god; and
in the first case, Penelope declared categorically that the vision was false, in
the second, she thought at first that it was false." This second instance to
which Highbarger refers is Penelope's dream in 4.795 ff. This dream was

nowhere attributes this dream to a god; she expresses skepticism about it only by saying that she thinks it came through the Gate of Ivory. If she had also, simultaneously, said that it had been sent by a god, the passage might indeed be confirmation of Highbarger's hypothesis, but, as it is, it can only arouse further doubt about the validity of his argument.

Shorn of its repetitions and irrelevant embellishments, Highbarger's argument may be reduced to the following. The Greeks believed that all dreams came from the gods, but that some dreams were false and some true. Only the false dreams come through the Gate of Ivory, which is also the Gate of Olympus; true dreams are really ghosts which issue through the Gate of Horns, which is the Gate of Hades. As Highbarger admits, however, Homer never makes either identification explicit. Nor does Highbarger ever resolve the logical inconsistency that both all dreams and only false dreams come from the gods. Furthermore, out of ten dreams in the Homeric poems, only one is a ghost (Patroclus), who is specifically described as coming from outside the gates of Hades, not through them; only one is unequivocally a false dream sent by a god, but it is not said to pass through the gate of Olympus, although it occurs in a passage of extremely full and leisurely narrative, and the dreamer (Agamemnon) does not suspect it to be false; only one dream is conjectured to come through the Gate of Ivory, but it

indeed sent by a god, Athena, and Highbarger seems totally unaware that it *dis*proves his thesis, for Penelope's original skepticism is dispelled by the dream figure's assurance that Athena sent her (4.825–32). This could hardly be made plausible by Homer if it was generally believed, as Highbarger asserts, that false dreams came from the gods. P. 36: "Penelope's dream of the eagle and the geese seemed too strange for her to believe *although* [italics mine] it had been sent by some god, as she thought"; again Highbarger seems in a muddle: it is not true that Penelope thought her dream about the geese was sent by a god, but if it were, and if Highbarger's thesis were right, surely he should say that Penelope distrusted the dream *because* it was sent by some god, as she thought. On p. 42, finally, Highbarger straightens out his logic, though still not his facts: "Penelope did not trust the allegorical dream sent to her by the unknown god."

is in fact a true dream, and it is never attributed to a god either by the dreamer (Penelope) or by Homer.

It is hard to imagine that anyone who has read Highbarger's book carefully admires it; it is even harder to believe that anyone who admires it can have read Homer carefully.[17] It is time to confess then that far from being a definitive treatment of the problem of the Gates of Dreams, as is often implied in references to it, Highbarger's book only adds confusion and erroneous notions to any consideration of the origin and meaning of Penelope's words about the Gates of Dreams.

As far as I am aware, only one other attempt to elucidate the passage has been made in recent times.[18] This is a brief argument by Rhys Carpenter in his Sather Lectures of 1946. He suggests that the passage must have been written in the last quarter of the seventh century when the Syrian ivory trade, which had begun in the late eighth century, was interrupted by a Scythian raid in 626 B.C. and ended by the fall of Nineveh in 612. As Carpenter puts it:

> In the Aegean world *ersatz* ivory had thenceforth to be made out of horn or bone.... The pointed antithesis between the two materials should stem from the late seventh century when good honest native horn or bone was perforce replacing expensive Oriental Ivory.[19]

Carpenter is concerned not so much to explain the passage as to use it to support his contention that the *Odyssey* was not composed until the end of the seventh century. Whatever one may

17. E.g. Stanford, *ad loc.*, "For a full discussion see E. L. Highbarger." Joseph Fontenrose reviewed Highbarger twice, once in *AJP*, 64 (1943), 278–85, once in the *Journal of Aesthetics and Art Criticism*, 5 (1942), 65–6; he is quite critical of the book in both reviews, but not particularly in reference to the Homeric portions.

18. Géza Róheim, *The Gates of the Dream* (New York 1942), a book on "psychoanalytic anthropology," takes its title from Vergil's lines and suggests that the gates represent "a vagina" or "a wide-open jaw" (pp. 279–83).

19. Rhys Carpenter, *Folk Tale, Fiction and Saga in the Homeric Poems* (Berkeley and Los Angeles 1946), p. 101.

think of his other evidence for this date, the passage at hand is surely a frail link in the chain. First of all, it rests on the quite improbable assumption that the idea of a Gate of Ivory "could not antedate the Syrian ivory trade of the late eighth century" (p. 101). There is abundant evidence that ivory was known in Mycenaean times; and it is likely that many passages in Homer contain material that dates back to that period.[20] Second, it is hard to see why a "pointed antithesis" between horn and ivory would only arise in a period when "horn or bone" had to replace ivory. Third, even if it did, the process which Carpenter postulates to explain the antithesis is the exact opposite of what usually happens in such circumstances. If a native product has to replace an imported one, it is the native replacement, however "good" or "honest" it may be in itself, which acquires the connotations of "artificial, false, inferior, *ersatz*" (to use Carpenter's own tell-tale adjective). "Real" is the word used to distinguish "expensive Oriental" silk from rayon or nylon, which, whatever their virtues, are not advertised as "good honest native" substitutes. Therefore, even granting Carpenter's other assumptions, his theory would probably have led to the association of horn or bone with deceit, rather than the other way around.

20. See Lorimer, *op. cit.* p. 32, and Frank H. Stubbings, "Crafts and Industries," Alan J. Wace and Frank H. Stubbings, *A Companion to Homer* (London 1962), pp. 533–4. Carpenter falls into the common fallacy of confusing the date of composition of a passage in Homer with the date at which some object mentioned in the passage was most current in the Greek world, but it is obvious that the idea behind Penelope's speech could have been formulated at any time between the first appearance of ivory in the Greek world and the latest date one chooses to assign to the final bard of the *Odyssey*. See G. S. Kirk, "Objective Dating Criteria in Homer," *Language and Background of Homer*, edited by G. S. Kirk (Cambridge 1964), pp. 189–90. Kirk warns against this fallacy, although his argument is directed more against the inverse fallacy of assuming an early date for a passage containing "an archaism, whether material or linguistic," for Mycenaean relic-hunting has replaced the popular nineteenth-century sport of condemning "late interpolations." On p. 195 Kirk remarks of another instance of ivory (the simile in iv.141–5, for which see pp. 46–8) that "this particular piece of information might conceivably have been acquired at almost any date."

It would seem, then, that little if any progress has been made since the days of the scholiasts in interpreting Penelope's speech as a bit of dream lore. The kinds of interpretation reported by Eustathius have in fact been abandoned by most modern scholars as fruitless speculation. But the hypotheses of Highbarger and Carpenter are hardly anything more. It may be that some day some material will be unearthed by archaeologists or assembled by folklorists which will shed light on the genesis of the idea and on the source from which Homer took it, if indeed he did not invent the whole idea. The lines certainly sound as if they reflect some popular belief, but in our present state of ignorance we cannot prove that this is so; it is not beyond the bounds of possibility that Homer himself, or some bardic predecessor, simply invented the striking image which is, in our *Odyssey*, put into Penelope's mouth. Until researches into early Mediterranean religion provide some definite evidence that the lines reflect a pre-Homeric legend about the gates of dreams, it seems better to admit that we do not possess enough evidence to make even a convincing guess about the background of Penelope's speech, and therefore to refrain from constructing dubiously founded and fraily joined conjectures about the origin, date, and extra-Homeric significance of the gates of horn and ivory.

But we need not, therefore, abandon all attempts to elucidate the passage, for there are other lines of investigation that have remained largely unexplored. First, we can examine more carefully than Highbarger did the language which Penelope uses in book 19, to make as sure as possible that we understand exactly and fully what she says in its immediate context. Then we can reflect about the significance of the gates of horn and ivory within the *Odyssey* as a whole. These lines of investigation at least have the merit of resting on a substantial body of evidence, for we have a complete poem as a framework for the second, and both the *Iliad* and the *Odyssey* to help us interpret the meanings of the words Penelope uses.

As a first step, let us place Penelope's speech in its immediate
context and then examine closely, not just the verses on the gates
themselves, but all that she says pertaining to dreams. It is dark,
the suitors have gone. Penelope has finished the first part of her
interview with the stranger dressed in beggar's rags, who is
really Odysseus. She has turned aside while Eurycleia washed
his feet and recognized him. When the beggar draws near the
fire again after this interlude, Penelope briefly touches on her
sorrows and mentions her inability to decide whether to wait
longer for Odysseus to return or to marry one of the suitors, so
that her son Telemachus may inherit his estate before it is con-
sumed by her wooers. Then very abruptly, without apparent
transition, she says, "but come listen to this dream and interpret
it for me"—ἀλλ᾽ ἄγε μοι τὸν ὄνειρον ὑπόκριναι καὶ ἄκουσον
(19.535).

She says that in her dream a great eagle swooped down from
the mountains, killed all her pet geese and soared away. Then,
as she was weeping, still in the dream, the eagle returned, and
in a human voice said that he was Odysseus come to take
revenge on all the suitors. Waking up, she looked around eagerly,
but saw the geese still alive, where they always were. The beggar
replies that Odysseus himself has already predicted what will
happen, and it is not possible to interpret the dream differently.
In return, Penelope makes the speech about the gates of horn
and ivory:

560 ξεῖν᾽, ἦ τοι μὲν ὄνειροι ἀμήχανοι ἀκριτόμυθοι
   γίγνοντ᾽, οὐδέ τι πάντα τελείεται ἀνθρώποισι.
   δοιαὶ γάρ τε πύλαι ἀμενηνῶν εἰσιν ὀνείρων·
   αἱ μὲν γὰρ κεράεσσι τετεύχαται, αἱ δ᾽ ἐλέφαντι·
   τῶν οἳ μέν κ᾽ ἔλθωσι διὰ πριστοῦ ἐλέφαντος,
565 οἵ ῥ᾽ ἐλεφαίρονται, ἔπε᾽ ἀκράαντα φέροντες·
   οἳ δὲ διὰ ξεστῶν κεράων ἔλθωσι θύραζε,
   οἵ ῥ᾽ ἔτυμα κραίνουσι, βροτῶν ὅτε κέν τις ἴδηται.
   ἀλλ᾽ ἐμοὶ οὐκ ἐντεῦθεν ὀίομαι αἰνὸν ὄνειρον
   ἐλθέμεν· ἦ κ᾽ ἀσπαστὸν ἐμοὶ καὶ παιδὶ γένοιτο.

Dreams, she begins by saying, turn out to be (γίγνονται) ἀμήχανοι and ἀκριτόμυθοι. In later Greek ἀμήχανος often has the meaning "helpless, weak," as in the Homeric Hymn to Apollo where men are said to live foolish and helpless—ζώουσ' ἀφραδέες καὶ ἀμήχανοι (193). But this passage is the first appearance of this meaning in Greek literature. In Homer ἀμήχανος originally refers to a person who is impossible to deal with in some way: irresistible in might, or unpersuadable, or simply incomprehensible. There is always some emphasis on the reactions of others faced with the person who is ἀμήχανος. In the few passages where the adjective is applied to a thing rather than to a person, as in Penelope's speech, the meaning is not substantially different; ἀμήχανος denotes a thing which appears intractable in some way to someone. For example, in the *Iliad* there appears twice the formula "then there would have been a disgrace and ἀμήχανα events would have happened"—ἔνθα κε λοιγὸς ἔην καὶ ἀμήχανα ἔργα γένοντο. In the first instance (VIII.130) the reference is to the rout of the Trojans by Diomedes from the Trojan point of view. In the second (XI.310) Hector is imagining the reactions of the Greeks if they had been driven back to the ships, as they would have been if Odysseus and Diomedes had not made a stand.[21]

Neither this line nor any other in Homer furnishes a very close

21. Other passages in the *Iliad* where ἀμήχανος occurs are: x.167, XIII. 726, xv.14, xvI.29, and xIX.273; all come in a direct address by one person to another, except the last where Achilles in speaking about his reaction to Agamemnon's seizure of Briseis calls the king ἀμήχανος. Once Sleep says to Hera νῦν αὖ τοῦτό μ' ἄνωγας ἀμήχανον ἄλλο τελέσσαι (XIV.262) in a line analogous to VIII.130=XI.310. In the *Odyssey* we have only one use of the adjective besides the one under consideration and that in an interesting passage which seems to furnish the transition between the original and later meanings. Eurycleia apostrophizes her absent (as she thinks) master: ὤ μοι ἐγὼ σέο, τέκνον, ἀμήχανος· ἦ σε περὶ Ζεὺς | ἀνθρώπων ἔχθαιρε (19.363). Here, since ἀμήχανος is transferred to the person feeling, Eurycleia is saying "I feel helpless in the face of your extraordinary misfortune," and the usage approaches the later one of "helpless," whereas in the strict earlier usage Eurycleia would have said that Odysseus was ἀμήχανος to her because he was so unfortunate. Cf. also ἀμηχανίη (9.295).

parallel to the use of ἀμήχανος in Penelope's speech, but the Homeric Hymn to Hermes contains several instances that show how easily the adjective could be transferred from people and events to things hard to cope with either physically or emotionally. Once there is a reference to unbreakable chains— ἀμήχανα δεσμά (157). When Apollo hears Hermes' lyre the longing that comes upon him for the instrument is called ἀμήχανος:

$$\text{τὸν δ' ἔρος ἐν στήθεσσιν ἀμήχανος αἴνυτο θυμόν.} \quad (434)$$

A little later Apollo, in praising this same marvel, asks "what art (is this), what song for cares that are ἀμήχανοι?":

$$\text{τίς τέχνη, τίς μοῦσα ἀμηχανέων μελεδώνων;} \quad (447)$$

Finally, in another passage Apollo threatens to hurl Hermes into Tartarus, whose darkness he describes as ἀμήχανος—ῥίψω... εἰς ζόφον αἰνόμορον καὶ ἀμήχανον (257). The Hymn to Hermes must be later than Homer, but the usage of ἀμήχανος in it shows meanings whose development from the Homeric usage is easy to understand.

The expression ὄνειροι ἀμήχανοι...γίγονται is unusual, but not incomprehensible, if we assume a development in the meaning of ἀμήχανος similar to that seen in the Hymn to Hermes. Penelope means that dreams are bewildering things and hard to understand; confronted with them, the dreamer tends to feel helpless. It should be noted that at this point she is speaking of dreams in general, not just those which come through the gates of ivory.

The exact sense in which dreams are hard to deal with is further clarified by the other predicate adjective, ἀκριτόμυθος, which Penelope uses. In Homer ἄκριτος already has its several connotations of unseparated, indiscriminate, and numberless.[22]

22. The basic sense of "indiscriminate" appears most clearly in the passage where Nestor proposes that the Achaeans heap up a single τύμβον... ἄκριτον over the pyre of those killed in the day's battle (VII.335–6 = 434–5). All passages naturally include some idea of "numberless," since there must be a plurality of things to be indiscriminate. Helen and Thetis both say

It is combined with some word for "speech" in three other places. In the *Iliad*, after Thersites has made his speech attacking Agamemnon, Odysseus, in rebuking Thersites' confused and ill-considered oratory, addresses him as ἀκριτόμυθε:

Θερσῖτ' ἀκριτόμυθε, λιγύς περ ἐὼν ἀγορητής. (ΙΙ.246)

Later in the same book, when Iris goes to announce to the Trojans that the Achaeans are mustering, she finds them in council debating and speaks chidingly to Priam: "Old man, ἄκριτοι speeches are always dear to you, as they were once in peace":

ὦ γέρον, αἰεί τοι μῦθοι φίλοι ἄκριτοί εἰσιν. (ΙΙ.796)

The third passage occurs in the *Odyssey*. In summarizing the song which Demodocus, the Phaeacian bard, sings about the wooden horse, Homer says that while the horse stood in front of Troy, the Trojans sitting around it debated many ἄκριτα:

ὣς ὁ μὲν ἑστήκει, τοὶ δ' ἄκριτα πόλλ' ἀγόρευον. (8.505)

Here, since the idea of number is already conveyed by πολλά, ἄκριτα must signify the uncertainty and confusion of the different courses of action being proposed about the horse. In the other two passages, there seems to be an implication of "endless" in ἄκριτος, but the primary significance is, as in the *Odyssey* passage, that the speeches designated as ἄκριτοι are confused and indiscriminate, having no application to reality.

In Penelope's speech, then, the first clause means that all dreams, by their very nature, are perplexing, leaving the

ἔχω δ' ἄχε' ἄκριτα θυμῷ (ΙΙΙ.412 = XXIV.91) when they feel indecisive and confused as well as overwhelmed at the extent of their woes. Hera refers to the ἄκριτα νείκεα of Oceanus and Tethys in a context which implies that her parents quarrel not only constantly, but also without clearly discernible grievances (XIV.205 = 304). In the *Odyssey* there twice appears after an injunction to stop grieving the formulaic explanation ἐπεὶ κάκιον πενθήμεναι ἄκριτον αἰεί (18.174 = 19.120). Palmer translates "to grieve incessantly makes matters worse" (p. 226), but the idea of constancy is adequately expressed by αἰεί, and ἄκριτον refers to a generalized grief about woes that come all together, as is made particularly clear by the context on the second occasion (19.117–19).

dreamer in a quandary, because they are full of messages among which it is impossible to discriminate and choose the one which indicates the dream's significance in real life.

She goes on to say that—if we take πάντα as Eustathius does to mean everything that is said or happens in dreams—not by any means will everything in them come true, or be fulfilled for men, or in men's experience. The middle of τελέω is used regularly thus in Homer of a speech, prediction, or wish which comes true.[23] To take just one example, a few hundred lines above, the beggar has repeated to Penelope the prediction he had earlier made to Eumaeus, that Odysseus is safe and on his way home. He adds an oath that all this will come true just as he has said—
ἦ μέν τοι τάδε πάντα τελείεται ὡς ἀγορεύω (19.305).

Penelope then amplifies her opening statement by adding that there are two gates of ἀμενηνῶν dreams, one made of horn (or horns), and one of ivory. The adjective ἀμενηνός was apparently obscure even in antiquity, for in fragment 222 of Aristophanes' *Banqueters* a young man is asked its meaning as a test of his learning. The two most commonly proposed derivations for it are: alpha privative plus μένος, strength; or alpha privative plus μένω, remain. It is therefore usually taken to mean either "feeble, insubstantial" or "fleeting." Liddell and Scott, as often, propose the first derivation and then translate for the most part as if from the second. As in the case of all such debatable words, our best guide to the meaning is actual usage. In the Homeric Hymn to Demeter, Hermes tells Hades that Zeus has sent him to take Persephone back to the upper world because Demeter is threatening to destroy the ἀμενηνά tribes of earth-born men—φθῖσαι φῦλ' ἀμενηνὰ χαμαιγενέων ἀνθρώπων (352). Here, and in Penelope's speech, either meaning seems at first sight possible. All the other usages in Homer, however,

23. The crucial point is that τελείομαι is not a precise equivalent of the English "fulfil" or "accomplish," as is often assumed, because the English verbs can be used to refer to finishing something which is already begun, whereas in Homer τελείομαι is used only in reference to a preceding mental or verbal wish, command, and so on. The evidence is both too abundant and too clear to be set forth here; see Marzullo *s.v.*

make it certain that the first meaning, "lacking physical strength" and therefore "incorporeal" is the correct one.

The phrase νεκύων ἀμενηνὰ κάρηνα is used four times in the *Odyssey* (10.521, 536; 11.29, 49). Even here it is often supposed that the word could mean "fleeting," but the question can be decided by a closer scrutiny of what Homer says about the dead. There is never any suggestion that the ψυχαί do not remain eternally in Hades once they arrive there, whereas there is considerable stress on the fact that they have lost the μένος that the body possessed when it was alive. As Odysseus' mother Anticleia explains when he tries unsuccessfully to embrace her, the sinews no longer hold flesh and bones together, for the blaze of the funeral pyre destroys them whenever the θυμός has left the white bones and the soul has flitted away (from earth) (11.218 ff.).[24]

The two other uses of the adjective are completely unambiguous. Once in the *Iliad* Ares complains to Zeus that if he had not leaped aside, Diomedes would have wounded him, and he would be living ἀμενηνός, that is, enfeebled:

$$\text{ἤ κε ζὼς ἀμενηνὸς ἔα χαλκοῖο τυπῇσι.} \qquad \text{(v.887)}$$

Similarly, in the Homeric Hymn to Aphrodite, when Anchises wakes and realizes that he has made love to a goddess, he appeals to Zeus in asking Aphrodite not to let him live ἀμενηνόν among men, for a man who lies with a goddess, he says, becomes not βιοθάλμιος, that is, not hale:

$$\text{μή με ζῶντ' ἀμενηνὸν ἐν ἀνθρώποισιν ἐάσῃς}$$
$$\text{ναίειν, ἀλλ' ἐλέαιρ' · ἐπεὶ οὐ βιοθάλμιος ἀνὴρ}$$
$$\text{γίγνεται, ὅς τε θεαῖς εὐνάζεται ἀθανάτῃσι.} \qquad \text{(188–90)}$$

Anchises' life will be fleeting in any case, as is all men's; what he is asking is not to be enfeebled, robbed of his strength. The verb ἀμενηνόω, also, plainly means "make powerless," not

24. Highbarger (p. 44) stresses this comparison because he thinks that it supports his equation of true dreams and ghosts, but he ought to have observed that the adjective ἀμενηνός links the ψυχαί which Odysseus meets in Hades to all dreams, not exclusively to those which come through the gate of horn, as his theory demands.

"make fleeting." In its only occurrence, Poseidon takes away the power of the spear of Adamas as he attacks Antilochus, so that half of the spear falls to the ground, while the other half sticks in the shield: ἀμενήνωσεν δέ οἱ αἰχμήν (XIII.562).

Returning to Penelope's speech, we notice next that High-barger was right in observing that horns is in the plural and ivory in the singular (see p. 7 above). Whether or not he was justified in banking so much on the distinction is another matter. For in every other respect the use of horns and ivory in this passage is parallel. First, there is an almost exact gram-matical balance in the contrasted clauses which follow. Secondly, the use of ξεστῶν, polished, as an adjective analogous to πριστοῦ, sawn, or carved, for ivory seems to suggest the sub-stance horn, not horns still on a bull who is guarding a gate, as Highbarger's hypothesis requires. Finally, as we shall see below (p. 43), the only other time in either poem that κέρας is used parallel to another substance, and not of an actual horn or horns of an animal, the plural is also used, though the other substance is in the singular, just as ivory is here. We observe too that the verb used with κεράεσσι is the perfect of τεύχω, the verb regularly used in Homer for working on or fabricating from substances.[25] On Highbarger's hypothesis there would be an unlikely zeugma, with the usual meaning "wrought of" with ἐλέφαντι, ivory, and an unparalleled meaning "adorned with" or "guarded by" with κεράεσσι, horns. Let us then provisionally accept the regular view that κεράεσσι and ἐλέφαντι are the sub-stances from which the gates, presumably the doors of the gates, are made. The meaning of the contrast will then most probably be suggested by some difference in the two substances.

Next, it should be noted that, in spite of Eustathius' distinc-tion between dreams as ἀληθεῖς, true, and ψευδεῖς, false, and

---

25. Again the evidence for the normal meaning of τεύχω is abundant and clear; see Marzullo. The developed meaning "prepare" is also frequent; unusual instances, such as I.4, occur, but there is nothing analogous to the meaning κεράεσσι τετεύχαται would have to have if Highbarger were right.

unlike the Vergilian passage, in Homer the dreams themselves
are not described adjectivally as "true" and "false."[26] Instead
the dreams are distinguished by verbal phrases, pertaining to
what they do after they have come through their contrasted
gates. One set of dreams ἐλεφαίρονται; the other ἔτυμα κραίνουσι.
The first question is, what does ἐλεφαίρομαι mean? Turning to
Liddell and Scott, if only to see where others may have gone
astray in reading the passage, we find this definition:

> cheat with empty hopes, said of the *false* [italicized by
> L & S as if it translated some word in the *Odyssey*] dreams
> that come through the ivory gate...generally, cheat,
> overreach.

But only two other references are cited, one in the *Iliad*, and one
in Hesiod.

The first passage describes an exciting moment in the chariot
race at the funeral games of Patroclus. Diomedes was just about
to overtake the mares of Eumelus, who was ahead in the race,
and he would have succeeded, if Apollo, who bore him a
grudge, had not dashed the whip from his hands. Diomedes
broke into tears of rage as he saw Eumelus' horses pull far ahead,
while his own were slowed or hindered (ἐβλάφθησαν) because
they ran without the whip. But, says the poet, Apollo did not
escape Athena's notice ἐλεφηράμενος the son of Tydeus:

> οὐδ᾽ ἄρ᾽ Ἀθηναίην ἐλεφηράμενος λάθ᾽ Ἀπόλλων
> Τυδεΐδην.   (XXIII.388–9)

Athena then handed Diomedes back his whip, put μένος in his
horses, and overturned Eumelus, thus seeing to it that Diomedes
won after all. Here the aorist participle of ἐλεφαίρομαι can
scarcely mean "cheat with empty hopes," for Diomedes is not

26. Eustathius' reformulation of Homer's passage has been particularly
misleading because of the difference between ἀληθής in Homer and later
Greek; see pp. 24 f. Similarly, Highbarger's discussion of the Homeric
passage is distorted throughout because he is thinking of Vergil's *veris umbris*
and *falsa insomnia* and does not notice the significant difference between this
formulation of the antithesis and Homer's.

in any way mentally deluded. It could mean something like "frustrate" or "take away something expected," but it does not necessarily do so, for there is no clear reference to any expectation on Diomedes' part. It need mean no more than "harm, cause damage to."

Hesiod uses ἐλεφαίρομαι of the lion whom Hera reared and settled in the hills of Nemea as a source of pain and destruction (πῆμα) to men. "There then he ἐλεφαίρετο the tribes of men native to the place":

ἔνθ᾽ ἄρ᾽ ὃ οἰκείων ἐλεφαίρετο φῦλ᾽ ἀνθρώπων. (*Theog.* 330)

Here the verb cannot possibly mean anything like "delude"; it must mean that the Nemean lion used to prey upon the inhabitants. Since the meaning "cause damage to" is necessary here and quite possible and suitable in the *Iliad* passage as well, there is no reason to suppose that ἐλεφαίρομαι ever meant anything like "delude."

For what it is worth, the meaning "damage" is compatible with one of the etymologies proposed for ἐλεφαίρομαι. Liddell and Scott say that it is "perh[aps] connected with ὀλοφώϊος," although, as with ἀμενηνός, they proceed to translate not on the basis of the etymology they prefer but on the one they reject, in this case ἔλπω, cause to hope. Hesychius says that ὀλοφώϊος means "destructive" and it is so used in Alexandrian times, by Theocritus (xxv.185) and Nicander (*Theriaca* 327). This meaning is compatible too with Homer's application of ὀλοφώϊος to the magic arts of Proteus and Circe.[27]

If we consider the matter without prejudice, the meaning "damage" also fits ἐλεφαίρομαι as it is used by Penelope. The idea that she uses it to mean "delude" would seem to have

27. 4.410, 460, and 9.289; cp. 17.248. Hjalmar Frisk, *Griechisches Etymologisches Wörterbuch* (Heidelberg 1960), and E. Boisacq, *Dictionnaire étymologique de la langue grecque* (3rd ed. Paris 1938), both connect ἐλεφαίρομαι with ὀλοφώϊος, but neither gives an etymology, and neither gives a satisfactory account of Homeric usage. As a general principle I prefer in determining the meaning of words to follow Homer's usage, whenever that is clear and consistent, rather than etymological speculations.

arisen primarily from Vergil's *falsa insomnia* (see above, n. 26). This meaning might be defended, even though it is at variance with the other instances of ἐλεφαίρομαι in Homer and Hesiod, if it were needed here to make sense of Penelope's words, but it is not. She can mean simply that dreams which come through the ivory gate are dangerous, that they are likely to bring men harm. The sense in which dreams may be said to do this will become clear as soon as we examine the participial phrase which amplifies ἐλεφαίρομαι.

The dreams that come through the ivory gate are dangerous, Penelope says, because they bring messages that are ἀκράαντα— or simply "when(ever) they bring" such messages (if the participial clause here is strictly parallel to the ὅτε clause in the corresponding line (19.567) about dreams from the horn gate). ἀκράαντος, in its only other occurrences in Homer, may once be translated "unfinished," when Agamemnon tells the army that the enterprise (ἔργον) for which they came (that is, the recovery of Helen and the sack of Troy) is ἀκράαντον:

$$\ldots\mathring{α}μμι\ δὲ\ ἔργον$$
$$αὔτως\ ἀκράαντον,\ οὗ\ εἵνεκα\ δεῦρ᾽\ ἱκόμεσθα.\quad (\text{II}.137\text{–}8)$$

In the other passage it refers to the future; Eurymachus tells the seer Halitherses that the suitors pay no attention to the prophecy which he is babbling ἀκράαντον, that is, idly, in a manner not destined to be fulfilled, or ineffectively, not supported by fact:

$$οὔτε\ θεοπροπίης\ ἐμπαζόμεθ᾽,\ ἣν\ σύ,\ γεραιέ,$$
$$μυθέαι\ ἀκράαντον.\quad\quad\quad\quad\quad\quad (2.202\text{–}3)$$

The second meaning is adequate for Penelope's speech, but its connotations can be determined more precisely in the light of κραίνουσι in the contrasted clause.

For Penelope goes on to say that dreams which come through the gate of polished horn ἔτυμα κραίνουσι, whenever anyone of mortals sees (them). Now ἔτυμος and ἀληθής are often translated as if they were synonyms, but ἀληθής in Homer has only one meaning, "honest, candid." It is always used with some verb of speaking except in one simile, where the battle line holds as even as the scales on which an ἀληθής (that is, honest) widow weighs out wool (xii.432 ff.).[28] ἔτυμος, on the other hand, signifies objective truth, facts, things that have really happened. For example, when Antilochus passes Menelaus in the chariot race by a bit of reckless driving, Menelaus angrily shouts, "Damn you, we Achaeans were wrong when we thought you were sensible":

ἔρρ', ἐπεὶ οὔ σ' ἔτυμόν γε φάμεν πεπνῦσθαι 'Αχαιοί. (xxiii.440)

That is, they thought he was sensible, but his action has just proved that they were mistaken. In contrast οὔ σ' ἀληθές γε φάμεν would mean: "We said you were sensible, but we didn't mean it, we spoke dishonestly."

Curiously enough, however, ψευδής and ψεύδομαι are used as the antonyms of both ἀληθής and ἔτυμος. Thus, for example, Eumaeus says that beggars, when they are in need of hospitality, often tell lies and are not willing to speak honestly:

ἀλλ' ἄλλως κομιδῆς κεχρημένοι ἄνδρες ἀλῆται
ψεύδοντ', οὐδ' ἐθέλουσιν ἀληθέα μυθήσασθαι. (14.124–5)

That is, beggars say what they think their hosts want to hear, not what they really think. But the formula ψεύσομαι, ἦ ἔτυμον ἐρέω; (x.534, 4.140) means not "Shall I lie or shall I tell the truth?" as it is often translated, but rather, "Shall I be wrong or shall I be proved right?" In both occurrences, the persons speaking, Nestor and Helen, are making a guess about something they have observed which is easily and quickly proved true or false. In the *Iliad*, Nestor thinks that he hears the

28. The decisive passages for ἀληθής, which occurs only eight times in Homer, are 17.15 and 18.342. In these two instances there is clearly no question of objective truth; ἀληθής with a verb of speaking means to say what one really thinks, to speak honestly, without concealment. And this meaning is possible in all the other passages: vi.382, 3.254=16.61, 13.254, 14.125. On the simile about the widow LSJ gives "not forgetting, careful," explaining that "the sense *honest* is post-Homeric." But this is quite inaccurate; the *meaning* "honest" is the only Homeric one; the simile is unusual only in that ἀληθής is used as an attributive adjective of a person rather than as an adverbial accusative with a verb of speaking.

thunder of horses' hooves when Odysseus and Diomedes are returning from their night expedition, and he is shortly shown to be right by their arrival. In the *Odyssey*, Helen wonders if their unexpected visitor is Telemachus, because she has never seen anyone who looks so much like Odysseus; Peisistratus replies that his friend is in fact (ἐτήτυμον) Odysseus' son.[29]

In Penelope's speech, then, ἔτυμα is either used as a substantive, meaning "events, actual occurrences, facts," or it may be used adverbially, to mean "in reality, actually," depending on the meaning of κραίνουσι here. The verb κραίνω and its only compound in Homer, ἐπικραίνω, are most familiar in the meaning "accomplish, bring to pass." In this meaning, which is obvious in fourteen of the sixteen instances of the two verbs, its object is usually ἐέλδωρ (wish, prayer), although there are a few exceptions where an analogous word (ἔπος, ἐφετμή, ἀρή) is substituted. It is always, with one exception when Nestor speaks to his sons, addressed to a god.[30] In short, κραίνω is the

---

29. ἔτυμος occurs twice in the *Iliad*, and four times in the *Odyssey*; ἐτήτυμος occurs three times in the *Iliad* and ten in the *Odyssey*. The most ordinary use of both is as an adverbial accusative meaning "in fact." A formula καί μοι τοῦτ' ἀγόρευσον ἐτήτυμον, ὄφρ' ἐῢ εἰδῶ occurs seven times in the *Odyssey* (1.174, 4.645, 13.232, 14.186, 24.258, 297, 403); in contrast to the ἀληθής passages, this line always accompanies a request for objectively true information, which the person addressed can vouch for. Otherwise, the verbs with which the adjectives are used vary, though εἰμί is the most common: I.558 (κατανεῦσαι); XIII.111 (αἴτιός ἐστιν); XVIII.128 (οὐ κακόν ἐστι); 4.140, 157; 3.241 (all ἐστί); 23.26 (ἦλθ'). Once the predicate nominative appears; when Penelope refuses to believe Eurycleia's report that Odysseus has slain all the suitors, she says οὐκ ἔσθ' ὅδε μῦθος ἐτήτυμος (23.62). The other instances are quoted on pp. 25 and 43.

30. See Marzullo for the normal usage. The passage in which Nestor uses κρηήνατ' ἐέλδωρ to his sons, instead of addressing a god as in the normal usage, is 3.418. One of the two unusual instances is quoted on p. 28; in the other Nestor says to Agamemnon that since he is king, he above all ought to speak and to listen, but he ought also κρηῆναι for another, whenever his heart urges him to say something for (our) good: οὕνεκα πολλῶν | λαῶν ἔσσι ἄναξ...τῶ σε χρὴ πέρι μὲν φάσθαι ἔπος ἠδ' ἐπακοῦσαι, | κρηῆναι δὲ καὶ ἄλλῳ, ὅτ' ἄν τινα θυμὸς ἀνώγῃ | εἰπεῖν εἰς ἀγαθόν (IX.97–101). It may

regular transitive of τελείομαι (see n. 23 above), and most people accordingly take Penelope to mean that the dreams which come through the gate of horn accomplish real things (see, e.g., Palmer's translation, p. 3 above).

It should be observed, however, that both the syntax and the thought are strange for Homer, if we take κραίνουσι in Penelope's speech in its regular sense. First of all, ἔτυμα can hardly be an equivalent for the normal objects of κραίνω, because it refers to the action or result itself, and not to the thought, wish, or message to be accomplished. This anomaly is disguised in the English "dreams accomplish real things," but, if we remember that in Homer κραίνω strictly means to translate a wish, prayer, command, and the like into action, then the absurdity of saying "dreams translate real things into action" becomes evident at once. Second, it is odd for Homer to say transitively that dreams themselves accomplish real things. The normal idea is that dreams, or things in them, are translated into action, and the normal expression is τελείομαι, as line 561 illustrates (see pp. 15, 19 above). So too, in the *Iliad*, when Agamemnon is deceived by the οὖλος ὄνειρος sent by Zeus, Homer does not use a form of κραίνω to say that Agamemnon thought that the dream would translate into action the message which it had brought (that Agamemnon would take Troy immediately). Instead the poet uses τελείομαι and says that the dream left Agamemnon "thinking things in his heart that were not about to be accomplished" (see p. 10 above).

Since neither the subject nor the object of κραίνουσι in Penelope's speech is consonant with the normal Homeric usage,

be said that the only innovation here is the omission of the usual object of κραίνω. I would agree, if Nestor had said to Agamemnon, "You as king have the power to translate your wishes into actions"; then line 100 would mean "and translate into action too whatever any one else suggests." But in view of line 99, it seems possible that κρηῆναι here is closer in meaning to the way κραίνω is used in the passage quoted on p. 28, and the thought is: "You as king have the authority to speak and to listen to advice; now extend this authority to any one else who has a good suggestion in this crisis, and let him speak, and listen."

it seems likely that κραίνω here has an unusual shade of meaning.
A satisfactory sense is suggested by one of the other two unusual
instances already mentioned (see n. 30 above). Once, in the
Odyssey, Alcinous says that twelve glorious kings κραίνουσι in
the community (of the Phaeacians), and he himself is the
thirteenth:

> δώδεκα γὰρ κατὰ δῆμον ἀριπρεπέες βασιλῆες
> ἀρχοὶ κραίνουσι, τρισκαιδέκατος δ' ἐγὼ αὐτός.   (8.390–1)

In this passage, the meaning of κραίνουσι is plainly "rule" or
"have power." Though this meaning is not elsewhere paralleled
in Homer, it is easy to see how κραίνω, which usually refers to
gods executing a prayer, might be transferred to kings who have
the power to execute their own wishes.

In Penelope's speech also we may take κραίνουσι to be used as
absolutely and as vaguely as in Alcinous', and translate
"dreams have power." The thought is still somewhat strange
for Homer, but seems to me preferable to the alternative
"dreams accomplish." Then ἔτυμα becomes adverbial, as it is
in other passages (see n. 29 above), and Penelope is saying that
the dreams which come through the gate of horn have power,
or are effective, in reality. The previous contrasted phrase for
the dreams which come through the ivory gate, ἔπε' ἀκράαντα
φέροντες, will then mean that these dreams bring mere words,
without any consequences in actuality.

Penelope's last words on the subject of her dream are: "But
I think that it was not through here (that is, through the gate of
horn) that my αἰνόν dream came; (though) truly it would be
welcome to me and my son (if it had)." In this passage αἰνόν is
almost universally rendered "strange" or "odd," and some
have found the adjective inappropriate. For example, Stanford
remarks (*ad loc.*) that "αἰνὸν 'dreadful' seems rather pointless
here: Merry's 'uncanny' perhaps expresses the right nuance of
meaning."

As always when a word seems inappropriate in Homer, we
should re-examine our notion of what a word means to be sure

that it is not our understanding rather than Homer's usage that is at fault. In the case of αἰνός, together with its adverb αἰνῶς, most share Stanford's assumption that "dreadful" and "dreadfully" are fair equivalents, whether they are used with full force and seriousness, or exaggeratedly, as in our "terribly." But a closer examination reveals shades of distinction that are important.

First, it is only the adverb that has weakened in force, and that not so much as is popularly assumed. For it is most often used with a verb of fearing, and even when it is not, there is often a residue of the original force, as in the passage where Helen is said to look αἰνῶς like a goddess:

αἰνῶς ἀθανάτῃσι θεῆς εἰς ὦπα ἔοικεν.   (III.158)

The adjective αἰνός, which Penelope uses, appears to have lost none of its original force, for it is never used of nouns unless they signify something extraordinarily fearful or dangerous. The most common are combat (φύλοπις), slaughter (δηιοτής), grief (ἄχος), shuddering fear (τρόμος), anger (χόλος), and rancor (κότος). Even when it is used with κάματος, weariness, the significance is more than what we mean when we say "I'm terribly tired," for it is used of the weariness which overcomes Odysseus when he struggles half-dead onto the Phaeacian shore after swimming three days and nights in stormy seas:

. . .ὁ δ' ἄρ' ἄπνευστος καὶ ἄναυδος
κεῖτ' ὀλιγηπελέων, κάματος δέ μιν αἰνὸς ἵκανεν.   (5.456–7)

Even more important, the significance of αἰνός can be narrowed, for it does not correspond to our general "dreadful," but is more closely equivalent to "dire," since it is not used except where the consequences of something are dreadful, as well as the moment of experience. Thus, for example, Thetis refers not so much to the pangs of childbirth as to the bitterness of Achilles' fate when she says, "Alas, my son, why did I rear you, having borne you αἰνά?":[31]

ὤμοι, τέκνον ἐμόν, τί νύ σ' ἔτρεφον αἰνὰ τεκοῦσα;   (I.414)

31. See Marzullo for references to αἰνῶς and αἰνός.

We are now able to assess exactly what Penelope means by calling her dream αἰνός. First, it should be noted that she does not describe the dream itself as a nightmare; the term for that in Homer is κακὸν...ὄναρ, as when Diomedes kills Rhesus just as he is gasping in a nightmare which Athena has sent him (x.495 ff.).[32] Penelope means not just that the dream has disturbed her, but especially that the question of its interpretation is a serious one because the consequences of a mistake are likely to be disastrous in her situation. For the situation is not one in which she can simply wait and see whether events confirm her dream, as it might seem to us, who do not generally take dreams seriously as tokens of reality. In Homer dreams are regularly omens demanding some action, and it is clear that Penelope thus regards her dream, for she immediately goes on to say that she will set the contest of the bow to choose a new husband.[33] She is being pressed on all sides, as she has just told the stranger before narrating her dream, on the question of remarriage. The dream is a warning, as she regards it, that she cannot continue her delaying tactics with the suitors. The dream then demands action in a situation where any action is bound to entail difficulties. If it has come through the ivory gate, then Penelope's obedience to its demand for action will entrap her in the very snare she has been avoiding for so long, marriage to one of the

32. It may appear that since κακὸν...ὄναρ cannot compose a verse-end formula, αἰνὸς ὄνειρος was the term for "nightmare" in that position. But if Homer had wanted to say "nightmare" and could not use κακὸν...ὄναρ at the end, he would simply have framed his line differently; he would not have used a formula that had a different connotation. There is an instructive example in book xx. After her interview with the stranger, Penelope dreams that Odysseus lay beside her, looking as he did when he went to Troy (20.88–9). The dream is so vivid (20.90) that it wakes her up, and she complains, saying that formerly her grief was endurable because she slept nights—αὐτὰρ ἐμοὶ καὶ ὀνείρατ' ἐπέσσευεν κακὰ δαίμων (20.87). This dream is emotionally disturbing, but it has no consequences for the future, so it is not called αἰνὸς ὄνειρος as is her ominous dream about the geese.

33. See Anne Amory, "The Reunion of Odysseus and Penelope," *Essays on the Odyssey*, edited by Charles H. Taylor, Jr. (Indiana 1963), pp. 102–6.

suitors and disloyalty to Odysseus. Even if the dream has come through the gate of horn, the consequences of acting on it are dire enough, as the rest of the *Odyssey* shows—a terrible slaughter and a psychological readjustment for Penelope that is painful as well as desired.[34]

Let us now draw together our discussion of the words and phrases in Penelope's speech and sum up accurately what she says:

> Stranger, truly dreams are by nature perplexing and full of messages which are hard to interpret; nor by any means will everything [in them] come true for mortals. For there are two gates of insubstantial dreams; one [pair] is wrought of horn and one of ivory. Of these, [the dreams] which come through [the gate of] sawn ivory are dangerous to believe, for they bring messages which will not issue in deeds; but [the dreams] which come forth through [the gate of] polished horn, these have power in reality, whenever any mortal sees them. But it was not through here, I think, that my dread dream came, [though] I assure you that it would be welcome to me and my son [if it had].

This examination of Penelope's speech has produced several small but important revisions in the usual translation, and these help clarify her meaning. It has incidentally illustrated a general truth which deserves wider recognition, that words in Homer tend to be more severely restricted in their connotations than they are in later Greek. It is to some extent this precision in meaning that gives Penelope's speech its characteristically Homeric finish, the impression of tautness and lucidity, which we feel often in reading Homer, even if we do not always stop to define the sources of the impression. We should notice also the rhetorical art, which again is often found in the speeches of Penelope and Odysseus. The description of the two gates in particular is couched in clauses carefully balanced in thought, but skillfully varied in length, order, and phrasing. The initial

34. *Ibid.* pp. 106–7.

contrast in materials in 563 is stated simply and directly, with τετεύχαται set nearly in the middle of the line and serving in meaning for both materials, but syntactically only with horn, so that the second clause is shorter than the first. Then in 564 and 566 both prepositional phrases consist of διά with an adjective followed by a noun, but the order of the phrases is reversed, so that the verb ἔλθωσι is chiastically arranged in the two lines; the second is varied further by the addition of θύραζε. In 565 and 567 the two relative clauses are in the same position, but the single verb ἐλεφαίρονται is balanced by the phrase ἔτυμα κραίνουσι; in the second half of each line a subordinate clause describes the circumstances for each kind of dream, but the first is a nominative participle modifying "dreams," the understood antecedent of οἵ, and the second is a subjunctive clause in which dreams are the understood object.

In sum, Penelope's speech does not seem, upon careful examination, to lend any support to a thesis such as Highbarger posits, that there are two radically different kinds of dreams. The impression given is rather that she is expressing metaphorically the common belief that some dreams predict the future and come true, while others merely seem to predict, but do not come true in reality, although both kinds of dreams are hard to interpret. In cases where action is called for by a dream, it is necessary, in spite of the difficulty, to try to distinguish between ones that will prove true and ones which do not truly predict the future, because if you believe in the latter and act accordingly you will come to grief. Furthermore, it is clear that Penelope especially wants to believe this dream, and therefore is especially cautious about believing it (cf. p. 55 below).

The question now becomes: why are horn and ivory chosen to symbolize this difference between dreams? I agree with the ordinary assumption that Penelope's speech implies a legend or a popular, proverbial belief, not a sudden inspiration on her part or on the poet's, but I do not think it possible to determine the ultimate origin of the idea. The most we can say is that the phrasing of the passage strongly suggests that the notion took its present shape under the influence of two main factors, the paronomasia already noticed (p. 4 above), and some contrast in the physical properties of horn and ivory. Some readers have rested content in the belief that the paronomasia alone accounts completely for the contrast, but it is hard to believe this, for the verbs used to match κέρας and ἐλέφας are hardly an obvious and natural pair. They have rather an air of having been carefully devised to reinforce an already existing antithesis.

The problem is to discover which of the possible contrasts between horn and ivory determined the antithesis. An association between horn and eyes on the one hand, and between ivory and teeth on the other, may well have played a part in the development of the idea, as the second interpretation quoted from Eustathius (pp. 5 f. above) suggests, for the subordinate clauses in the passage, ἔπε' ἀκράαντα φέροντες and βροτῶν ὅτε κέν τις ἴδηται, associate speech with the ivory gate and sight with horn. Moreover, as we shall see shortly, eyes and horn are associated in another passage in the *Odyssey*. But the connection scarcely seems obvious enough to have been the sole factor in forming the antithesis; and there is the further problem that the symbolism as interpreted by Servius does not quite fit the situation. That is, in waking reality, the testimony of an eyewitness is more trustworthy, usually, than hearsay; but in a dream, is not sight just as deceptive as hearing? So Penelope implies when she contrasts her waking glimpse of the live geese with her dream vision of the eagle killing them (19.551–3). Nor does she indicate that she finds either the dream vision or the waking glimpse more convincing than the verbal interpretation offered first by the eagle-Odysseus in her dream and then by the stranger at her side in the hall. Eustathius shows some embarrassment at this very difficulty, and tries to circumvent it, but not very successfully (see the quotation, above, and n. 10).

Surely one needs some more direct connections between horn and dreams that come true and between ivory and dreams that prove vain. And Eustathius' third suggestion, that horn is semi-transparent, while ivory is totally opaque, deserves more

serious consideration than it has received. Once one accepts the
notion of gates of dreams as a reasonable image to begin with,[35]
then horn and ivory are not unsuitable as substances for the
gates through which different kinds of dreams come. For the
fact that neither substance is completely transparent corresponds
to the fact that all dreams are by nature obscure, as Penelope
says at the beginning of her speech. But those whose meaning is
relatively perspicuous may reasonably be said to come through
a gate of horn, which is semitransparent, while ivory, an opaque
substance, is suitable for the gates through which come those
dreams whose meaning is very difficult to see. That some such
association lies behind the antithesis is perhaps indicated by the
adjectives used of horn and ivory in Penelope's speech, for
ξεστός, applied to the smooth polished simple substance of
horn, and πριστός, used of the intricately carved and decorated
substance of ivory, both reinforce the contrast in transparency
between the two materials.[36]

35. The image was apparently a traditional one, for once Penelope when
she addresses a dream-figure is said to be slumbering ἐν ὀνειρείῃσι
πύλῃσιν (4.809). Similarly, at the beginning of the second Nekuia, Hermes
and the suitors' ghosts pass παρ' Ἠελίοιο πύλας καὶ δῆμον ὀνείρων (24.
12). Highbarger, pp. 3–6, relies on this passage for his identification between
the gate of horn and the horned gate of the setting sun, but again fails to
observe that dreams in general are implied, not just true dreams. In any
case, if dreams were thought of as inhabiting a δῆμος, the idea of their
issuing through gates was a natural one.

36. The verb ξέω in Homer is used only of planing wood (5.245, 17.
342 = 21.44, 23.199); cp. the description of Odysseus' bed, p. 45, and
v.81. But the three adjectives derived from it, εὔξεστος, εὔξοος, and
ξεστός, are used of a large variety of objects or structures made of wood,
stone, metal, and horn—javelins, wagons, baths, porticos, chariots, stools,
spear-stands, rudders, oars, stones, thresholds, chariot poles, adzes, doors,
bows, tables, chests, and mangers (see Marzullo). The adjectives, therefore,
mean "smooth, polished," whether made so by lopping, or rubbing, or
whether naturally so. The verb πρίω = saw does not occur at all, and the
adjective πριστός only twice, at 18.196 and 19.564 (νεόπριστος occurs
at 8.404). This is often translated "sawn," but this need not refer to the
sawing of ivory from the tusk of an elephant. Homer never mentions the
source of ivory (see n. 5), and the archaeological evidence also indicates that

This seems to me to be as much as can plausibly be guessed about the origin and development of the idea of horn and ivory gates. But it remains only a guess; we can scarcely be said to have solved the problem of the genesis of the idea. As remarked earlier, however, this problem is essentially insoluble on the evidence available to us, so it is fruitless to discuss it further. On the other hand, one of the tasks that is possible, namely to clarify our understanding of the real import of Penelope's speech, has, I hope, been accomplished, at least partially, by the preceding detailed examination of the words which Penelope uses.

We are now free to consider the other line of investigation suggested earlier: the relevance, if any, of Penelope's speech to the rest of the *Odyssey*. Most scholars, in their concentration on the problem of the provenance of the idea of the gates of dreams, have ignored the poetic aspects of Penelope's speech, assuming tacitly that Homer makes Penelope refer to an old legend merely to express in a picturesque way her skepticism about her dream. But the meaning of her speech would not be exhausted by a full account of the genesis of the legend behind it, just as it has not been fully illuminated by a discussion of its component words, limited as that discussion was to the immediate context of her speech. Like Achilles' equally famous words about the jars of good and evil (xxiv.525–33), Penelope's speech is more than a striking bit of proverbial lore; each has wider implications for the poem in which it occurs.

At this point, however, we enter one of the most treacherous areas in present Homeric scholarship, the question of Homer's artistry, for no one has as yet satisfactorily and fully met the challenge which Milman Parry's work offers to those who wish to discuss the *Iliad* and the *Odyssey* as poems. I do not presume to rush in where some of the most eminent Homeric scholars of

Greece received ivory as a substance, and often already decorated; see n. 20. Wace and Stubbings, Plates 27 *a*, *b*, 32 *a*, *b*, 36 *a*, *b*, and Figures 61 *a*, *b*, illustrate the kind of decorated ivory that would have been familiar to epic poets.

today have feared to tread, by discussing this problem at any
length, but I should like to offer a few observations and a
modest statement of my working assumptions, before returning
to discussion of the specific text at hand.

Even if we believe that Homer was an illiterate bard working
entirely within an oral tradition, we do not have to deny him
control over his material to the extent that some recent critics
seem inclined to do,[37] for some of the current uneasiness about
the degree of art which we may impute to an oral poet rests on
false premises. For example, scholars often write as if oral composition precludes any previous rehearsal or even acquaintance
with the material sung, whereas it is obvious that Homer must
have sung many, many times the songs out of which he ultimately shaped the *Iliad* and the *Odyssey*. (I follow the current
practice of using "Homer" to refer to the poet or poets who
may be assumed to have put our *Iliad* and *Odyssey* into the shape
they now possess.) Given the formulaic nature of epic diction
and the exigencies of any specific performance, a singer may
not be able to choose individual words as carefully and freely as
a writing poet,[38] but he has compensating advantages in the

37. Perhaps the most pessimistic statement of the aesthetic difficulties
raised by the implication of Milman Parry's work is to be found in F. M.
Combellack, "Milman Parry and Homeric Artistry," *Comparative Literature*,
xi (1959), 193–208. Parry himself, particularly perhaps in his early work,
did not make the mistake of equating the technique with the quality of
poetry. See e.g. *A comparative study of diction as one of the elements of style in early
Greek epic poetry* (unpublished Master of Arts Thesis, Berkeley 1923), p. 11:
the technique of oral composition "might be learned parrot-like by men of
little genius who added nothing to their inheritance, [but] it was also a technique which furnished inexhaustible material for genius"; and p. 25: "despite
the native richness of the tradition, it required a great poet to turn it into great
poetry. Both Homer and Hesiod followed the set scheme, but while one
breathed a divine life into it, the other could hardly make it open its eyes."

38. But the extent to which a bard was restricted by the formulaic system has
been exaggerated both by M. Parry himself and by his followers. Many of the
instances of inappropriate epithets which are adduced to prove the exigencies
of oral composition rest on misunderstandings of the meaning of epithets,
as I hope to show soon in a study of ἀμύμων and other traditional epithets.

treatment of theme. Since his material is almost entirely traditional, he sings the same stories repeatedly during his working years, and he may therefore, if his talents and interests allow, continually deepen his understanding of his subjects and correspondingly refine his treatment of them to bring out the significance he perceives. These advantages of the oral bard have not been, it seems to me, sufficiently appreciated by those who currently feel hesitation in attributing artistry to Homer because they have been convinced by the work of Parry and Lord, and by some of the implications of their work.

It is true, as Parry and Lord have shown, that the singer who is called upon, casually, for a song as an evening's entertainment cannot ordinarily invest his song with the same degree or kind of art as a poet who has the solitude to polish and revise his work. But we are at present (and may be always) totally ignorant of the conditions under which the *Iliad* and the *Odyssey* were produced; all we know is that the conditions were somehow extraordinary, for it is obvious that neither poem is a natural result of the common conditions of oral composition, whether as described in the *Odyssey* or as observed in Yugoslavia. However demonstrably oral the style of both poems may be, the monumental scale of the *Iliad* and the *Odyssey* makes it clear that each poem resulted from an unusual effort. Moreover, in neither case is the unusual length achieved by a loose stringing-together of episodes, but it is rather the result of careful selection and disposition of legends and themes about the Trojan war and its heroes. We can therefore (indeed must) imagine Homer to have devoted a great deal of preliminary care, thought, and rehearsal to the poems, even though the final singing of the poems might not have allowed him scope for revision of details.[39]

Several other assumptions of dubious validity are likely to lurk in the arguments of those who insist that Homer, being an oral bard, cannot be credited with artistry. Thus it is sometimes

39. See Adam Parry, "Have We Homer's *Iliad?*" in this volume, pp. 177 ff. and compare George E. Dimock, Jr., "From Homer to Novi Pazar and Back," *Arion*, 11 (1963), 40–57.

stated, and even more often tacitly implied, that because Homer
could not write, he was incapable of complex construction or
subtle characterization.[40] A literate person accustomed to use
writing as an aid to memory might be unable to construct a
poem of any complexity without making notes, but surely a
master bard working in a rich and elaborate tradition, with
perhaps twenty or thirty years of practice in his art, could well
produce, through repeated singings, oral epics as intricate in
structure as any written ones. As for the gift of portraying
characters as vivid and complex as those in Homer, this talent
is equally inexplicable and rare, but it is certainly not dependent
on literacy.

Then there is the notion that because the surface of a bard's
mind must be taken up with the difficulties of framing hexameter verses for his narrative he had no attention or energy left
for anything else, together with the corollary assumption that
full conscious attention is a prerequisite of artistic effects. Those
who praise the artistry of Homer currently risk attack on the
ground that Homer could not consciously have devised the
felicity of expression, significant juxtaposition, suggestive echo,
or whatever stroke of art is being admired. But the question of
how conscious a poet is of his art is equally irrelevant for bard
and for writer. If poetic effects can be demonstrated with
reasonable clarity and in detail by a close and accurate discussion of a text, we should not ask the critic to undertake the
otiose, and in any case impossible, task of demonstrating that
the poet produced these effects in full consciousness of what he
was doing.

Similarly, it is often thought that Homer must have been
unable to indulge in subtle effects or profundities of meaning,

40. This point of view is eloquently represented by Denys Page, e.g. in
The Homeric Odyssey (Oxford 1955), pp. 141–2, at the end of which he says,
"Subtlety of soul, complexity of character, true portrayal of personality—
for these we must wait until the practice of the art of writing affords the
poet the necessary leisure and the necessary means for reflection, for planning
the future in some detail, and for correcting the past."

even if he had been capable of producing them, because no one in his audience would have been able to appreciate his art. This assumption may be correct for run-of-the-mill bards, just as writers of television dramas do not often write beyond the presumed capacities of their audience, but can we fairly say the same of a poet who possessed the talent to compose the *Iliad* or the *Odyssey*? Any poet with confidence in his own skill composes, not according to what he thinks his audience can grasp, but to the full limit of his own capacities; and in the case of a poet whose confidence is justified, this limit may be well beyond what a critic might think possible. It is clear that the Homeric poems far exceed, in scope if in nothing else, the regular items in a bard's repertory. If we grant to Homer (as we must, if we assume that a single poet composed each poem more or less as we have them) the ambition and skill to transcend the tradition in which he worked, enough to conceive and execute a monumental poem which could not be absorbed by an audience in a single sitting, we are surely justified in granting him also the ambition and skill to surpass the ordinary expectations of his audience about the meaning of his poem.

My basic assumption, therefore, is that one bard, a master of the traditional oral epic songs, composed our *Odyssey*, not "in profuse strains of unpremeditated art," but in accordance with a deliberate and complex design which had probably taken shape gradually during the years in which he must have sung the tales of Odysseus' wanderings and homecoming. I do not mean that each and every detail of this design was consciously worked out by the bard beforehand. Once he had decided what parts of the traditional material he would use, in what order he would put them, what view of the main characters he would present, above all which of the possible themes inherent in the episodes he had chosen he would emphasize, and so on, then the artistry with which the details of the main design were executed would be a result largely of his native talent and long years of practice. The conditions of oral composition would prevent a singer from giving to each moment of his poem the same kind of

time and attention which a writing poet might expend line by
line, but they would not necessarily preclude artistry of a high
order. The expression of the important moments of the song
could well have that unconscious rightness of choice which
seems a divine inspiration but is largely the result of self-
training, just as the famous words imply which Homer puts in
the mouth of the Ithacan bard Phemius: "I am self-taught, and
the god implants all kinds of songs in my mind":

> αὐτοδίδακτος δ᾽ εἰμί, θεὸς δέ μοι ἐν φρεσὶν οἴμας
> παντοίας ἐνέφυσεν.   (22.347–8)

Just such an important moment in the *Odyssey* is surely the
first interview between Odysseus and Penelope, and within that
scene one of the details which seems most likely to have received
the full benefit of the poet's artistic powers is Penelope's speech
about the gates of dreams. So far we have been concerned with
the idea of gates of horn and ivory and with the speech itself, in
relative isolation. The use of horn and ivory to distinguish
between different kinds of dreams has been shown to be at least
partially explicable on the grounds that a difference in transparency in the substances corresponds to a difference between
dreams that are easy or hard to interpret. We found also that the
words of Penelope's speech are admirably precise and specific in
their connotations and are arranged so as to secure the maximum rhetorical effect. But neither the impressive imagery of
the idea, nor the rhetorical elegance with which it is expressed,
accounts sufficiently for the mysterious power and suggestive-
ness of the passage as a whole, for Homer seems somehow to
have endowed Penelope's speech with a resonance that extends
beyond the immediate import of her words.

It is time to consider the speech as one detail in a larger
artistic whole, and to see if we can arrive at a more specific
understanding than a vague "somehow" of the ways in which
Homer has exercised his art to make the speech not only a
memorable fragment, but a part which contributes significantly
to the whole poem. If we can, then we will have made some

progress toward providing the concrete documentation which the general question of artistry in oral poetry needs.

Some of the power of the passage doubtless derives from the fact that dreams themselves always hold a certain fascination for the rational mind. Then in the *Odyssey* dreams and omens in general play an important role because they are used to delineate some of the main themes of the poem, such as the growing up of Telemachus, the revenge of Odysseus on the suitors, and the reunion of Odysseus and Penelope.[41] It is evident that Penelope's speech gains significance because it is part of this larger thematic pattern, for the speech occurs during the first interview between her and the disguised Odysseus, in a scene which is the crucial pivot between the earlier separate references by Odysseus and Penelope to each other and the final reunion scene in book 23.[42]

But these general considerations, that dreams are fascinating in life and important in the *Odyssey* and that Penelope's speech is significantly placed, no more explain the effect of the passage to our entire satisfaction than the previous discussions of the idea and the language. There is another element, to which we have perhaps given insufficient attention: the poetic effect of horn and ivory themselves. Does not the peculiar effectiveness of the passage depend partly on the sensuous imagery evoked by the two phrases διὰ πριστοῦ ἐλέφαντος and διὰ ξεστῶν κεράων? This is a subjective matter, and there is no doubt immense variation in readers' reactions, but I think that most people reading or hearing the passage feel, however obscurely and subliminally, some response to the physical qualities of the materials. Both are relatively hard, cool substances more like each other to the touch than other possible materials for gates to be made of—wood and stone, say. But there are differences between them too; one explicit—horn is described as smooth and polished, and ivory as carved (see n. 36); and one implicit—

41. Anne Amory, *Omens and Dreams in the Odyssey*, an (unpublished) Radcliffe dissertation, 1957, explores further Homer's poetic use of dreams.

42. See Amory, "Reunion," n. 33 above.

horn is dark in color and ivory is white. In addition, there is the very strangeness and unreality of the materials chosen for the gates; even if we do not clearly visualize actual gates, surely the imaginative appropriateness of using for the gates of dreams materials out of which gates are not ordinarily built influences our response to the passage.

Finally, there is yet another possibility which seems to be worth exploring, namely that a further contribution is made to the poetic effect of the passage by the associations with which these two substances are endowed in other passages in the *Odyssey*. There are in fact a number of these, which we should survey briefly.

Some of the references in the *Odyssey* are to actual horns on animals. In the third book, after Athena reveals that she has been accompanying Telemachus, the awed Nestor promises a special sacrifice, of a heifer whose horns are tipped with gold. A formula describing the gilding appears three times, with appropriate syntactical variations; once when Nestor promises the sacrifice, once when he gives specific orders for it, and once when it is performed.[43] Together with these, there is a reference to two of Nestor's sons leading in the heifer for the sacrifice, holding her by the horns (βοῦν δ' ἀγέτην κεράων, 3.439). In addition, in a simile about a fisherman, a reference is made to some device connected with a fishing line, the exact nature of which is not clear.[44] All these we may ignore.

But two references to horn as a substance deserve fuller attention. First, Odysseus' bow is made of horn, as we learn

43. τήν τοι ἐγὼ ῥέξω χρυσὸν κέρασιν περιχεύας (3.384); ὄφρα βοὸς χρυσὸν κέρασιν περιχεύῃ (3.426); ὁ δ' ἔπειτα βοὸς κέρασιν περίχευεν (3.437; 3.384=x.294).

44. ἐς πόντον προΐησι βοὸς κέρας ἀγραύλοιο 12.253; cp. ἥ τε κατ' ἀγραύλοιο βοὸς κέρας ἐμβεβαυῖα (xxiv.81). See Alexander Shewan, "Fishing with a Rod in Homer," *Homeric Essays* (Oxford 1935), pp. 427–40, where he argues with odd vehemence that κέρας throughout Homer refers not to horn, but to hair (he does not mention either of the passages in 19, for obvious reasons). See also D. B. Monro, *Homer, Iliad* (4th ed. Oxford 1897), p. 432 (postscript on xxiv.80–2).

when he examines it carefully to make sure that termites (or whatever ἶπες should be taken to mean) have not eaten into it while he was gone:

$$...ὁ \; δ' \; ἤδη \; τόξον \; ἐνώμα$$
$$πάντῃ \; ἀναστρωφῶν \; πειρώμενος \; ἔνθα \; καὶ \; ἔνθα$$
$$μὴ \; κέρα \; ἶπες \; ἔδοιεν \; ἀποιχομένοιο \; ἄνακτος. \quad (21.393–5)$$

The other instance occurs in the first part of Odysseus' interview with Penelope, before her speech about the gates of dreams; the beggar tells her that he is a Cretan named Aethon, and that he had entertained Odysseus in Crete on his way to Troy. He told all these lies so convincingly, says the poet, that they seemed like things that had really happened:

$$ἴσκε \; ψεύδεα \; πολλὰ \; λέγων \; ἐτύμοισιν \; ὁμοῖα. \quad (19.203)$$

His story melts Penelope's frozen grief and she weeps as snow melts in the spring. Odysseus pities her as she weeps, but by craft he represses his own tears and keeps his eyes motionless between their lids, fixed as if (made) of horn or iron:

$$ὀφθαλμοὶ \; δ' \; ὡς \; εἰ \; κέρα \; ἔστασαν \; ἠὲ \; σίδηρος$$
$$ἀτρέμας \; ἐν \; βλεφάροισι· \; δόλῳ \; δ' \; ὅ \; γε \; δάκρυα \; κεῦθεν.$$
$$(19.211–12)$$

This is the passage referred to earlier (p. 21 above), where the plural of κέρας, namely κέρα, is clearly used as a substance, parallel to iron.[45]

Six passages in the Odyssey mention ivory, mostly as an expensive decorative material. First, when Telemachus is

45. Iron may be added here to horn simply because it too is a hard substance, but there are two other places where iron also intrudes into the horn–ivory antithesis. Iron is associated with Odysseus' bow in that the contest for which the bow is used involves shooting through twelve axes. Exactly what this means has never been satisfactorily explained, but it is at least clear that the axes are iron (21.81, 97, 114, 328). Then, in the final recognition scene, Odysseus, just before he is forced to reveal the secret of the ivory-inlaid bed, exclaims that Penelope has a heart harder than iron— ἦ γὰρ τῇ γε σιδήρεον ἐν φρεσὶν ἦτορ (23.172). But this association is not nearly so marked as that between horn and ivory, and it is not, of course, connected with the gate of dreams.

entertained by Menelaus he calls Peisistratus' attention, in awed
tones, to the gleam of bronze, gold, amber, silver, and ivory in
the hall, imagining that the house of Zeus must be similar:

> χαλκοῦ τε στεροπὴν κὰδ δώματα ἠχήεντα
> χρυσοῦ τ' ἠλέκτρου τε καὶ ἀργύρου ἠδ' ἐλέφαντος.   (4.72–3)

The second passage is a description of the sword which
Euryalus gives to Odysseus in apology for having insulted him.
It is solid bronze, with a silver handle, and it has a sheath
either made of or rimmed around with ivory, and is very
valuable:

> δώσω οἱ τόδ' ἄορ παγχάλκεον, ᾧ ἔπι κώπη
> ἀργυρέη, κολεὸν δὲ νεοπρίστου ἐλέφαντος
> ἀμφιδεδίνηται· πολέος δὲ οἱ ἄξιον ἔσται.   (8. 403–5)

The third instance occurs in the prelude to the famous scene
in which Penelope extracts gifts from the suitors. When the
queen first suggests going to the hall, the old nurse Eurynome
encourages her, but says, "Do wash the tear stains off your
face first" (18.170–6). Penelope refuses, saying that the gods
destroyed her beauty when Odysseus went to Troy. But then
while Eurynome is gone to fetch the handmaids who will
accompany the queen to the hall, Athena puts Penelope to
sleep, cleanses her face with the same divine, fragrant cosmetic
which Aphrodite uses, and makes her bigger, taller, and whiter
than carved ivory:

> λευκοτέρην δ' ἄρα μιν θῆκε πριστοῦ ἐλέφαντος.   (18.196)

Fourth, when Penelope enters for the long-delayed interview
with Odysseus, the chair she sits in is described in detail. It is
inlaid with spirals of ivory and silver; the craftsman Icmalius
made it; it has an attached foot-stool and is covered with a
fleece:

> τῇ παρὰ μὲν κλισίην πυρὶ κάτθεσαν, ἔνθ' ἄρ' ἐφῖζε,
> δινωτὴν ἐλέφαντι καὶ ἀργύρῳ· ἥν ποτε τέκτων
> ποίησ' Ἰκμάλιος, καὶ ὑπὸ θρῆνυν ποσὶν ἧκε
> προσφυέ' ἐξ αὐτῆς, ὅθ' ἐπὶ μέγα βάλλετο κῶας.   (19.55–8)

The fifth passage in which ivory is mentioned describes the key which Penelope uses to open the storeroom when she goes to get the horn bow of Odysseus. The key is beautiful, properly curved, made of bronze, and has an ivory handle:

εἵλετο δὲ κληῖδ᾽ εὐκαμπέα χειρὶ παχείῃ
καλὴν χαλκείην· κώπη δ᾽ ἐλέφαντος ἐπῆεν.   (21.6–7)

The final mention of ivory in the *Odyssey* occurs in Odysseus' description of the marriage bed which he made with his own hands. It has for a bed post the living trunk of an olive tree, which Odysseus smoothed and polished skillfully all round with bronze:

κορμὸν δ᾽ ἐκ ῥίζης προταμὼν ἀμφέξεσα χαλκῷ
εὖ καὶ ἐπισταμένως, καὶ ἐπὶ στάθμην ἴθυνα.   (23.196–7)

Then, after constructing the rest of the bed, he decorated it with gold, silver, and ivory:

δαιδάλλων χρυσῷ τε καὶ ἀργύρῳ ἠδ᾽ ἐλέφαντι.   (23.200)

Are these passages anything more than quite incidental and conventional bits of adornment? First, for comparative purposes, let us look at the *Iliad*. The word κέρας occurs seven times in various cases. Five instances refer to horns on animals; of these one refers to gilding the horns of a sacrificial cow, and one to holding a cow by the horns, and both are reminiscent of lines in *Odyssey* 3 (see n. 43). The sixth also is like the *Odyssey*; it refers to the fishing device made of horn (see n. 44). The seventh is debated, but refers either to a bow or to a hair style.[46] Horn as a substance is never mentioned in the *Iliad*, but one of the five references to actual horns involves the bow of Pandarus. When Athena first inspires him to break the truce, he takes from its

46. Diomedes taunts Paris with τοξότα, λωβητήρ, κέρᾳ ἀγλαέ, παρθενο-πῖπα (xi.385). The theory that this refers not to Paris' bow, but to a sort of love-lock, goes back to Aristarchus, and is said by Walter Leaf, *The Iliad of Homer* (London 1900–2) *ad loc.*, to have been proved by Helbig; but there is nothing in Homer's usage to support this, whereas it is possible, from the use of κέρας elsewhere, that it might mean "bow" in this context.

case "his well-polished bow, made of a wild goat" (perhaps a chamois):

αὐτίκ᾽ ἐσύλα τόξον ἐΰξοον ἰξάλου αἰγός.　　　　　(IV.105)

The fact here implied, that the bow was made of the horns of the goat, is made explicit a few lines later. Pandarus himself had shot the goat, "whose horns grew from his head to a length of sixteen palms":

τοῦ κέρα ἐκ κεφαλῆς ἑκκαιδεκάδωρα πεφύκει.　　　　(IV.109)

Then an artisan described as "horn-polishing" made the bow:

καὶ τὰ μὲν ἀσκήσας κεραοξόος ἤραρε τέκτων.　　　　(IV.110)

There is no passage in the *Iliad*, however, remotely similar to the one in the *Odyssey* which compares Odysseus' eyes to horn (see p. 43 above).

Ivory is mentioned only twice in the *Iliad*, once very briefly. In the description of the death of Mydon, the charioteer of the Paphlagonian king, we find: "and from his hands the reins white with ivory fell to the ground in the dust":

...ἐκ δ᾽ ἄρα χειρῶν
ἡνία λεύκ᾽ ἐλέφαντι χαμαὶ πέσον ἐν κονίῃσι.　　　(V.582–3)

The other instance is more impressive. When Menelaus is wounded by Pandarus, an elaborate simile describes how blood stained his legs: "as when some Maeonian or Carian woman stains ivory with crimson, to be a cheek-piece for horses; it lies in a store-room, and many horsemen desire it to wear, but it lies as a treasure for a king, both an ornament for the horse and a source of pride to the driver":

ὡς δ᾽ ὅτε τίς τ᾽ ἐλέφαντα γυνὴ φοίνικι μιήνῃ
Μῃονὶς ἠὲ Κάειρα, παρήϊον ἔμμεναι ἵππων·
κεῖται ἐν θαλάμῳ, πολέες τέ μιν ἠρήσαντο
ἱππῆες φορέειν· βασιλῆϊ δὲ κεῖται ἄγαλμα
ἀμφότερον κόσμος θ᾽ ἵππῳ ἐλατῆρί τε κῦδος.　　　(IV.141–5)

These passages comprise all the references to horn and ivory in the Homeric poems: in the *Iliad* six or seven references to horn (depending on how we take the disputed one; see n. 46), and two to ivory; in the *Odyssey* (counting Penelope's speech as one reference each for the two materials), eight to horn, and seven to ivory. These are not numerous, but they are enough to enable us to make some reasonably safe generalizations. Homer has little occasion to mention horn as a substance. Nine of the fourteen or fifteen occurrences of κέρας refer to the horns of cattle; four or five more refer to useful objects: two to bows (or three, if we take the disputed instance thus; see n. 46), and two to a fishing device. Against this background the references to horn in Penelope's speech and in the comparison of Odysseus' eyes to horn appear all the more extraordinary.

Ivory, in contrast, appears only as a substance. If Homer knew that it was the tusk of an exotic animal, he kept that bit of lore to himself. Ivory is, moreover, purely a decorative material, and an expensive one, associated primarily with royalty, as is shown with especial clarity by the simile in the last quotation, and as is also implied by the other reference in the *Iliad* and most of those in the *Odyssey*. To some extent, therefore, the references to ivory in the *Odyssey* are conventional; the kingship of Odysseus is stressed, as it is not in the *Iliad*; the role of Penelope as queen is prominent; it is natural that in describing the possessions and dwelling of the royal pair Homer should several times adorn them with ivory.

The question is to *what* extent are these references conventional; are the objects made of horn and ivory merely pretty details chosen by the poet at random from the thesaurus offered by the oral tradition of formulae for describing the appurtenances of warrior-kings and their palaces? Such indeed seems to be more or less the case in the *Iliad*. It contributes nothing to the poem except a bit of ornamental variation that Pandarus' bow is specifically said to be made of horn as well as μέγας, ἀγκύλος, καμπύλος, and ἐΰξοος, whereas Helenus' bow is called only ἐΰξοος, and the others in the *Iliad* who have bows—Alexander, Teucer, Dolon, Odysseus, and Artemis—have to content themselves with bows either totally unadorned or called mostly ἀγκύλος, καμπύλος, and παλίντονος, although Apollo is granted the epithet ἀργυρότοξος. Similarly, we are surely not to suppose that Mydon, alone of the charioteers killed in the *Iliad*, has the distinction of reins white with ivory for any special reason, although it is true that he also has the distinction of serving one of the most notorious revenants in Homer, for his king Pylaemenes is killed along with Mydon (v.576 ff.), but turns up mourning his son some books later (xiii.643).

Of all the gallons of blood shed in the *Iliad*, Menelaus' uniquely flows like the crimson used to stain an ivory ornament fit for a king. The sensuous imagery of the white ivory and crimson dye gives Menelaus' treacherously inflicted wound an extra vividness, and thereby helps to set this episode, in which Pandarus symbolically recreates the original offense which led to the war, apart from all the others in which men are wounded in the course of regular battle.[47] But the presence of ivory here does not alter our understanding of the *Iliad* as a whole.

In short, the *Iliad* contains only three significant references to horn and ivory. Two of these, Pandarus' bow and the simile describing the wound it makes in Menelaus, occur close together and are, as it were, reciprocally related. But this collocation, however effective it is in its particular scene, awakens no echoes; it has no effect on the rest of the poem; it has no connection with the main hero of the poem, nor does it have any discernible contribution to make to any of the main themes of the *Iliad*. The third reference, to ivory, has no connection with the first two, and appears to be entirely incidental.

In the *Odyssey*, however, the situation is somewhat different, for even without counting Penelope's speech, the references to horn and ivory are not only more numerous than in the *Iliad*,

47. As often, the details within the simile, although apparently irrelevant to the action, have an indirect emotional appropriateness; so here, the ἄγαλμα laid away suggests the other ἀγάλματα which Menelaus once had laid away in his palace before they were taken by Paris when he took Helen. I am indebted here to a study of the artistry of Homer's similes done by Peter Westervelt at the Center for Hellenic Studies, Washington, D.C., in 1964–1965.

but most of them are also more significantly placed. The first two references to ivory, Telemachus' comment on the splendor of Menelaus' palace in book 3 and the sheath of the sword Euryalus gives to Odysseus in book 8, may be discounted as merely ornamental, like Mydon's reins in the *Iliad*. All the other instances of horn and ivory, however, are connected with Odysseus and Penelope, and they are not widely scattered: one in book 18, two in 19, two in 21, and one in 23. To these we must add Penelope's speech, which occurs exactly in the middle of the series, and which antithetically associates horn and ivory in a passage whose strangeness and beauty make it hard to overlook. These eight passages, moreover, are all intimately and intricately connected with one or both of two major themes in the *Odyssey*, the reunion of Odysseus and Penelope, and the revenge of Odysseus on the suitors. The bow and the key are connected primarily with the revenge theme, but also with the reunion. All the instances in 19 bear on the reunion theme, but the gates of dreams passage is connected also with the revenge theme, for Penelope sets the contest as a result of her dream. Penelope's beauty, her chair, and the bed involve the reunion theme.

Did Homer insert these passages at random, as purely decorative details? Here we meet again the dilemma of the artistry of the oral poet. Decorative descriptive passages were obviously part of the oral tradition, and the phrases of which these passages are composed may be almost wholly formulaic. Just as the poet of the *Iliad* has an array of phrases in which to describe arms and armor, so the poet of the *Odyssey* must have drawn from a stock of expressions describing the furnishings of palaces. But the poet in both poems had a choice among phrases and a choice about where to insert a passage of this sort. The description of Achilles' armor is different from and more significant than all the other short decorative passages describing armor in the *Iliad*. In the same way the poet of the *Odyssey* was not bound by tradition to concentrate his references to horn and ivory around the figures of Odysseus and Penelope. He

presumably chose to specify that Odysseus' bow was made of
horn, while leaving unsung the composition of the bows of
Philoctetes and Heracles (8.219, 11.607). It may be appropriate for Penelope as a queen to sit in an ivory-inlaid chair and
use a key with an ivory handle, but it is not necessary. The poet
does not mention ivory in connection with either Helen or
Arete, although he describes Helen's expensively decorated
work basket in some detail (4.131–5), and although he has
several occasions on which he could have provided one or both
queens with chairs and keys like Penelope's, had he so desired
(4.136; 7.141; 8.439; 15.99 ff.).

In fact the *Odyssey* has many descriptive passages in which the
bard was free to expand, contract, and specify decorative
details as he wished. All of them have a general artistic purpose:
they contribute to the picture of an ordered, luxurious, peace-
time, domestic world which is the necessary scenery for the
major theme of hospitality, just as the battle vignettes in the
Iliad provide the background which is essential for the display
of heroic valor to have its full effect. Individually, also, many of
them have the same kind of artistic finish that we saw in the
simile about Menelaus' wound. The passages involving horn
and ivory likewise are both charming in their individual scenes
and satisfying in their generic domesticity. But in the horn and
ivory passages, I believe, the poet has taken the further step of
deploying them so that they reinforce each other. This arrange-
ment may have been quite instinctive and without any deliberate,
conscious, artistic purpose; the poet's awareness of what he is
doing should be irrelevant, for what he has in fact done should
be visible in the text, although interpretation of what is or is not
visible must remain partly a matter of subjective judgment.

In this particular case it seems to me that the passage about
the gates of dreams has exercised a sort of magnetic effect on the
surrounding decorative passages, and that these are phrased in
such a way and so placed as to complement and clarify the
meaning of the dreams passage. The result is that in the
Odyssey horn is associated with plainly recognizable truth and

with Odysseus, while ivory is associated with deceptive truth and with Penelope.[48] To see how far this hypothesis is true, let us consider in more detail the passages quoted above (pp. 42–5).

Both horn passages are clearly associated with Odysseus, and both associate horn with truth, though not in obvious ways. First, the bow is of course the instrument with which Odysseus accomplishes his revenge on the suitors, and it is used throughout the *Odyssey* as a symbol of Odysseus' valor. Even when he is *incognito* he tells the Phaeacians that he is skilled in handling the well-polished ($\varepsilon\ddot{v}\xi oos$) bow, and that among the Achaeans only Philoctetes excelled him in archery (8.215 ff.). More specifically, at the end of the poem the bow vividly represents one facet of the $\dot{\alpha}\rho\epsilon\tau\dot{\eta}$ of Odysseus, for which Penelope loves him (see 18.205), toward which Telemachus strives, short of which the suitors so conspicuously fall, and by the exercise of which he re-establishes his right to his wife and home. It is, finally, the token by which Odysseus reveals his true identity to the suitors and forces them to admit, for the first time, the real nature of their crimes (22.45–9).

The other instance of horn is the unusual passage in book 19 in which Odysseus' eyes are compared to horn. The passage invites attention to several points. First, at line 203, there is an opposition between plausible lies and facts, $\ddot{\epsilon}\tau\upsilon\mu\alpha$—the same word which Penelope uses of dreams that come through the horn gate. Second, there is a marked contrast between Odysseus' behavior and Penelope's, although their emotions are the same. Third, horn is associated with the eyes, just as in the allegorical

---

48. In the original conception of the gates of horn and ivory it seems likely that the antithesis was a simple one between horn (true dreams) and ivory (false dreams). But as Homer uses the passage, the antithesis is a paradoxical one, for even in 19 the dream about which Penelope expresses skepticism by implying that it must have come through the gate of ivory is in fact a true dream. In the other passages also, ivory is associated not with real falsehood, but with deceptive truth. The same proposal has been made in connection with Vergil's imitation; see Otis, n. 10 above, and T. J. Haarhoff, *Vergil: The Universal* (Oxford 1949), pp. 10–11.

interpretation found in Servius and Eustathius. Fourth, the
hardness and fixity of horn are perhaps intended to recall the
endurance and steadfastness of purpose which have marked
Odysseus all through his wanderings and toils. Finally there is
an association between horn and truth, though it is a paradoxical one. Odysseus keeps his eyes as steady as horn by deceit
(δόλος), by hiding his tears. But he is enabled to do this, while
Penelope weeps like snow melting, only because he, unlike his
wife, knows the real truth, that he has in fact safely returned.

Let us turn now to the ivory passages. The one in which
Athena makes Penelope's skin whiter than ivory is not a conventional descriptive passage but, like the one about Odysseus'
eyes, a comparison unique in Homer. The association between
ivory and deceptive truth appears in the sequel when Penelope
descends to the hall. The beauty with which Athena has
endowed her enchants the suitors (18.211–12), but Penelope
insists that the gods destroyed her beauty when Odysseus went
to Troy, although she admits that if he were to return, her fame
would become greater and fairer (18.251–5). But Odysseus
in fact has returned, and is in the hall looking at his wife for the
first time in twenty years. Athena's action then is a preview, so
to speak, of the real and enhanced beauty which Penelope says
she will recover when Odysseus returns, but the ivory-like
beauty is at the same time deceptive, for Penelope does not
herself fully realize the situation, but thinks that the spectators
are deceived.

This same beauty still attends Penelope when she enters the
hall again for the interview with the stranger later that night.
Just before describing her ivory-inlaid chair, the poet compares
her to Artemis or golden Aphrodite (19.54), and the mention
of these two goddesses recalls the episode in 18 where Penelope, after having been anointed with Aphrodite's cosmetic,
wakes and prays to Artemis for death (18.201–5). The chair
itself is associated with unrecognized truth, for as Penelope sits
in it talking to the stranger she has not yet recognized Odysseus
in his disguise.

The passage about the key brings ivory and horn together, for beyond the simple fact that the key opens the storeroom in which the bow is kept, the descriptions of Penelope using the key and Odysseus the bow are curiously similar. Penelope shoots back the bolts, aiming straight in front, and the doors let forth a sound like the roar of a bull:

ἐν δὲ κληῖδ' ἧκε, θυρέων δ' ἀνέκοπτεν ὀχῆας
ἄντα τιτυσκομένη · τὰ δ' ἀνέβραχεν ἠΰτε ταῦρος
βοσκόμενος λειμῶνι. (21.47–9)

When Odysseus tries the string of the bow, it sings like a swallow under his touch:

δεξιτερῇ δ' ἄρα χειρὶ λαβὼν πειρήσατο νευρῆς ·
ἡ δ' ὑπὸ καλὸν ἄεισε, χελιδόνι εἰκέλη αὐδήν. (21.410–11)

Then he shoots an arrow straight through the axes, aiming right in front:

αὐτόθεν ἐκ δίφροιο καθήμενος, ἧκε δ' ὀϊστὸν
ἄντα τιτυσκόμενος, πελέκεων δ' οὐκ ἤμβροτε πάντων. (21.420–1)

One critic has seen in this parallel an instinctive use of sexual symbolism,[49] but even if we reject this comment as fanciful, it is true that the passages put Odysseus and Penelope into a similar situation, with the crucial difference that horn is connected with Odysseus, who knows the complete truth, while ivory is associated with Penelope who does not. For Penelope, in getting the

---

49. Gabriel Germain, *Homer*, translated by Richard Howard (London 1960), pp. 148–9: "It is curious that Penelope's gesture of thrusting the key into the lock when she goes to the treasury for her husband's bow should be expressed by the same words, aiming straight in front of her, which, later on, applied to Ulysses when he aims at the slender target formed by the holes of the twelve axes lined up one before the other. If there is a sexual symbolism in the bowman's exploit, the bard must have been unconscious of it (he has not invented the trial by archery, an old kingly rite); but, instinctively, he has doubled it with a parallel symbol, bearing witness to this symmetry by slipping into a useless formula (for one does not aim at a keyhole one is used to)."

bow and announcing the contests, acts on the inspiration of
Athena (21.1–2), without being fully aware of the true situation. There has been much scholarly debate about Penelope's
motivation at this crucial point in the story,[50] but for our
purposes it is sufficient to note the indisputable fact that, whatever reasons Penelope may have for acting as she does, her
action itself is exactly the right one from Odysseus' point of
view, for her setting the contest allows him to get hold of the
bow with which he kills the suitors. As in 18, therefore, Penelope acts in accordance with the true situation but without herself completely recognizing the truth, so that once again ivory,
in being associated with her, is associated with a deceptive-
seeming truth.

The last reference to ivory in the *Odyssey* occurs in the description of the marriage bed of Odysseus and Penelope. Since the
bed is the token by which Penelope recognizes Odysseus (or
more accurately, since it is by Odysseus' description of the bed
that Penelope is brought to admit that the stranger really is
Odysseus), the bed has an obvious relevance to the theme of the
truth, plain or hard to recognize, that haunts the other horn and
ivory passages. But here the association of ivory with Odysseus
and Penelope is far more complex than in the previous passages.
First of all, the usual situation is reversed, and it is Penelope
who knows the truth, while Odysseus is in the dark. When
Odysseus, finally growing impatient at Penelope's long delay in
recognizing him, tells the nurse to make up his bed, Penelope
tells Eurycleia to make up the bed outside the marriage cham-
ber. This is a false speech, and Odysseus, for once in the poem,
is the deceived rather than the deceiver. In his anger he reveals
the μέγα σῆμα of the bed which he built around an olive tree so
that it could not be moved. In so far as he made the bed,
decorating it with ivory, and in so far as it is he who describes
it, ivory is here associated with Odysseus, rather than with
Penelope, but rightly, since here it is he who fails to recognize
the truth.

50. See Page, *op. cit.* pp. 114–15 and Amory, "Reunion," pp. 112–16.

But the bed is not associated with Odysseus alone, for it is a marriage bed, and Penelope has slept in it, with and without Odysseus, for more than twenty years. The bed, both in its fixity and in the intricacy of its decoration, is reminiscent of the characteristics which Odysseus and Penelope share, that is, of their constancy and steadfastness of purpose on the one hand, and, on the other, of their wiliness and inventiveness. This final instance of ivory, then, subsumes and provides a clue to the other passages which we have been discussing.

Odysseus and Penelope, in spite of their similarities, and in spite of the ὁμοφροσύνη between them, look at the world in very different ways. Odysseus observes most things unwaveringly, as he does Penelope's tears in 19, for example; and what he sees is immediately recognized by him as real. He sees what is around him and can reason about it. Accordingly, he usually has a firm grip on what is true and what he is inventing, and he is master both of the actual situation and of his own lies with which he deceives others. The chief exceptions are occasions during his adventures when he is at the mercy of powers which seem to symbolize either the unconscious, infra-rational forces in man, or the non-rational forces of the natural world over which man has no control.[51] Another exception is his first landing on Ithaca, which he does not at first recognize, and which he refuses to believe is really Ithaca, even after Athena has told him that it is. Here his profound suspicion is the counterpart of the extreme caution which Penelope displays in deciding whether or not the beggar is really Odysseus.

In contrast to the way in which Odysseus reasons about his experiences and reaches out to become master of his circumstances, Penelope is passive and intuitive. She looks at things only intermittently; she is always holding a veil in front of her face, or looking away from things. She does not notice Telemachus' absence at the beginning of the poem (see 4.680 ff.), nor does she observe Eurycleia's recognition of the beggar

51. See Charles H. Taylor, Jr., "The Obstacles to Odysseus' Return," Taylor, *op. cit.* pp. 87–99.

(19.478). When she finally comes to Odysseus after the suitors
are dead, she cannot look directly into his face (23.106–7).
What she does see is not exactly false, but it is often mysterious,
and its truth is not, and cannot be, instantly apparent. Moreover, she tends to deny or deprecate the truth of what she really
does see and feel. Yet her perceptions are ultimately accurate,
and the actions which she undertakes on the basis of her half-
glimpsed, intuitive, tentatively acknowledged feelings always
turn out to be exactly the right ones.

In sum, I suggest that the *Odyssey* shows considerable artistry
in the disposition of some decorative passages which were in
themselves probably entirely traditional and incidental (although one may suspect that the passage in which Penelope's
skin is compared to ivory and Odysseus' eyes to horn are in a
somewhat different category). Many of the horn and ivory
passages are connected with each other; they center around and
reflect some light on the gates of horn and ivory passage; they
enhance and decorate two major themes of the poem; finally,
they seem to be adapted to a vision of the opposite but comple-
mentary natures of Odysseus and Penelope. In doing this, the
poet may have been aided by some associations which lie outside the realm of the poem. Horns, especially bull horns, were in
many Mediterranean lands a symbol of vital masculine energy.[52]
In their simplicity of form and surface, which is reflected in the
epithet "polished," they are fittingly associated with Odysseus'
capacity for direct action and his clear-headed perception of
facts. Ivory, on the other hand, is an expensive and delicate
decoration whose intricately cut and carved surface is suitable
to Penelope's more sheltered circumstances, her more involuted,
indirect perception, and her more hesitating commitments to
action.

52. See Levy, p. 100, and Onians, pp. 238–44 (cp. n. 13 above).
There is also the possibility of a color association, just as men's skins
are often painted brown and women's white in Minoan and early Greek
art.

Without the extraordinary passage about the gates of horn and ivory, the others might remain ornamental fragments. But once Homer put that speech in Penelope's mouth, once he had her address it to Odysseus during their first interview, once he made the occasion for the speech a means of leading to the climactic action of the poem, then he had the catalytic agent necessary to precipitate the other decorative passages into an artistic compound.

Thoughtful Hesiod

ERIC A. HAVELOCK

Thoughtful Hesiod

Οὐκ ἄρα μοῦνον ἔην Ἐρίδων γένος, ἀλλ' ἐπὶ γαῖαν
εἰσὶ δύω· τὴν μέν κεν ἐπαινέσσειε νοήσας,
ἣ δ' ἐπιμωμητή· διὰ δ' ἄνδιχα θυμὸν ἔχουσιν.
ἣ μὲν γὰρ πόλεμόν τε κακὸν καὶ δῆριν ὀφέλλει,
σχετλίη· οὔ τις τήν γε φιλεῖ βροτός, ἀλλ' ὑπ' ἀνάγκης   15
ἀθανάτων βουλῇσιν Ἔριν τιμῶσι βαρεῖαν.
τὴν δ' ἑτέρην προτέρην μὲν ἐγείνατο Νὺξ ἐρεβεννή,
θῆκε δέ μιν Κρονίδης ὑψίζυγος, αἰθέρι ναίων,
γαίης ἐν ῥίζῃσι, καὶ ἀνδράσι πολλὸν ἀμείνω·
ἥ τε καὶ ἀπάλαμόν περ ὁμῶς ἐπὶ ἔργον ἔγειρεν·   20
εἰς ἕτερον γάρ τίς τε ἰδὼν ἔργοιο χατίζει
πλούσιον, ὃς σπεύδει μὲν ἀρώμεναι ἠδὲ φυτεύειν
οἶκόν τ' εὖ θέσθαι· ζηλοῖ δέ τε γείτονα γείτων
εἰς ἄφενος σπεύδοντ'· ἀγαθὴ δ' Ἔρις ἥδε βροτοῖσι.
καὶ κεραμεὺς κεραμεῖ κοτέει καὶ τέκτονι τέκτων,   25
καὶ πτωχὸς πτωχῷ φθονέει καὶ ἀοιδὸς ἀοιδῷ.
ὦ Πέρση, σὺ δὲ ταῦτα τεῷ ἐνικάτθεο θυμῷ,
μηδέ σ' Ἔρις κακόχαρτος ἀπ' ἔργου θυμὸν ἐρύκοι
νείκε' ὀπιπεύοντ' ἀγορῆς ἐπακουὸν ἐόντα.
ὤρη γάρ τ' ὀλίγη πέλεται νεικέων τ' ἀγορέων τε   30
ᾧ τινι μὴ βίος ἔνδον ἐπηετανὸς κατάκειται
ὡραῖος, τὸν γαῖα φέρει, Δημήτερος ἀκτήν.
τοῦ τε κορεσσάμενος νείκεα καὶ δῆριν ὀφέλλοι
κτήμασ' ἐπ' ἀλλοτρίοις· σοὶ δ' οὐκέτι δεύτερον ἔσται
ὧδ' ἔρδειν· ἀλλ' αὖθι διακρινώμεθα νεῖκος   35
ἰθείῃσι δίκῃς αἵ τ' ἐκ Διός εἰσιν ἄρισται.
ἤδη μὲν γὰρ κλῆρον ἐδασσάμεθ', ἄλλα τε πολλὰ
ἁρπάζων ἐφόρεις μέγα κυδαίνων βασιλῆας
δωροφάγους, οἳ τήνδε δίκην ἐθέλοντι δίκασσαν.
νήπιοι, οὐδὲ ἴσασιν, ὅσῳ πλέον ἥμισυ παντὸς   40
οὐδ' ὅσον ἐν μαλάχῃ τε καὶ ἀσφοδέλῳ μέγ' ὄνειαρ.

Hesiod, *Works and Days* (Rzach), 11–41

If Hesiod is to be considered an oral poet in the same sense, and
to the same degree, as Homer,[1] the metrics and vocabulary of
these hexameters would be expected to obey Homeric rules of
formulaic composition. In fact, they may contain hints to the
contrary,[2] which might raise interesting questions concerning
the technical conditions of composition. Rather than pursue
these, I propose to focus on the character and content of the
argumentative structure,[3] always bearing in mind that if this on
examination shows a degree of novelty, in comparison with the
habits of narrative epic, then parallel divergences in metrics
and vocabulary would not be unexpected. Argumentation of
course abounds in Homer, primarily in the speeches. The
present passage, however, reads like an attempt to expound a
formal thesis with a certain degree of logical rigor which
measured by epic standards is unusual; it is to this attempt that
present attention will be turned.

On the face of it, and making some concessions to the
"roughness" of Hesiod's style, the content of these lines can be
interpreted with reasonable coherence in the following paraphrase:

There are two varieties of contention among men; one of
them is negative, provoking war, the other positive, rousing
men to work through competition. Emulation of rich neighbors
illustrates this kind of competition, (so does) quarreling between
craftsmen and resentment between beggars or bards. You,
Perses, must learn this lesson and so avoid wasting your time in
(the wrong sort of) contention, which means listening in on the

1. J. A. Notopoulos, "Homer, Hesiod, and the Achaean Heritage of
Oral Poetry", *Hesperia*, 29 (1960), 177–97.

2. For example, ἰθείῃσι δίκης (36), with word-end at position 3½, may
be un-Homeric (but cf. Kirk, pp. 97 ff. below); the sense of ὀφέλλει (14) is
Homeric, but ὀφέλλοις (33, the MS. reading, which may well be correct)
might exemplify an adaptation of the Homeric formula for protreptic purposes (cf. also *W.D.* 213). ἐπιμωμητή (13), a *hapax leg.*, looks like a coinage
formed to assist the poet's essay in definition.

3. For a recent discussion, see H. Munding, *Hesiods Erga in ihrem Verhältnis
zur Ilias* (Frankfurt 1959).

wrangles in the agora. Sustenance is seasonal and must be adequately accumulated as a prerequisite for indulgence in disputes (of which, of course, I disapprove) aimed at the property of others (that is, of me). You (Perses) will not have a second chance to act in this way (that is, at my expense). We (Perses and I) should settle our wrangle (that is, lawsuit) justly. The allotment (I mean our patrimony) we (you and I) divided up (between us), but you (Perses) made off with much more (than your share), after honoring (that is, bribing) judges who like giving this kind of (that is, unjust) justice. Fools are they (the judges, the litigants, or Perses?), ignorant of the advantages of moderation (that is, legal compromise between Perses and me) and of a frugal diet (in preference to Perses' acquired wealth).

Suppose this is the sense and connection intended by the poet.[4] An initial difficulty then arises concerning the portrait of Perses who, on the one hand, it would appear, is exhorted to avoid the dangers of poverty, and on the other is accused of excessive acquisition. This inconsistency tends to support those who have argued that Perses, though he may have been a real brother, is used as a lay figure in this poem. This, though probable, is not the issue with which I wish directly to deal.

Behind the problem of personal identity in this passage lies another which cuts deeper. The air of logical connection which appears in our translation depends for its effect upon the bracketed portions added as supplements to the Greek text. Read without them, the argument tends to loosen up and even disintegrate. This is not true of the first fourteen lines (11–24), ending in examples of rivalry for wealth. But to these are then subjoined two aphorisms occupying a line each, the intent of which, taken by themselves, can be viewed as satirical: (*a*) the first object of a craftsman's criticism is always his fellow craftsman; (*b*) beggars resent each other, as do bards (hence, either: resentment is universal or: bards are like beggars). These rather

4. To assist this interpretation, the Loeb translator adopts the emendation τὰ for τε at line 37, and prints ἀλλὰ not ἄλλα.

cynical sentiments are linked to the previous gospel of work, but the logic of the connection is not very tight. Such activities would rather be proof of time-wasting than of hard work, that is, of the negative strife rather than the positive, especially in view of the implicit distinction previously drawn between *deris* and *zelos.*

At line 28, to maintain continuity with the previous passage, we have to interpret *eris kakochartos* as equivalent to the negative strife described in 13 ff., and as excluding the good strife of 24. But without this interpretation, the Greek more naturally reads as initiating a fresh argument, to the effect that strife of any kind can menace hours of labor; this happens if its attraction can lure one into joining the audience at disputes in the market-place. On this showing, the poet at this point has abandoned the formal division with which he had begun.

Lines 33 and 34*a*, again, can be connected logically to the preceding by assuming that they are ironical, expressing a policy which from Hesiod's standpoint is immoral. But taken by themselves, without benefit of such moralizing interpretation, they could be read as another piece of proverbial cynicism advising the would-be aggressor in acquisition to be sure to have a secure financial basis from which to proceed.

From 34*b* onward, the continuity suggested depends on identifying the second person singular in the Greek as addressed to Perses, and the first person plural as including Hesiod and Perses. The *kleros* (37) then becomes their common patrimony, and the *neikos* of 35 becomes a lawsuit between Hesiod and his brother in which Hesiod had been worsted. The text supplies none of these clues. If they are withdrawn, the connection between 34*a* on the one hand, and 34*b* plus 35*a* on the other, falls apart, as is also true of the connection between 35*a* and 35*b* ff. and between 36 and 37, and between 39 and 40, and between 40 and 41.

It is not our intention to reduce the whole passage to a meaningless series of phrases, but rather to indicate that the poet is in fact aiming at an argumentative unity but that his unity is very difficult for him to achieve; the reason being that he is working with disjunct bits and pieces of verse drawn from his oral reservoir which he is trying to put together in a new way. However, before suggesting his method, it is fair to ask: How far, supposing the original material does consist of disjunct pieces of verse, can the process of disintegration of context be pushed?

A good many units making up this composition consist of self-contained proverbs. This is true of 23 *b* plus 24 *a*, of 25 plus 26—a pair linked by parallel syntax and assonance—of 28 (plus 29 if desired), of 30 plus 31, and of 40 plus 41. If syntax were manipulated, one or two others could emerge from the text. This is true of 22 (plus 23 *a* if desired) if *plousion* were changed to the nominative, and of 32 if the first two words were changed to the feminine and the last to the nominative, perhaps of 33 plus 34 *a* if for the first three words some substitute were proposed: *plouton ktesamenos*, though unlikely, would do. Further manipulation might produce similar effects on lines 20, 36 and 39. Not the actual existence, but the latent possibility of such proverbs is the point to be stressed.

Let us now return to what one feels to be the poet's sustained intention. Though the passage can be analyzed and broken down into these bits and pieces, when read as a whole it conveys the impression of a single thread of sustained meaning, but the thread, so to speak, is in spots very frayed, and almost broken. The original impression is fixed for us by the first fourteen lines, after which logical coherence begins to give way at 25 and disintegrates faster as the poet proceeds. In these opening lines he establishes quite firmly the antithetic concepts of a praiseworthy and good *eris* and a blameable and bad *eris* (lines 12–13). To each is attached a series of appropriate descriptive formulae. The bad *eris* is a rouser of war, intractable, unloved, a burden prized perforce (14–16). The good *eris* enjoys cosmic parentage and divine status, is far better for men, and is a rouser of men to work through emulation (17–24). So far, so good. But this paragraph of fourteen lines in fact exhausts the capacity of the poet (*a*) to maintain his antithesis with clarity and logic, (*b*) to define adequately its second half, that is, the functions and effects of good strife. The reasons for this double limitation will be suggested in a moment.

Thereafter, two things happen to the exposition. At first, Hesiod attempts to embark further on the attributes of the good strife, but the attempt breaks down into partial irrelevance (lines 25–7). Then he abandons the antithesis altogether and his verse is allowed to flow into a description of the evils of strife in general (28). But this strife is now viewed as centering not on war, but on litigation in the market-place (29); and it is to this topic that those formulas which fill up lines 30–2 attach themselves. Less clearly, the same topic seems to control lines 33–9, with 40 and 41 added as an appendix.

What is the reason for the initial failure of connection—the failure, that is, to sustain argument coherently beyond fourteen lines? I suggest the following: The oral reservoir, so to speak, as we can determine from Homer and from the *Theogony*, supplied our poet with familiar images of strife as the spirit of combat and of contention between individuals, as the child of Night, and as a dangerous element in human life. He applies his own creative genius to these formulas in order to split the single conception into two types, which he calls *gene*, and this constitutes a mental leap forward. The effect is to call into being a new topic of discourse, namely a good strife, a novel conception and one which he wishes to develop as a moral principle necessary to the economy of an agricultural society. But his formulas do not readily support either the antithesis or the existence of this new concept and he has to fight, as it were, mentally against the tradition, and his effort finally collapses. He becomes the prisoner of familiar formulas which have taken shape in an epoch of minstrelsy which was innocent of such a distinction, or at least had never formally recognized it; but he never entirely loses the thread of his new conception.

The first fourteen lines, then, give expression to a thesis which can be accepted as an act of new creation and a successful one.

They would nevertheless be expected to obey that familiar law of oral composition whereby any act of poetic originality is carried out by remodeling or reorganizing previously used formulas. The antecedents of these lines lie initially in those contexts of the *Iliad* where *eris* is portrayed as arousing the combative instincts of men in battle. Her Homeric image is a little complex. She is an affliction (*argalee*) and also possessed of passionate energy (*amoton memauia*), yet also is beneficial (*laossoos*). She casts *neikos* into the midst and arouses *ponos* and increases *stonos*, but she also puts *sthenos* into men's hearts. In particular, she encourages and enjoys an equal contest. Zeus and the gods generally let her loose on men. She can grow till she treads earth and strikes heaven.[5] Nor should we forget her role as that initial contention aroused by Apollo which sets the machinery of the *Iliad* in motion, particularly as Homer later makes a point of this when he represents his hero as condemning and discarding this *eris*.[6]

Echoes, as it were, of these attributes penetrate into Hesiod's divided account. As she who treads over the earth, the original *eris* turns into twin figures who do this (11–12). As the spirit of combat, afflictive (σχετλίη) and also god-directed (ἀθανάτων βουλῇσιν), she becomes the bad strife. But equally as the source of energy in the fighter and as the participant in equal contest and the source of *ponos* she helps to suggest the attributes of the Hesiodic good strife (20–4). Finally, as the source of *neikos*, she supplies a prototype for the lines following the antithesis which discuss or portray litigation in the agora.

Between the Homeric description of *eris* and the dichotomy achieved by Hesiod there intervenes the genealogy of *eris* supplied in the *Theogony* (225–32). The truth seems to be that the *Iliad*, the *Theogony*, and the *Works and Days* deal successively

5. iv.440–5 raging ceaselessly, a little wave which then extends from earth to heaven, casting equal *neikos*, fostering *stonos*; v.517–18 arousing *ponos*, raging ceaselessly; xi.3–12 *argalee*, discharged by Zeus, putting great *sthenos* in the heart; xi.73 *polustonos*; xviii.535 companion of *kudoimos* and *ker oloe*; xx.48 arising as the gods mingle in battle, *kratere*, *laossoos*.

6. i.6, 8; xviii.187; xix.58, 64.

with *eris* as a topic of some significance and each enlarges on the preceding. Homer had described her as the spirit of war. In almost cosmic terms, she grows to such stature that she strides on earth while her head is against heaven. Her companions are *deimos, phobos, kudoimos,* and *ker oloe*. She is also the sister of Ares *androphonos*. She presides over or brings about *polemos, mache, neikos,* and *ponos*. The *Theogony*, rationalizing, we suggest, these images of *eris*, works her into the genealogical scheme by assigning her parentage to Night, thus giving her cosmic extension, and gives her a list of brothers and sisters which includes *Ker* (211), and a list of children which includes *Androktasiai, Ponos, Machai, Phonoi,* and *Neikea* (226–9). She herself is *karterothumos* (225), consistent with her Homeric portrait as the source of combative energy in men: altogether, a formidable and oppressive figure in the genealogical gallery of the *Theogony*.

Our present passage, then, begins by correcting this genealogy.[7] There are two *gene* of strifes, not one. But in using *genos* in this way, the bard has insensibly shifted its meaning. Two *gene* of *eris* (in the singular), if he had so phrased it, would mean two different generations or sets of children derived from *eris*. A man can have only one ancestral *genos*, but conceivably his descendants could number several *gene*. This would have been a genealogical correction, and in part Hesiod may mean this, since he is probably thinking of a strife who has good children as against the list of bad children in the *Theogony*. However, he does not say this. He speaks of "two *gene* of strifes" (in the plural) which can mean only two different strife-families, that is, two different people born (with the name) strife. The implication is that they are children of a common parent—either twins or at least sisters. Now this is not strictly a genealogical correction, but a typological one. *Genos* is being transmuted from its previous familial meaning into that of class or kind, and this is achieved by a change in the context in which an existing word

7. First noted in the commentaries *ad loc.* of Mazon (1914) and Wilamowitz (1928); see also other references in Munding, *op. cit.* p. 31, n. 41.

is used, not by using a new word. Once he has managed to double the name *eris* in this way, Hesiod splits one from the other conceptually by praising one and blaming the other. *Epimomete*[8] as an epithet is suggestive. An act of genuine mental creation has occurred and he is somehow aware of it. Is this why he insists on the participle *noesas* to indicate the effort of (mental) attention required? After that it becomes easy to muster some Homeric formulae, previously used to describe the combative *eris*, and here attach them to the blameworthy type, and to recall in the same context the Homeric designation of the gods, Zeus (xi.3) and Apollo (1.8–9) in particular, as the originators of *eris*. The divine *boulai* (*W.D.* 16) may even be another reminiscence of the preface to the *Iliad* (1.5).

But the sister *eris*, whose separate existence he so far tenaciously retains in his mind, requires a separate definition, and a more sophisticated one. This is his own mental creation,[9] and it is important, so he grounds the definition in that genealogy supplied in the *Theogony*, and then, remembering that Night is extended triple round Tartarus, above which grow roots of earth (*Theogony* 726–8), he exalts the importance of his new *eris* by giving it cosmic extension, thus preparing for the parallel assertion of the importance of its role in human life ("for men it is far better"). To define this role, he then successively attaches to the cosmic figure the formulas of three proverbs applicable to agriculture but recalling the Homeric spirit of emulation in combat which still lurks in the back of his mind as a contextual reference. Then, as if to reaffirm his mental grip on this dawning conception, he reasserts in a formulaic variant the importance of the role for men of this particular ($\H{\eta}\delta\epsilon$) *eris*.

If at this point his connection begins to give out and his coherence to fade, we can measure his partial failure against the initial success achieved by remustering traditional formulas in order to construct a new pattern, something we can properly

8. Cf. n. 2 above.

9. Munding, *op. cit.* p. 56, finds the notion of a good *eris* (but not the word) in the epic athletic contest.

style a new idea. A concept has been born, or rather given linguistic expression, which is the main battle. The effort is not sustained very long. The tight logic gives out because, we suggest, he is compelled to draw upon a vocabulary which is intractable for the purpose.

Lines 33–9, on any interpretation, offer conundrums. 34*b* plus 35*a* are suspended in a vacuum. Do 35–6 appeal for a settlement out of court, as opposed to one adjudicated by a prince (39)? Would any such alternative be likely in Hesiod's society? The formulas of 36 surely refer to the normal administration of justice. And how could successful and greedy acquisition confer great prestige on princes, unless they were the beneficiaries?

A clue to these obscurities may lie once more in the *eris* theme of the *Iliad*.[10] Hesiod has moved from the good *eris* to *eris*-in-general by way of the agora. As *eris* is transplanted from the fields to the speaking place, she becomes the principle and process of litigation. The *eris* of the *Iliad* erupts and then subsides in two scenes laid in the agora.[11] Hesiod's participant in the agora, after gaining his fill, proceeds to provoke *neikos* and *deris* by going after other people's property. But he will not be able to do so twice. A distribution has been made, but he has made off with more. Honor is due to princes who are gift-gobblers.

With these sentiments compare some of the statements made by Achilles to Agamemnon:

> Ἀτρεΐδη κύδιστε, φιλοκτεανώτατε πάντων,
> πῶς γάρ τοι δώσουσι γέρας μεγάθυμοι Ἀχαιοί;
> οὐδέ τί που ἴδμεν ξυνήϊα κείμενα πολλά·
> ἀλλὰ τὰ μὲν πολίων ἐξεπράθομεν, τὰ δέδασται.　　(1.122–5)

> καὶ δή μοι γέρας αὐτὸς ἀφαιρήσεσθαι ἀπειλεῖς　　(1.161)

> 　　　　　　　　ἀτὰρ ἤν ποτε δασμὸς ἵκηται,
> σοὶ τὸ γέρας πολὺ μεῖζον　　　　　　　　　　(1.167)

10. So Munding, pp. 25–41.
11. 1.54, 305; xix.45, 276.

ἦ πολὺ λώϊόν ἐστι κατὰ στρατὸν εὐρὺν Ἀχαιῶν
δῶρ᾽ ἀποαιρεῖσθαι ὅς τις σέθεν ἀντίον εἴπῃ·
δημοβόρος βασιλεύς,[12] ἐπεὶ οὐτιδανοῖσιν ἀνάσσεις·
ἦ γὰρ ἄν, Ἀτρεΐδη, νῦν ὕστατα λωβήσαιο.   (1.229–32)

τῶν δ᾽ ἄλλων ἅ μοι ἐστί θοῇ παρὰ νηΐ μελαίνῃ,
τῶν οὐκ ἄν τι φέροις ἀνελὼν ἀέκοντος ἐμεῖο·
εἰ δ᾽ ἄγε μὴν πείρησαι, ἵνα γνώωσι καὶ οἵδε.   (1.300–3)

As for the proposal in Hesiod's lines that litigation between
two parties (διακρινώμεθα) be settled, and the reference to the
legal functions of princes, one may again compare, from the
same scene in the *Iliad*, Nestor's unavailing attempt at media-
tion, including his remarks to Achilles:

μήτε σύ, Πηλεΐδη, ἔθελ᾽ ἐριζέμεναι βασιλῆϊ
ἀντιβίην, ἐπεὶ οὔ ποθ᾽ ὁμοίης ἔμμορε τιμῆς
σκηπτοῦχος βασιλεύς, ᾧ τε Ζεὺς κῦδος ἔδωκεν,   (1.277–9)

as well as the formal reconciliation offered by Achilles at *Iliad*
XIX, where the *eris* now to be concluded is given thematic
significance:

Ἀτρεΐδη, ἦ ἄρ τι, τόδ᾽ ἀμφοτέροισιν ἄρειον
ἔπλετο, σοὶ καὶ ἐμοί, ὅ τε νῶί περ ἀχνυμένω κῆρ
θυμοβόρῳ ἔριδι μενεήναμεν εἵνεκα κούρης;   (XIX.56–8)
                    αὐτὰρ Ἀχαιοὺς
δηρὸν ἐμῆς καὶ σῆς ἔριδος μνήσεσθαι ὀΐω.   (63–4)

Acceptance of this offer is accompanied by the transfer of
compensation previously promised (lines 140 ff., 238 ff.).

Are these echoes so slight as to be fortuitous? Or do they add
up to a pattern of reminiscence? We recall the suggestion
earlier made that, as Hesiod proposes the notion of a fruitful
competitive strife, he may have the preface to the *Iliad* in his
memory, among other contexts. Then he lets go of the antithesis and treats *eris* under another guise, as a single principle. But

---

12. Munding (p. 28) notes the coincidence between δῶρ᾽ ἀποαιρεῖσθαι
(230), δημοβόρος βασιλεύς (231), and βασιλῆας | δωροφάγους (*W.D.* 38–9).

in doing so, he does not simply repaint the epic portrait of her. Instead, she is translated into a legal context. The *neikos* which she arouses becomes akin to the principle of litigation, a topic complementing the notion of competition. Both are so to speak additions to the conceptual apparatus. But litigation has its epic prototype conspicuously in the engagement between Achilles and Agamemnon, a *neikos* to be settled not by war but by negotiation; it had launched the plot of the *Iliad*. Hesiod is using the same theme to launch his own poem. And so, as Hesiod proceeds to portray litigation, his phraseology evokes the scenes, of quarrel and reconciliation, between the two heroes.

If this be acceptable as an explanation of these puzzling lines, we see revealed another facet of the poetic process by which Hesiod, working within a fairly tight oral tradition, achieved his own creative ends. Besides the manipulation of epic vocabulary to yield fresh dichotomies, besides the loose grouping of aphorisms to furnish continuous discourse, we perceive also the evocation and exploitation of whole situations or scenes in the epic prototype, and ones which are familiar.

Ultimately, the method of Hesiod can be viewed as one of topicalization carried on within the existing matrix of narrative oral poetry. This is still some distance away from logically organized discourse, let alone abstract definition and analysis. The linguistic materials are still oral. They can be rearranged and regrouped and as it were "translated" to produce the semblance of discourse. Within these limits, the achievement of thoughtful Hesiod is surely not inconsiderable.

Studies in Some Technical Aspects of Homeric Style

G. S. KIRK

Studies in Some Technical Aspects of Homeric Style

PRELIMINARY NOTE

One of the fundamental aspects of Homeric style is the use of formulas, which plays little part in the investigations which follow. Detailed analysis and much more work are needed before the implications of formulas are fully understood; at present a vagueness over definitions and an excessive concentration on the name-epithet system are causing difficulties. Meanwhile other and neglected aspects of the style of the *Iliad* and *Odyssey* deserve attention, notably their rhythmical structure, and the relation of the verse and its component parts to the sentence and lesser units of meaning. A fuller understanding of these topics may well be a prerequisite for any serious advance in our knowledge of formular techniques; and it seems *a priori* probable that in many respects, though not all, rhythm and verse-structure conditioned formular practice rather than *vice versa*.

I. THE STRUCTURE OF THE
HOMERIC HEXAMETER

Hermann Fränkel was the first to see, in 1926, that the Greek
hexameter tends to fall into four word-groups, separated by
three regularly placed caesuras.[1] These caesuras, or cuts
between words, are the main caesura in the third foot, the
"bucolic" caesura (strictly diaeresis) between the fourth and
fifth feet, and the caesura in or before the second foot (most
commonly after its first syllable). Of these cuts, only the central
one is almost invariable—it occurs in nearly 99 out of every 100
Homeric verses; but that means that there are as many as 329
verses in all in which the central caesura is missing, is bridged
over, often with so common a form as διογενὲς Λαερτιάδη
πολυμήχαν' 'Οδυσσεῦ. The bucolic caesura occurs in something
over 60 of every 100 Homeric verses (and becomes still commoner in later hexameter poetry); and so does the caesura after
the first longum of the second foot.[2]

Fränkel had begun by considering the reverse aspect of the
caesura, the inhibitions on word-end in particular positions in
the verse which had been recognized by nineteenth-century
scholars for the most part. These are: no word-end at position 6
unless a word-end has preceded at 5 or $5\frac{1}{2}$; no word-end at $7\frac{1}{2}$
unless word-end at 7 or 8; no word-end at $3\frac{1}{2}$ or 4 unless
previous word-end at 3 or 2.[3] The two last inhibitions are

1. "Der kallimachische und der homerische Hexameter," *GGN* (Phil.-
hist. Kl.), 1926, 197–229. This brilliant article is incorporated, in a somewhat
revised form, in the same author's *Wege und Formen frühgriechischen Denkens*
(2nd ed. Munich 1960), pp. 100–56; and a shorter description of the theory
appears in his *Dichtung und Philosophie des frühen Griechentums* (2nd ed.
Munich 1962), pp. 32 ff.

2. For this last caesura I rely on the figures for the 1000-line samples used
by H. N. Porter, *Yale Classical Studies*, 12 (1951), table II on p. 52. These are
a reliable guide since the Homeric colometry is remarkably consistent, and
Porter has been careful.

3. I adopt the convenient numeration used by Fränkel and Porter:

$$1 \ 1\frac{1}{2} \ 2 \ 3 \ 3\frac{1}{2} \ 4 \ 5 \ 5\frac{1}{2} \ 6 \ 7 \ 7\frac{1}{2} \ 8 \ 9 \ 9\frac{1}{2} \ 10 \ 11 \ 12$$
$$\underbrace{-\ \cup\ \cup}\ -\ \underbrace{\cup\ \cup}\ -\ \underbrace{\cup\ \cup}\ -\ \underbrace{\cup\ \cup}\ -\ \cup\ \cup\ -\ \cup$$
$$\qquad\quad A \qquad\qquad B \qquad\quad C$$

A, B and C mark the three areas of caesura.

versions of "Hermann's bridge" and "Meyer's law" respectively. Fränkel found that he could restate them in a positive sense, in terms of the regular caesuras and the four word-groups which they separate. The first of the three inhibitions amounts to no more than saying that, if there is no main caesura, a nearby caesura must not divide the verse exactly in half; this is so obvious that it is rarely stated. "Hermann's bridge," according to Fränkel, simply means that, if there is no word-end at position 8 (or its substitute, position 7), then there must be no ambivalent and misleading word-end in that region of the verse, to conceal the fact that the "regular" caesura has been bridged. "Meyer's law" states essentially that, if the regular caesura at 3 (or its substitute at 2) is missing in the first part of the verse, then the colon must continue without distracting word-breaks until the next caesura. The reason for the bridging of the caesuras in all three cases is regularly the presence of a "heavy word," a word which by its metrical length (at least that of a choriamb or a molossian, $- \cup \cup -$ or $- - -$) does not fit into the pattern of short cola, but which compensates by its weight and impressiveness for the departure from the normal colometric structure of the verse. Thus, according to Fränkel, the apparent inhibitions accord exactly with the fourfold colometric structure suggested by the regular caesuras.

It is part of the theory—and, as we shall see, one that leads to difficulty—that in each of the three regular areas of division between cola there is one commonest position for caesura and one or more substitute or secondary positions. Thus the "feminine" caesura after the third trochee is the commonest break near the middle of the verse; when it does not occur there is a "masculine" caesura instead, at position 5. The bucolic caesura is the commonest break near the end of the verse, and of the almost 40% of Homeric verses which do not have this break the majority have caesura at position 7, after the first syllable of the fourth foot. The commonest caesura in the first part of the verse is at position 3, but a break at position 2 is a quite frequent substitute. Fränkel also thinks that breaks at 1 or

1½ can serve as substitutes, where there is no break at 3 or 2. In this case, however, the first "colon" is reduced to the length of a trochee or even a single long syllable; and in the case of the secondary caesura at 7 following a feminine caesura in the middle of the verse we find, similarly, that Fränkel is compelled to envisage a third colon of one iamb.

This was one of the reasons which persuaded H. N. Porter, who in general accepts the four-colon theory, to propose certain amendments to it in his article "The Early Greek Hexameter" (*Yale Classical Studies*, 12 (1951), 3–63). Porter envisages that position 2 is the only viable alternative to 3 for the division between first and second colons; those (fairly common) Homeric verses which begin with a word-pattern like ἱστὸν ἐποιχομένην or Ζεὺς ὑψιβρεμέτης should be thought of, not as having an unrealistically meager initial colon, but as bridging the normal division between the first two colons. Moreover the alternative to the bucolic caesura cannot be at 7 (so as to make an iambic third colon), but must be at 9, after the first syllable of the fifth foot. Porter accepts the idea that word-groups which must be of standard length and not ambiguously divided adequately explain the apparent restrictions on word-end; but he is inclined to see an additional motive for the inhibitions in the first and third cola in the effort to avoid an adonius ($- \cup \cup - \cup$), which smacks of the verse-end: "The adonic cadence, which has a 'dying fall,' was appropriate to the end of the line and to the end of the first half line, the second colon, but any suspicion of it was avoided in the first and third cola of the line" (*op. cit.* p. 13).

I should like first to question the scope of Porter's additional motive. It is possible that it operates in the case of word-end at 3½ without previous break at 3 or 2: for example in verses like *Iliad* 1.1, Μῆνιν ἄειδε, θεά (where the sense-pause before the vocative may accentuate the status of Μῆνιν ἄειδε as a separate rhythmical unit).[4] In general terms it may be agreed that

4. It has been argued by Fränkel (*GGN* (Phil.-hist. Kl.), 1926, 215), however, with some support from Wackernagel, *Indogermanische Forschungen*, I (1892), 424f., that interposed vocatives like θεά in this verse cause little or

adonic sequences were carefully used so as not to cause ambiguity about where the verse-end actually does occur—though no one can have thought that it was likely to occur in the second foot. Possibly, too, the repetition of the pattern at the beginning of a verse, immediately after the end of the preceding verse, was felt to be undesirable. But this kind of motive certainly does not apply (as Porter believes) in the third colon, since, even with the avoided word-end at $7\frac{1}{2}$ (without accompanying word-end at 8 or 7), the closest that we can get to an adonic sequence is $\cup \cup - \cup$ (with a masculine caesura preceding) or $\cup - \cup$ (with a feminine). Now $\cup \cup - \cup$ is a very different matter from $- \cup \cup - \cup$, and I think it altogether improbable that it was avoided in these circumstances because of possibility of confusion with the verse-end "signature." This is largely a matter of personal opinion; but at the very least it must be agreed that the argument here is not a particularly strong one.

Moreover I am inclined to doubt the validity of the suggested motive even for the first part of the verse. Another possibility is that, since two of the three avoided positions for word-end (discounting the obvious position 6, when there is no break at 5 or $5\frac{1}{2}$), and the two which are in any case allied because they involve trochaic cuts, are symmetrically disposed about the most common and important division of the verse, that is, the feminine caesura, then their motives are corresponding ones. To put it schematically, the inhibitions on trochaic word-ends operate in the following positions, relative to the frequent and pivotal trochaic cut of the feminine caesura:

$$\overset{\quad\quad\quad 3\frac{1}{2}\quad\quad 5\frac{1}{2}\quad\quad 7\frac{1}{2}}{- \cup \cup - \cup \cup - \cup \,|\, \cup - \cup \cup - \cup \cup - \cup}$$
$$\quad\quad\quad\quad \wedge \quad\quad\quad\quad\quad \wedge$$

no break in the stream of sound, but are very closely attached to the word which precedes them. I do not see how we can tell which was the practice of the Homeric singers. On the whole it seems to me more likely that there *was* a break before the invocation. The normative effect of the commoner rhythmical pattern may have minimized the break in ostensibly irregular or unusual verses like the one under consideration; but that is a different matter.

If avoidance of a clausula does not help to explain the inhibition at $7\frac{1}{2}$, then on this view it would also be irrelevant to word-end at $3\frac{1}{2}$ (or, at the most, a purely secondary consideration).

However, Porter's adonic-sequence argument is itself supplementary; the main reason for the restrictions, in his view, is that the surrogate caesuras at 2 and 9 (for that is where he, unlike Fränkel, places the C^2 caesura, C^2, A^2, B^2 being the notation adopted for the secondary caesuras) "are not themselves adequate to express the form [i.e. of the colon] but must receive the negative support of avoided word-ends" (*op. cit.* p. 16). Fränkel, as we have seen, expresses the matter somewhat differently, mainly in terms of his "heavy words" which bridge the usual division between cola; but essentially he and Porter agree in believing that the reason for the word-end inhibitions is the need either to maintain, or unambiguously to bridge, the regular cola into which the verse was felt to fall. Yet even against this basic idea the hypothesis of corresponding motives for inhibitions at corresponding trochaic positions might have some force. It is easy to see, from Fränkel's picture, that a "heavy word" which bridges over the usual caesuras at either 8 or 7 must *eo ipso* bridge over the possible division at position $7\frac{1}{2}$, which intervenes. It is not so easy to see why a "heavy word" which bridges over the usual caesuras at 3 or 2 must necessarily bridge over the possible division at $3\frac{1}{2}$, since that division lies outside, and not within, the range of usual word-ends. Fränkel thinks that since the usual positions for caesura have been bridged, then the bridge must be extended to the next main caesural point, but there seems to be no real *reason* for this belief. If, in his view, position $1\frac{1}{2}$ is a possible alternate for 3 or 2, as a point at which cola can be envisaged as dividing, then why should not $3\frac{1}{2}$ be an alternate too? Perhaps that is arguing too much *ad hominem*; for I, like Porter, am not happy about Fränkel's desire to extend the A caesura to positions $1\frac{1}{2}$ and 1. But, even accepting Porter's amendment here, it is difficult to see why

e.g. $- \cup \overset{1\frac{1}{2}}{\big|} \cup - \cup \cup -$ should be acceptable and $- \cup \cup - \cup \overset{3\frac{1}{2}}{\big|} \cup -$

not so—though here Porter adduces his adonic-cadence argument. That is a different kind of argument, of course, quite unconnected with the idea of the four cola; and I shall later suggest that other rhythmical considerations (of a general kind) might be considered as alternative explanations of the word-end inhibitions.

One feels sympathy with Porter's view that a third colon of trochaic or spondaic value merely, as entailed by Fränkel's feeling that position 7 must be the alternative C caesura, is unrealistic, and prejudicial to the idea of a colon as any kind of word-group.[5] Yet Porter's own suggestion that the alternative C caesura falls not at 7 but at 9 is equally unsatisfactory, though for different reasons. The truth is that word-end at 9, where there is no preceding word-break either at 8 (agreed to be the regular C caesura) or at 7, occurs in only 8·8 % of Iliadic, 8·2 % of Odyssean verses.[6] Thus it is very difficult to consider 9 as a regular position for a significant caesura, since this proportion of occurrences is just about equal to that from which the A caesura, for example, is missing altogether by Porter's count (his Table I (*b*), p. 51). Thus those verses which have word-end at 9 but not at 7 or 8 should probably be envisaged, as by Fränkel, as verses in which the third and fourth cola coalesce. Moreover of verses which have word-end at 9 but not 8, almost half have word-end at 7 as well (Porter's Table XX (*b*), p. 61). In fact 7 is a common position for word-end, unlike position 9: 45·4% of Iliadic, 51·7% of Odyssean verses have word-break there (Table XVII (*a*) and (*b*), p. 60). Furthermore 19·8 % and 25·4 % of verses respectively from each poem have word-end at both 7 and 8 (Table XIX, p. 61), so that approximately 25 % of verses in each case have word-end at 7 when there is no C[1]

---

5. Admittedly L. E. Rossi, *Studi Urbinati*, 39 (1965), 239 ff., has shown that in some cases the short cola (on the Fränkel hypothesis, which he substantially accepts) bear special emphasis. But I doubt whether the majority of instances can be justified in this way.

6. On the basis of Porter's 1000-line sample of each poem; see his Table IV (*c*) and (*d*), *op. cit.* p. 54.

caesura at 8. If there is a secondary position for division between the third and fourth cola, then Fränkel is undoubtedly right that it must be in the fourth foot, at position 7, and Porter is undoubtedly wrong in pressing for the statistically negligible position 9. But that still leaves us with the difficulty that Fränkel's third colon, in the case of C^2 caesura at 7, is absurdly short, not really a colon at all.[7] Finally anyone who distrusts statistics (which are the only reliable means of control, in fact, in cases like this; we may be thankful to Porter for providing them, even though they do not on this occasion support his own case) can resort to the much inferior test of reading verses with word-end at 9 and not at 8 or 7 (or of course $7\frac{1}{2}$): however he reads such verses, he will not (I believe) find that their latter parts fall into two cola of any kind whatever.[8]

The result seems to be that neither Fränkel nor Porter can suggest satisfactory alternative positions for the caesuras separating their first two, and their last two, cola. In the case of their C^2 caesuras either we must accept Fränkel's unnaturally short third colon, if the break is to be envisaged at position 7, or we must accept Porter's statistically unsatisfactory break at position 9. Alternatively, of course, we can say that there *is* no "alternate" to the bucolic caesura, and that in the nearly 40% of Homeric verses which do not have that caesura the latter part of the verse does not in practice normally fall into two word-groups. Similarly in the case of the A^2 caesura: Fränkel's device of extending it to positions $1\frac{1}{2}$ or even 1 gives an unnaturally short first colon, and Porter is surely right in rejecting this solution. On the other hand his concession that verses with word-end at $1\frac{1}{2}$ or 1, and not at 3 or 2, involve a bridging-over of the first two cola, necessary though it seems to be, implies that something over 8% of Homeric verses (without counting those that do not observe the inhibitions at $3\frac{1}{2}$ and 4) depart

---

7. Though see note 5 above.

8. Take for example xvi.18, νηυσὶν ἔπι γλαφυρῇσιν ὑπερβασίης ἕνεκα σφῆς, or xvi.36, εἰ δέ τινα φρεσὶ σῇσι θεοπροπίην ἀλεείνεις, or xvi.41, αἴ κ᾽ ἐμὲ σοὶ ἴσκοντες ἀπόσχωνται πολέμοιο.

from the assumed colometric structure. That is not very serious, perhaps, and the impediments to the theory in the first part of the line are not in this respect so substantial as those that seem to apply in the second; but more will be said later about word-break in the first part.

It is time to consider the essential question of what is meant by a "colon" in this context. Is a colon a unit of meaning? Or is it simply a rhythmical unit, unconnected with semantic divisions within the verse? Fränkel's answer is plain, that it is in essence a unit of meaning. Yet this does not really accord with the facts. Many Homeric verses, even among those which show the common pattern of A^1, B^1, C^1 caesura, simply do not fall into four sense-units. Moreover Fränkel's own very short first and third cola (in the event of A^2 or C^2 caesuras), which are relatively frequent, for the most part form sense-units only in so far as any single word is a sense-unit. It is true that in this case they are not non-units or anti-units, as a collocation of two or more words may be; but they do not really fit in with the idea of the verse as composed of four word-groups. Now it would clearly be wrong to be too exigent about what composes a "unit of meaning"; we cannot expect that the hexameter verse should be composed of four complete utterances. A unit of meaning should be envisaged, rather, as a clause, or a phrase, or the subject of a sentence (with or without epithet), or its predicate, or its verb (with or without adverbial material), or its object (with or without epithet). Sometimes an epithet, or group of epithets, might form a colon separate from that which contained or included their noun (though normally only if the sense is predicative); and adverbial material may clearly stand on its own, in a colon separate from that of the verb. Thus xvi.2, Πάτροκλος δ' $\overset{A^1}{}$ Ἀχιλῆϊ $\overset{B^1}{}$ παρίστατο, $\overset{C^1}{}$ ποιμένι λαῶν, could justifiably be envisaged as having four cola (three of them, as it happens, consisting of a single word, if δ' be not counted) which are units of meaning in this sense, and not just in the more restricted sense in which any word is a unit of meaning. But what about e.g. XVI.4, ἥ τε κατ' αἰγίλιπος πέτρης δνοφερὸν χέει

$\overset{A^2}{}$ $\overset{B^2}{}$ $\overset{(C^2)}{}$ $\overset{(C^2)}{}$

ὕδωρ? Here the separation of αἰγίλιπος from its noun πέτρης (and
of both from their preposition) is disruptive of the sentence;
and so, if we accepted Porter's C² caesura, is the separation
of δνοφερὸν from ὕδωρ. In the case of XVI.6, καί μιν φωνή-

$\overset{A^2}{}$

$\overset{B^2}{}$ $\overset{(C^2)}{}$

σας ἔπεα πτερόεντα προσηύδα, the attempt to establish a semantic
division between καί μιν and φωνήσας is hardly a happy one;
moreover Fränkel's analysis means that ἔπεα is to form one
colon, while its epithet falls within another. That is out of the
question in this instance; either ἔπεα πτερόεντα must be taken
together as one colon, προσηύδα as another (but that is to be
rejected since 9½ is not a statistically viable position for colon-
division), or the whole second part of the verse, from the main
caesura onward, is to be taken as a sense-unit.

It does not take long, or the examination of many Homeric
verses, to see that the four-colon theory, if it is to stand at all,
cannot stand if "colon" is to imply "semantic unit," *tout simple*.
This, indeed, is another point at which Porter is able to improve
on Fränkel's theory, for he argues that the four cola are in
origin rhythmical cola (and that their divisions are not, as
Fränkel called them, "Sinneseinschnitte"). Each of them is "an
expected sequence of syllables produced by a brief rhythmical
impulse" (*op. cit.* p. 17); that was how the hexameter verse
came into being, and to ask why the first colon has that particular
length "is like asking why a glyconic may not be substituted for
the first line of a Sapphic strophe" (p. 37). We are at least free
here from the attempt to "explain" the structure of the hexameter in terms of the compiling of shorter verse-units, though I
doubt whether it is necessary to be quite so agnostic as Porter.
Porter is more plausible in his contention that these brief
rhythmical impulses must have had what he terms a "normative
effect," that they must have affected the semantic articulation
of the verse and imposed their own divisions (which were
indeed word-end divisions) upon the sense of the sentence. Thus

the cola frequently end up as sense-units *in effect,* and the kind of articulation of the meaning which we find when we read Homeric verses with awareness of the *rhythmical* cola is what was actually attained by singers in antiquity.

Since the colon is normally limited by word-end, which determines the pitch at the end of the colon and thus the pitch-pattern of the colon as a whole, there is an initial attraction in Porter's supplementary idea that "It is quite possible...that a result of the colometric structure of the line was a four-cycle pitch-pattern which constituted the melody of the line" (p. 26). That word-ends should be systematically disposed throughout the verse partly in order to determine and regularize a basic pitch-melody is barely conceivable; but, if this was an original motive for the colometric division, it must have ceased to operate as the hexameter developed, or Alexandrian accentuation must have been very faulty as a means of revealing archaic τόνος, since there seems to be no correspondence in the pitch-pattern at the ends of assumed cola in Homer.

That the four apparent cola are rhythmical in essence but very often have a normative effect on meaning is hard to disprove, since cases in which the articulation of sense does not correspond with the colon-limits can be explained as cases in which the normative tendency did not operate; after all, normative tendencies do not function invariably, and it is a fact that the effects of rhythm on meaning in Shakespeare, for example, are frequent but not by any means invariable or consistent. In order to test the four-colon theory further (and, as we have seen, it has already displayed some internal difficulties) it is prudent to try to answer the following questions:

(1) How common *is* the four-colon verse, and how often can verses which have word-end in the A, B, C positions be equally well, or better, explained as two- or three-colon verses (using, in this case, the reasonable articulation of sense as the criterion of "better")?

(2) Are there other factors which might explain, as well as or better than the four-colon theory, the prevalence of word-end in

certain positions in the verse, and also the inhibitions on word-end in other positions?

Before attempting to settle these questions I should say that they have already been answered, briefly but firmly, by A. M. Dale in her survey-article in *Lustrum*, 2 (1957), 29 ff. Professor Dale thinks that "as a mode of hearing the hexameter and of apprehending its grace and the unending subtlety of its metrical in relation to its rhetorical content, F.[ränkel]'s contribution is of the highest value" (p. 32), but that nevertheless "the older idea that the fundamental division of the hexameter is into two cola stands the test better than F.'s postulate of a fourfold line." She also considers that the inhibitions, at least, should be explained by factors other than the divisions between cola; for example the rarity of the amphibrach word-type ($\cup - \cup$) is due to three factors, of which one is "the avoidance of contiguous trochaic cuts with their famous 'bouncing' effect (λ 598)."[9] This, as will be seen, is a fruitful idea; though her other suggested factors, namely avoidance of even single trochaic cuts (except at positions $1\frac{1}{2}$ and $5\frac{1}{2}$) and mere observance of "Hermann's bridge," are not so happy. Professor Dale emphasized one further point in the course of her trenchant and all too brief criticism: that Fränkel's claim in favor of his four-colon theory, that it gave a *positive* explanation for the word-end inhibitions without the need for rules or taboos, has not much force (except perhaps to a modern logician); there is no reason why the epic singers should not have observed certain rhythmical taboos, even if the original reasons for those taboos had been forgotten. I think that Dale is correct here, and that Fränkel's theory, however ingeniously it succeeds in reducing the structural laws of the hexameter and abolishing prohibitions like Meyer's law

9. *Op. cit.* p. 34. The case of *Od.* 11.598 will be considered below, p. 97. Dale and Porter (*Yale Classical Studies*, 12 (1951), 9f.) rightly refute the error of E. O'Neill, Jr. (*ibid.* 8 (1942), 103 ff.) in thinking that e.g. the rarity of amphibrach words was necessarily the cause rather than the effect of broader structural characteristics of the hexameter verse; but see p. 104 below.

and Hermann's bridge, is not therefore made more probable in itself and must stand on its other merits.

The first question can be answered in part from Porter's statistics: the A^1, B^1 and C^1 caesuras each occur in about three out of five lines of Homer (*op. cit.* p. 10); they all occur together in about one out of four lines (*ibid.* Table I, p. 51), and seven out of ten lines have combinations of A, B and C caesuras either primary or secondary.[10] Even when these figures are somewhat amended to take account of overoptimism about a C^2 caesura, they are still impressive. Certainly the occurrence of word-end at certain positions throughout the verse cannot simply be due to chance; though whether it is due to a single factor or cause, and that a tendency to divide the verse into regular rhythmical cola, is not yet proved. Not much more progress can be made in this particular direction by purely statistical examination; but before we turn to the second of our two questions it is worth examining more closely the relation of possible sense-divisions to those implied by the four-colon verse. The criteria are necessarily somewhat subjective; one would like to be able to present a factual examination of an adequate sample of verses; but in order to avoid giving even the appearance of a scientific approach to what cannot be presented or decided scientifically, I am simply going to examine a shorter passage, in what seems to be fairly typical Iliadic language, from book XVI.[11] Vertical strokes mark off the rhythmical cola

10. *Ibid.* Porter in his statistics is naturally taking his own C^2 and A^2 positions (at positions 9 and 2 respectively), not those of Fränkel (at 7, and 2, $1\frac{1}{2}$ or 1). Since he seems to be wrong about C^2, though right about A^2, his results cannot be accepted without reserve. My own position is that there is nothing that can be accepted as a regular C alternate in default of the bucolic caesura, and therefore that the proportion of verses containing a C caesura is about six out of ten only. Porter's other proportions, cited above, have to be reduced accordingly.

11. Most of my examples are drawn from this book, which is also the sample used for the following study (on pp. 105 ff.) of enjambment and associated phenomena. Its qualities as a sample are outlined on pp. 117 f. The analysis on p. 146 shows that the present passage is low in part-verse cumulation, high in verse-end strong stops.

according to the Porter view, though without C² caesura and usually with preference for A¹ and B¹ over A² and B². Underlining marks off what seem to be sense-cola, in a fairly liberal sense of the term, and with some concession to the idea that rhythmical cola may impose themselves, in certain cases, on the sense. To the right of each verse are two numbers: the first the total of the rhythmical cola, the second of the sense-cola. Square brackets around the second indicate that the sense-cola, though the same in number as the rhythmical, do not exactly correspond.

	῏Η ῥα, καὶ ἐξ | ὀχέων | σὺν τεύχεσιν | ἆλτο χαμᾶζε.	4:[4]
	Πάτροκλος δ' | ἑτέρωθεν, | ἐπεὶ ἴδεν, | ἔκθορε δίφρου.	4:4
	οἱ δ' ὥς τ' | αἰγυπιοὶ | γαμψώνυχες | ἀγκυλοχεῖλαι	4:2
	πέτρῃ ἐφ' | ὑψηλῇ | μεγάλα κλάζοντε μάχωνται,	3:2
430	ὥς οἱ | κεκλήγοντες | ἐπ' ἀλλήλοισιν ὄρουσαν.	3:3
	τοὺς δὲ ἰδὼν | ἐλέησε | Κρόνου πάις | ἀγκυλομήτεω,	4:3
	῞Ηρην δὲ | προσέειπε | κασιγνήτην ἄλοχόν τε·	3:3
	"ὤ μοι ἐγών, | ὅ τέ μοι | Σαρπηδόνα, | φίλτατον ἀνδρῶν,	4:4
	μοῖρ' ὑπὸ | Πατρόκλοιο | Μενοιτιάδαο δαμῆναι.	3:[3]
435	διχθὰ δέ μοι | κραδίη | μέμονε φρεσὶν | ὁρμαίνοντι,	4:3
	ἤ μιν | ζωὸν ἐόντα | μάχης ἄπο | δακρυοέσσης	4:2
	θείω ἀναρπάξας | Λυκίης ἐν | πίονι δήμῳ,	3:2
	ἦ ἤδη | ὑπὸ χερσὶ | Μενοιτιάδαο δαμάσσω."	3:[3]
	Τὸν δ' ἠμείβετ' ἔπειτα | βοῶπις | πότνια ῞Ηρη·	3:2
440	"αἰνότατε | Κρονίδη, | ποῖον τὸν | μῦθον ἔειπες.	4:2
	ἄνδρα | θνητὸν ἐόντα, | πάλαι πεπρωμένον αἴσῃ,	3:2
	ἂψ ἐθέλεις | θανάτοιο | δυσηχέος | ἐξαναλῦσαι;	4:3
	ἔρδ'· ἀτὰρ | οὔ τοι πάντες | ἐπαινέομεν θεοὶ ἄλλοι.	3:[3]
	ἄλλο δέ τοι | ἐρέω, | σὺ δ' ἐνὶ φρεσὶ | βάλλεο σῇσιν·	4:3
445	αἴ κε ζὼν | πέμψῃς | Σαρπηδόνα | ὅνδε δόμονδε,	4:3
	φράζεο | μή τις ἔπειτα | θεῶν ἐθέλῃσι καὶ ἄλλος	3:[3]
	πέμπειν | ὃν φίλον υἱὸν | ἀπὸ κρατερῆς ὑσμίνης·	3:2

πολλοὶ γὰρ | περὶ ἄστυ | μέγα Πριάμοιο μάχονται   3:[3]

υἱέες | ἀθανάτων, | τοῖσιν κότον | αἰνὸν ἐνήσεις."   4:2

(xvi.426 ff.)

As already stated, some concession has been made, in the marking off of possible sense-cola, to the normative effects of the assumed rhythmical cola; but it is impossible to present more than a personal, fallible and possibly inconsistent conjecture here. Thus line 435, for instance, might obviously be regarded as falling into different sense-groups from those suggested above; perhaps I should have granted more to the normative effect of the A caesura and given κραδίη independent status, or linked it with its verb; and equally the second half of the verse might be regarded as a single sense unit. Similarly the long epithets of 428 might deserve separate status, and the close linking of μεγάλα κλάζοντε and μάχωνται in 429 is admittedly influenced by the lack of the C-break. Indeed all the verses marked here as having only two sense-units could, obviously, be envisaged as having additional subdivisions; though I believe the suggested bipartite division is a natural one. There may be mistakes here and elsewhere, but I hope that the general trend of my analysis might be roughly correct. The results (which convey a hint rather than an established conclusion) are interesting: only 12 of the 24 verses are divided into the assumed four cola;[12] and only two verses, 427 and 433, have four rhythmical cola which can reasonably be regarded as corresponding exactly with possible sense-divisions. Even if we allow the dubious C² caesuras (both together), only one or two more verses can be added to this latter total of two. Now it is the degree of noncorrespondence between reasonable sense-units and the assumed cola that is worrying; more allowance for normative effect could be made than has actually been made,

12. If we were to allow the Fränkel C² caesura at position 7, another five verses could be transferred from the three-colon to the four-colon category, making 19 out of 24 verses, i.e. just about the 7 out of 10 average (p. 87 above).

in some verses, but there are several others (e.g. 426, 436, 440), in which this could not be done. The same disagreement between rhythmical and sense cola applies in the three-colon verses. Of course many of the assumed colon-breaks *are* also sense-breaks. That is not surprising in the cases of the main B caesura and of the bucolic caesura; we know that there is often a sense-break in those positions without having to have it proved by a colometric theory and statistics. But the four-colon theory implies a high degree of correspondence between sense and rhythm; for, even on Porter's view that the cola are in origin and essence rhythmical cola, their predominant normative effect is an inevitable consequence. Moreover at the one point which is not in a sense "obvious," namely the A caesura, at least half of the verses in our short sample passage fail to show a correspondence between assumed rhythmical break and possible sense-break. Finally it may be observed that nine verses show a plausible division into *two* cola, separated by the main B caesura—and this without invoking the possible normative effect of a two-colon system, which would certainly increase the proportion.

Thus it seems that the answer to question (1) on p. 85 above is not altogether favorable to the four-colon theory; that, if the unsatisfactory C^2 caesura is discounted, then the number of verses which must be regarded as four-colon (rather than three- or two-colon) verses is not significantly high, especially when the evidence of natural or possible sense-divisions is brought to bear. With this in mind one proceeds with greater interest to the attempt to answer question (2): "Are there other factors which might explain, as well as or better than the four-colon theory, the prevalence of word-end in certain positions in the verse, and also the inhibitions on word-end in other positions?"

I believe that there is a certain *combination of factors* which can stand as a reasonable alternative to the four-colon theory, and which avoids that theory's disadvantages. (Again I emphasize that the apparent unity and simplicity of Fränkel's theory is not necessarily in its favor in a problem like that of the aetiology of a complicated metrical form.) Let us take the apparent positive word-end rules first, and the inhibitions later. Porter asserted, on p. 10 of his article, that "The assumption that the hexameter is composed of short cola is forced by the fact that word-ends occur in certain positions within the line much more frequently than would be expected *ceteris paribus*." This, of course, to some extent begs the question; but first it is useful to be reminded that the positive tendencies are restricted to the main, central caesura at position 5 or 5½, to the bucolic caesura at 8, and to the apparent A caesura at 2 or 3.[13] Of these the first is a very strong tendency indeed: the hexameter verse normally had to have word-end just before but not at its central point. Very often that division coincides with a sense-articulation, and we may properly speak of at least a two-colon verse. The bucolic caesura occurs in just over six verses out of ten, and is closely associated, by position at least, with the verse-end sequence or signature. Could not that be its justification—that the charac-teristic rhythmical sequence at the end of the verse tends to be reinforced by a minimal semantic articulation (that is, a division between words) at its starting-point? Whatever the structural development of the hexameter in historical terms, that seems quite probable. We can call those last two feet a "colon," if we wish; but it is not an invariable colon, and it has been seen that alternatives claimed by referring to word-end at 7 or 9 are not satisfactory. Word-end at 9 (and not at 7, 7½, or 8) is statistically negligible, on the one hand. Word-end at 7 (and not at 7½ or 8), on the other, is bound to be fairly frequent *simply because of the common lengths of available word-units* (that is, of Greek words). For the moment I am assuming that word-end at 7½, and not in the adjacent positions, was avoided for reasons of euphony unconnected with any colometric structure; that assumption will be considered later. That being so, in verses where there is no bucolic caesura at 8, in order to avoid word-

13. Word-break at position 7 almost qualifies, but not quite. It occurs in almost half the total of Homeric verses (p. 81 above); but this is largely due to word-length probabilities, on which see below.

end at 7 the poet had to produce a word of the minimum value
$--\smile\smile-$ (with masculine central caesura) or $\smile-\smile\smile-$ (with
feminine). But words of this length are comparatively rare in
the poetical vocabulary (that is not quite so simple a statement
as it looks, but I think it may be accepted for the purposes of the
present argument); so that in practice we find word-end at 7 as
a quite frequent "alternative" to word-end at 8, without any
implications for a fixed colometric structure.[14]

So far we may agree that most verses fall into two cola at the
B caesura, and over half can be regarded as being further
divided, in the second of these cola, by the bucolic caesura: they
might therefore be envisaged as three-colon lines. Yet the
frequency of the latter division is not sufficient to justify any
theory about normative colometric structure. What, then, about
the A caesura in the first part of the verse, and the two short
initial cola which it is assumed, on the Fränkel–Porter view, to
mark off? It seems quite possible that word-length availability
provides the proper explanation here too, though not so neatly
as in the second half of the verse. An initial difficulty is that it is
extremely hard to arrive at a noncircular estimate of the
probabilities of word-end, in relation to available word-types,
at positions 2 and 3. As a preliminary it may be observed that
the absence of word-end from either position, if combined with
the assumption of a euphonic explanation of some kind for the
inhibitions at $3\frac{1}{2}$ and 4, entails the use of long words of a
minimum value of $\smile-\smile\smile-$ (that is, a mora longer than
Fränkel's minimum "heavy words"). Words longer than that
are very rare in Homer, quite rare in Greek; whereas words of
this minimum value, according to O'Neill's 1000-line samples
from the *Iliad* and the *Odyssey*, occur in about 15 % of Homeric
lines, in about 10 % in the required position ending at the
masculine (B^2) caesura. The result is, on this evidence, that
nearly nine verses out of ten will have word-end at either
position 2 or position 3, quite apart from any possibility of

14. O'Neill's tables 33 and 34 show the very severe drop in Homeric
words longer than 4 syllables or 6 morae; cf. p. 93.

colometric structure. Unfortunately this evidence is not decisive, since the apparent rarity or undesirability of such long words might itself be affected by a positive desire (caused, for example, by colometry) to have word-end at 2 or 3. Admittedly words of 7 morae and above are especially uncommon even in other parts of the verse; so that some probability remains that, if 3½ and 4 are avoided positions for word-end in many verses, then we are bound to find very frequent word-end at either 3 or 2.

There is a further possible difficulty in an explanation of this kind. Does the availability of word-types account for the predominance of word-end at 3 over word-end at 2? First of all we must ask how strong this predominance is. It is not so strong as the use of Porter's Table II might suggest: his first cola extending to the A^1 caesura (position 3) are about twice as numerous as those extending to the A^2 caesura (position 2), because where there is both an A^1 and an A^2 caesura he naturally counts the "primary" caesura, on his view, and not the secondary one. Thus many verses which have word-end at 3 also have word-end at 2. This is only to be expected, incidentally, from the availability of words composed of a single long syllable—by far the commonest of all word-types. The ratio of verses with word-end at 3 (and not at 2) to those with word-end at 2 (and not at 3) is in fact 364:291.[15] Thus there does seem to be a predominance of word-end at 3 over word-end at 2, but it is not a very marked one. Whether or not this predominance can be explained solely with reference to available word-types is very hard to answer with confidence: on the whole my guess is that it cannot, and that the total availability of word-types would favor neither position. No sort of calculation which I can devise on the basis of the O'Neill–Porter tables is free from the possibility of serious distortion, so it is fairer to make no claim here stronger than one founded on personal impression. But in any event, if some other factor is required to account for a

15. Each of these figures is a mean of the totals for the *Iliad* and *Odyssey*, and represents the number of occurrences in a 1000-line sample (Porter, *op. cit.* table II).

slight predominance of word-end at 3 over word-end at 2, it
need not be a factor involving the four-colon theory. Indeed it
is not hard to think of one obvious possibility: the desire to have
word-end within the metron rather than coinciding with its
terminus—in more technical language, to have caesura in its
narrower sense rather than diaeresis. The one obvious exception
to this is the bucolic diaeresis; but this seems to be a special case
in any event, and the separation of the last two metrical feet
into a distinctive colon seems to be connected with the special
rhythmical status of the end of the verse as a clausula. In other
parts of the verse, as in the B caesura, internal word-break may
well have been preferred (and, even in the first foot, word-break
after the first longum). This not only increases the subtlety of
the tension or interplay between the basic rhythmical element
(the dactyl) and the basic semantic element (the word), it also
avoids overemphasizing the basic rhythmical element at the
expense of the rhythmical unity of the whole verse by making it
coincide with a succession of word-divisions. Thus verses in
which word-end falls as follows were avoided:

$$- \smile\smile \mid - \smile\smile \mid - \mid \smile\smile \mid - \smile\smile \mid - \smile\smile \mid - \smile.[16]$$

If these general considerations are valid, then the reason for
predominance of word-end at 3 over word-end at 2 need not be
anything to do with colometric structure.[17]

We may now turn from the positive word-end tendencies to
the inhibitions on word-end. Ignoring the inhibition at position

16. Admittedly this is very difficult to check, because of the possible
interference of other factors. Also word-divisions like $- \smile\smile \mid$ and $\mid - \smile \smile \mid -\smile$
are obviously quite common (Porter, Tables II (*b*) and V (*a*)), though the
latter, for example, accounts for only about one-quarter of the possible
word-combinations from the bucolic caesura to the end of the verse.

17. There are, of course, other possible special factors: Mr A. M. Parry
points out, for example, that runover cumulation words (on which see
pp. 114 ff.) are often choriambic participles or patronymics, and that the
choriamb ending at position 3 provides "a strong rhythmical means of
passing from one verse to the next."

6, whose explanation is obvious, we may first consider the inhibition at 4. This is different in kind from those at $3\frac{1}{2}$ and $7\frac{1}{2}$ in that it does not involve a trochaic cut. The four-colon theory had an explanation here which applies also to $3\frac{1}{2}$: that if the main caesural area is to be bridged, then it must be firmly bridged and not prejudiced by word-division in adjacent positions. That explanation is less effective for 4 than for $3\frac{1}{2}$, in any case, and other possible deficiencies have already been noted on pp. 79 ff. I can offer two possible and different types of explanation for the inhibition at 4: first that it avoids the coincidence of word-end and metron-end, as described in the preceding paragraph; secondly that in the case of verses with B² (masculine) caesura it avoids ending the first part of the verse with a monosyllable. There is certainly an inhibition on monosyllables (except for special effects) at the end of the verse, and a similar feeling might have applied to the end of its first part or first major colon. That inhibition may then have affected, by extension, verses with feminine caesura too; among other things we must bear in mind here the schematizing influence of the formular language of the epic, which would tend to generalize the effects of particular rhythmical situations. Yet avoidance of the monosyllabic ending was not total: the inhibition was virtually abandoned if there was preceding word-end at 3, and reduced if there was preceding word-end at 2. Again, however, this detail is explicable in terms of euphony rather than of a fixed colometric structure, since the effect of final monosyllable is obviously more abrupt if the monosyllable is preceded by a heavy word. Thus e.g. $-\vdots\underset{\smile}{\smile}\smile-\mid\smile\smile\mid\overset{4}{-}\overset{5}{\mid}$ is permissible, and even $-\underset{\smile}{\smile}\mid-\smile\smile\mid\overset{4}{-}\overset{5}{\mid}$ can be tolerated on occasion, but $-\vdots\smile\vdots\smile-\smile\smile\mid\overset{4}{-}\overset{5}{\mid}$ is avoided.

The inhibitions at $3\frac{1}{2}$ and $7\frac{1}{2}$, being concerned with trochaic cuts equally disposed about the B¹ trochaic caesura at position $5\frac{1}{2}$, may well have a corresponding cause; probably, I would guess, do so. Yet they are very different in their severity:

apparent violations of the inhibition on word-end at $7\frac{1}{2}$ (except with accompanying break at 7 or 8) occur roughly once in a thousand Homeric verses, while violations of the inhibition at $3\frac{1}{2}$ (unless there is word-end at 3 or 2) are really quite common. Clearly the significant difference between the two positions in the verse lies not in their relation to the main caesura, but rather in the proximity of $7\frac{1}{2}$ to the bucolic caesura and to the introduction of the verse-end sequence. It may be that something close to the Fränkel type of explanation is correct here, for we have seen that in effect there *are* often two rhythmical cola in the second part of the verse. Thus if word-break is *not* to be observed before the final rhythmical sequence, then it might have seemed important to avoid a sequence only a single mora longer, masquerading, as it were, as the real thing. Yet is that really a plausible argument for such a stringent rule? After all, caesura at 7 is perfectly permissible, if there is no caesura at 8; and that is only a single mora earlier than caesura at $7\frac{1}{2}$. Surely the fact that $7\frac{1}{2}$ involves a *trochaic* cut must have something to do with the matter, after all.

What is there about trochaic caesuras which makes them different in effect from caesuras after the first longum? There is nothing improper about trochaic caesuras as such; indeed the main and most frequent of all caesuras in the hexameter verse is a trochaic caesura. Moreover trochaic cuts are quite common in the first and the fifth feet. The answer presumably lies in some general consequence like the "bouncing effect" said by Professor Dale to be produced by contiguous trochaic cuts (p. 86 above). Probably even "bouncing" goes too far. It may be an apt metaphor for the way such cuts sound when we recite the verse with our own habits of pitch and stress and our own ways of relating words to each other; yet it may be misleading for the sound of the verse as sung by an ancient Greek ἀοιδός. The "bouncing" metaphor is probably determined by the onomatopoeic effect of one of the most famous Homeric instances of contiguous trochaic cuts, an instance cited by Dale herself: *Od.* 11.598, αὖτις ἔπειτα πέδονδε κυλίνδετο λᾶας ἀναιδής.

The stone keeps bounding down the hill: that is the idea that most commentators have thought the verse, with its five dactyls, its three successive (and total of four) trochaic cuts, and its violation of the inhibition at $3\frac{1}{2}$, is meant to imply by its sheer sound and rhythm. But is it rather the jerkiness of the stone's progress, or alternatively the regularity and inevitability of its rolling downhill, time after time, that is intended? "Bouncing" implies going up and down, and suggests pitch-elevation; but we really do not know what effect word-end as such had on the stream of sound and its pitch-pattern. In short I feel confident, like Professor Dale, that contiguous trochaic cuts *could* produce a characteristic effect which for the purposes of ordinary expression was found to be unpleasant or distracting; but we cannot tell precisely what this effect was, even to the point of applying to it metaphors like "bouncing."

Ever since Giseke and then Meyer noticed some kind of inhibition on word-end at $3\frac{1}{2}$, scholars have been vague about the circumstances in which the inhibition does or does not apply.[18] "Meyer's law" is in a thoroughly confused state; and I am not altogether sure that Fränkel, O'Neill and Porter have properly clarified its scope, let alone its cause. As defined by them the inhibition applies when there is word-end neither at position 3 nor at position 2; but that still leaves so many exceptions that one wonders whether the inhibition has been properly identified. What are we to say of an "inhibition" which mysteriously fails to apply to such common formulas as
τὸν (τὴν) δ' ἠμείβετ' ἔπειτα (47× *Il.*, 24× *Od.*), – ◡ ὑπόδρα ἰδών (17× *Il.*, 9× *Od.*), οἱ δ' ἐπ' ὀνείαθ' ἑτοῖμα προκείμενα χεῖρας ἴαλλον (3× *Il.*, 11× *Od.*)? Even if we overlook these, on the barely possible ground that *elision*[19] or a *digamma* altered the effect of a trochaic cut, other exceptions are numerous enough

18. B. Giseke, *Homerische Forschungen* (Leipzig 1814), pp. 101ff.; W. Meyer, *Sitzb. Bay. Akad.* (1884), 1004; cf. also J. van Leeuwen, *Mnemosyne*, 18 (1890), 265ff.

19. Van Leeuwen, *op. cit.* p. 271.

to have called up some desperate remedies. Porter, for example, tries to neutralize other examples by claiming that short final vowels like -ι in datives plural, or -α and -ε in verbs, conjunctions, and adverbs, "are not essential to the meaning of the word," do not really count, and so cannot be considered as actually preceding a valid caesura (*op. cit.* pp. 37 f.). Rather than pursuing such fleeting shadows of possibility I prefer to consider whether the inhibition has been correctly framed— whether verses like i.1, Μῆνιν ἄειδε, θεά (and an embarrassing number of others in the opening book of the *Iliad*), are really to be considered irregular at all.

My method has been to study the instances of ἔπειτα in the first twelve books of the *Iliad*, relying on Gehring's index; because I think that this word must be by far the commonest of the amphibrach words in Homer, and it is these words which by their metrical shape give rise to two successive trochaic cuts unprejudiced by other intervening word-end. Discarding cases where ἔπειτα comes at the end of the verse (and so entails only one trochaic cut), and the numerous cases of the formula τὸν δ' ἠμείβετ' ἔπειτα (on which I have commented above), there are 45 verses containing ἔπειτα in the first half of the *Iliad*. ἔπειτα δέ $\overset{7\frac{1}{2}}{}\overset{8}{}$ (which incidentally involves no breach of the inhibition at $7\frac{1}{2}$) occurs five times. Of the remaining 40 occurrences, all in the first part of the verse, no less than 17 entail violation of the assumed inhibition (and of these nearly all are unaffected by possible palliatives like elision). Thirteen of these violations are caused by $\overset{3\frac{1}{2}}{ἔπειτα}$ (e.g. v.36 τὸν μὲν $\overset{3\frac{1}{2}}{ἔπειτα}$ καθεῖσεν, xi.422 αὐτὰρ $\overset{3\frac{1}{2}}{ἔπειτα}$ Θόωνα), the other four by $\overset{5\frac{1}{2}}{ἔπειτα}$ preceded by a single long word (e.g. i.449, χερνίψαντο δ' $\overset{5\frac{1}{2}}{ἔπειτα}$). Now where an amphibrach word ends at position $3\frac{1}{2}$, it is frequently followed by a feminine caesura, that is, another trochaic cut, to give a series of three trochaic cuts. Thus the commonest cause of a violation is the placing of the amphibrach word to end at position $3\frac{1}{2}$, and a frequent consequence of this is that there will be three, not merely two, successive trochaic cuts.[20]

Quite possibly it is this succession not of two but of three contiguous trochaic cuts which was found undesirable—of cuts, moreover, which were separated by whole words, and therefore felt with their full force (whatever precisely that force was) and without the palliation or diversion of other, intervening, word-ends. Yet we must be careful not to exaggerate the effects of amphibrach words in producing apparent violations of the inhibition, merely because they are convenient to identify and to handle. Of the 25 violations in the first book of the *Iliad*, six are caused by τὸν δ᾽ ἠμείβετ᾽ ἔπειτα, another 12 by other words *longer* than amphibrachs ending at position $3\frac{1}{2}$, and only seven by amphibrach words ending there. Yet, since the proportion of "violations" in this book (in 25 verses out of 611), and to a less marked extent in all other parts of the Homeric poems, is so high as to suggest that the "rule" has been exaggerated, it is quite possible that an inhibition was felt *only* against amphibrach words and their effects, and that heavy words ending at $3\frac{1}{2}$ should be accepted as regular.

So far this is mere conjecture; but there is one important piece of supporting evidence. Amphibrach words are infrequent within the verse, in comparison with other word-types of four

20. Indeed in the present sample *all* the cases of ἔπειτα$^{3\frac{1}{2}}$ are followed by a feminine caesura, whereas the average of masculine to feminine caesura is normally about 2:3. It might seem, therefore, either that there was a special inhibition on verses whose first halves exemplified the symmetrical pattern $- \cup \mid \cup - \cup \mid \cup -$, or that a sequence of two trochaic cuts, in this part of the line, tended to generate a third. But this is not the general case, as consideration of other amphibrach words like γυναῖκα or ἔθηκε shows; the opening line of the *Iliad*, too, has ἄειδε$^{3\frac{1}{2}}$ followed by male caesura. The distribution with ἔπειτα is an object-lesson in the need for large samples; for after 13/13 cases of feminine caesura after ἔπειτα$^{3\frac{1}{2}}$ in the first twelve books of the *Iliad*, the next four occurrences all have masculine caesura following, and in the last twelve books as a whole only six out of thirteen cases of ἔπειτα$^{3\frac{1}{2}}$ are followed by feminine caesura so as to give three successive trochaic cuts.

morae and three syllables; but if amphibrachs ending at the
verse-end are included, then the occurrence is very similar to
that of anapaestic and dactylic words.[21] There is nothing in the
nature of amphibrach words as such, then, or in their availability,
to deter the early hexameter poets from using them. Yet when
we compare the ratio of verse-end to internal uses with the
ratio for other word-types which can occur with a final short
syllable at the verse-end, there is a very marked discrepancy:

	Word-type	Occurrences within verse		Occurrences at verse-end	
		Iliad	*Odyssey*	*Iliad*	*Odyssey*
(i)	$- \cup$	735	761	98	122
(ii)	$\cup - \cup$	95	85	176	187
(iii)	$\cup \cup - \cup$	166	136	86	63
(iv)	$- \cup \cup - \cup$	40	28	38	36

These figures are based on O'Neill's 1000-line sample from
each poem, and derived from his tables 5, 9, 13, and 22 (for
internal occurrences) and table 29 (for occurrences at the verse-
end, i.e. in position 12). The amphibrach word-type (ii) is
unique in that it occurs about twice as often at the verse-end as
within the verse; (i) and (iii) occur much less frequently at the
verse-end (as, other things being equal, one would expect, since
the verse-end position is only one out of three or more possible
positions); while the relative figures for (iv) are approximately
equal (this reflects the fewer available internal positions for this
word-type, together with avoidance of its adonic sequence
except at the verse-end or at position $5\frac{1}{2}$). In other words,
amphibrachs behave unexpectedly in occurring with relatively
high frequency at the verse-end and relatively low frequency
within the verse.

As usual, the conclusion to be drawn from this phenomenon
is not entirely straightforward. The frequency of amphibrach

21. E. O'Neill, Jr., *TCS*, 8 (1942), tables 7, 8, 9 on pp. 141f. Spondaic
words are more than twice as frequent (table 6 on p. 141). The figures for
verse-end words are not precisely accurate since certain forms are ambiguous
in the length of their final syllable.

words at the verse-end is surely to some extent (perhaps to a large extent) due to the analogy of $\cup--$, and that is the commonest single form at the verse-end by a substantial margin. Putting it in another way, a trochaic caesura in the fifth foot was the commonest of all types of word-division after the bucolic caesura.[22] Therefore there was a special demand for amphibrach words at the verse-end. But the fact that this demand was satisfied suggests that such words were freely available. Why then were they definitely avoided (as the middle column of (i), (ii), (iii) above shows, and as is confirmed by comparison with the number of internal occurrences of $\cup\cup-$ and $-\cup\cup$, O'Neill tables 7 and 8) in the internal positions taken together? I think the answer must lie in their production of successive trochaic cuts; and that the uninhibited frequency at the verse-end is in part, at least, due to the fact that in this position, and this position alone, is only a single trochaic cut caused. I have already shown that there is some evidence for believing that a sequence of three cuts, not two, was found objectionable; and that such a sequence was avoided with particular care in the second part of the verse because it was liable to interfere with the effect of the verse-end sequence.[23]

Thus, to take another actual example of an amphibrach word, ἔθηκε(ν) occurs 40 times in the *Iliad*: 30 times at the verse-end, nine times at position $5\frac{1}{2}$, once at $3\frac{1}{2}$. The last case produces three successive trochaic cuts, since a feminine caesura follows: v.122, γυῖα δ' ἔθηκεν ἐλαφρά, πόδας καὶ χεῖρας ὕπερθεν. This produces a definite infringement of the inhibition, even in

22. Porter, *YCS*, 12 (1951), table V(*a*) on p. 54. Actually $-\cup\cup\mid-\overset{12}{\cup}$ and $-\cup\mid\cup-\overset{12}{\cup}$ occur about equally in the *Iliad*, but the latter is considerably more popular in the *Odyssey*.

23. Thus the notorious infringement of the inhibition at $7\frac{1}{2}$, Πηλεὺς θήν μοι ἔπειτα γυναῖκα γαμέσσεται αὐτός (ix.394), would be even more offensive if there were a trochaic cut at $9\frac{1}{2}$ rather than $7\frac{1}{2}$. I believe that Maas was correct in thinking that Aristarchus' reading, γε μάσσεται, cannot be accepted because of the strained or pointless γε (P. Maas, *Greek Metre* (Oxford 1962), tr. H. Lloyd-Jones, p. 60).

the stricter form I should like to impose on it.[24] Of the nine
occurrences at $5\frac{1}{2}$, three produce infringements of the standard
form of the inhibition:

καί μ' ἀφνειὸν ἔθηκε, πολὺν δέ μοι ὤπασε λαόν   (ix.483)
ἐν στήθεσσιν ἔθηκε, καὶ ἐξέλετο φρένας ἐσθλάς   (xvii.470)
αὐδήεντα δ' ἔθηκε θεὰ λευκώλενος Ἥρη.   (xix.407)

All these cases I regard as perfectly harmless, since they produce
only two successive trochaic cuts, not three (and the same will
be the case with i.1, Μῆνιν ἄειδε, θεά, and similar verses, in
which the dangerous amphibrach in position $3\frac{1}{2}$ is followed by
a masculine and not a feminine caesura). Certainly one does
not *feel* that these verses are rhythmically offensive.

The advantages of the four-colon theory are that many early
hexameters do fall into four parts; these are often not sense-
units, but Porter's theory of the "normative effect" on meaning
of a "pattern of (rhythmical) expectation" is quite satisfying;
and Fränkel's idea of "heavy words" which bridge the whole
area where caesura is to be expected—an idea which certainly
works in the case of verses in which the main B caesura is
bridged—provides an attractive principle by which to judge the
apparent inhibitions at $3\frac{1}{2}$ and $7\frac{1}{2}$. The disadvantages of the
theory are that the first and third colons often disappear, or
must be envisaged as unrealistically short; that in many verses
the sense-division is not into four parts, however much the
"normative effect" is stretched, but into two parts or three;

24. It is possible that the infringement is deliberate, to produce a stylistic
effect of lightness, corresponding with Athene's lightening of Diomedes'
limbs. On the whole I believe this sort of explanation should be used very
cautiously; Porter perhaps overdoes it (*op. cit.* pp. 38ff.). Thus I doubt
whether Ζεύς, ἐτάραξε δὲ πόντον, ἐπισπέρχουσι δ' ἄελλαι (5.304) should
be defended on the ground that its irregularity reproduces that of the sea;
indeed on my view there *is* no irregularity. The real and rare breach of the
inhibition at $7\frac{1}{2}$ at vi.2, πολλὰ δ' ἄρ' ἔνθα καὶ ἔνθ' ἴθυσε μάχη πεδίοιο,
may help to reproduce the confusion of the battle, as Fränkel, Porter, and
others have thought; or it may just be a careless verse in this respect—for,
although the verse expresses confusion, it is not clear to me that the ignoring
of the inhibition significantly helps in this effect.

that the "heavy word" idea does not explain why positions $3\frac{1}{2}$ and 4 should be bridged, as well as 3 and 2; and that it still leaves an untidy number of apparent violations unaccounted for. I have suggested as an alternative (and in some respects more attractive) way of explaining the phenomena a complex of causes, some obvious and others less so: the B caesura is a structural division of the verse primarily designed to integrate it and prevent it from falling into two equal parts; the C caesura tends to introduce a distinct verse-end sequence; the tendency to caesura around the middle of the first "half" of the verse is due primarily to the average lengths of Greek words available in the poetical vocabulary, with the preference for caesura at 3 due largely to the preference for internal caesura except before the verse-end sequence; the inhibitions on word-end at $3\frac{1}{2}$ and $7\frac{1}{2}$ are caused by the desire to avoid any strong possibility of three successive trochaic cuts, that on 4 being due to the desire to avoid a monosyllabic ending, especially after a heavy word, to a major part of the verse.

This complex of different kinds of suggested causes is very different from the "beautiful" simplicity of Hermann Fränkel's genuinely admirable conception, but it may account for more of the phenomena, and more accurately. It does so, admittedly, by invoking criteria like "the avoidance of anticlimactic final monosyllables" and "the avoidance of undesirable rhythmical effects" about which we can know very little in their ancient form, and about which our modern responses are liable to be misleading. We tend to apply very crude metaphorical language to the basic elements of pitch, quantity, stress, rhythm, and sense, and my only consolation here is that skilled metrists like Professor Dale fall victim to the same temptation—can hardly, indeed, avoid it. Moreover there are special difficulties, like that of estimating the availability of word-types on the basis of the very material for which we are seeking rules affecting word-type distribution; and like that of properly gauging the effects of formulas, which can seriously affect statistics based (as initially they must be) on a simple word-count. In this respect it may be salutary to observe that, although O'Neill was certainly wrong in his bland assumption that the structural laws of the hexameter depend upon the tendency for different word-types to gravitate to particular places in the verse, rather than *vice versa*, there *are* certain cases where word-localization cannot be explained by the normalities of sentence-structure and word-division, but seems to be determined by habit or other factors. Thus the very marked restriction of γενέσθαι, γένηται, γένοντο, γένοιτο to the end of the verse,[25] which greatly exceeds that of such word-types in general, is not due primarily to the recurrence of formular phrases (which is often a potent factor); word-order and the function of verbs provide some explanation, but, in addition, apparently singers *did* develop some kind of formular attitude to these particular forms, and tended to place them instinctively at the end of the verse.

This is but one example of one possible complicating factor. Nearly all one's assumptions in this kind of investigation are likely to be oversimplified, and many of our assumed causes may be mere incidental effects of other, unidentified causes. And there is always the question of what a colon is, what it implies. I have suggested explanations different from those of Fränkel, but have not denied that the verse tends to be punctuated by word-end at more or less strongly preferred points. Does that not leave three cola, at least? In a sense it does; but the distinction is that these cola are incidental, are not basic underlying elements of the hexameter, and need not be defended as such when they are absent. It is doubtful, indeed, whether "cola" is a particularly useful way of describing them; though this is not to deny that Fränkel's way of analysis has, indeed, greatly illuminated the complexity of the hexameter and the possibilities for significant interaction between its different elements.

25. Totals of the four words: at the verse-end, 53× *Il.*, 52× *Od.*; other positions, 6× *Il.*, 10× *Od.*

II. VERSE-STRUCTURE AND SENTENCE-STRUCTURE IN HOMER

Milman Parry was aware that the oral style of Homer depended not only on the use of formular phrases but also on the distribution of those phrases, and the sentences they composed, from verse to verse. In particular he devoted a brilliant article to "The distinctive character of enjambement in Homeric verse" (*TAPA*, 60 (1929), 200–20). This was supplemented by "Whole formulaic verses in Greek and Southslavic heroic song" (*TAPA*, 64 (1933), 179–97); and the use of enjambment in the ancient Greek and modern Yugoslav traditions was further compared by A. B. Lord in "Homer and Huso III: Enjambement in Greek and Southslavic song" (*TAPA*, 79 (1948), 113–24). These studies have not been often cited, nor have they given rise to kindred studies of much importance. Yet they are in a sense preliminary; and Parry's first article, which is the basic one, reports in only broad terms the statistics on which his (and some of Lord's) conclusions rest.

It is the purpose of the present article to re-examine the different types of enjambment and see if further analysis is possible on the lines indicated by Parry; and to carry on the inquiry into the effects of sentence-structure, in relation to the hexameter verse, on the style of the *Iliad* and *Odyssey*. I have made a detailed schematization of the 867 verses of book XVI of the *Iliad*, showing the occurrence of enjambment, internal stops, cumulation, and associated phenomena; this analysis, with the explanation of the symbols used, appears in the appendix (pp. 141 ff.) as Table A. Table B gives a summary of totals by 50-verse sections, while Table C is a reminder, for convenience, of the narrative content of the sample and the occurrence in it of speeches and similes. The purpose of such an analysis is to widen the basis of statistical knowledge about enjambment (and so on) on the one hand, and to present this knowledge in visually accessible form on the other. There is no additional advantage in such a schematic summarization of results, and reference to the Greek text should be made for confirmation of apparently significant sequences and concentrations of structural phenomena which show up from the schematization. No startling or particularly concrete results can be expected from this kind of inquiry; rather, at best, a heightened understanding of the complexity of Homeric style, of its relation to oral procedures, and of the interaction between rhythm and meaning. Parry wrote of his own inquiry (pp. 229 f. of his 1929 article) that "a study in style like the present one fulfills its aim as it goes ahead, forming for us bit by bit a clearer sense of the way in which a poet has fitted his thought to the pattern of his verses."

Enjambment is the carrying over of the sentence from one verse into the next, involving an overrunning of the verse-end. In the simpler forms of oral poetry (like the Southslavic) almost every verse contains a sentence, almost every sentence fills out a verse. There the style is simple, progressive, unperiodic: "paratactic" in a sense, since the thought is divided into parcels, as it were, which are delivered up successively and separately. More developed and accomplished singers, like those of the Homeric tradition, carry the thought, in varying degrees, from one verse into the next, and so produce much subtler and more complex effects both for rhythm and for meaning. Even in the *Iliad* and *Odyssey* such "enjambed" verses are barely in the majority (though that depends on how precisely one defines the sentence); in the literate hexameter epic of Vergil and Apollonius, on the other hand, the status of the verse-end as a semantic limit decreases significantly, and the strongest kinds of enjambment become far commoner than in any oral tradition.

There are different kinds and degrees of enjambment. Parry's main division was into "unperiodic" and "necessary." He applied the former to cases in which the sentence *could* have ended with the verse, but in fact is carried on into the succeeding verse by the addition of further descriptive matter (adverbial or epithetical) or of "a word or phrase or clause of the same grammatical structure as one in the foregoing verse" (*TAPA*, 60 (1929), 207). This kind of progressive extension of the

sentence is typical of what Parry called the "adding style" used
by singers. Parry's term for it, "unperiodic," is derived from
Dionysius of Halicarnassus. Its negative form makes it possibly
confusing, and I propose to use "progressive" instead. By
"necessary" enjambment, on the other hand, Parry referred to
cases where the sentence could not be considered complete by the
end of the verse, and *must* be carried on into the following
verse. He rightly subdivided this category into two types. The
first consists of cases in which a subordinate clause, for example,
fills one verse, and is succeeded by the main clause in the next.
In these cases we should normally expect to find weak punctuation, marking some degree of pause, at the point of enjambment. The second type consists of cases in which the sense runs
straight on from the end of one verse to the beginning of the
next; the former verse cannot be said to contain a whole
thought (even of the kind "when he had gone") or to describe
a completed action: rather it is of the "when he | had gone"
type, in which "had gone" comes in the succeeding verse. In
this second subdivision of "necessary" enjambment no punctuation of any kind can be envisaged at the end of the enjambed
verse. Of these two subdivisions, I propose to term the former
(for which Parry gave no special name) "periodic," since it is
involved in that kind of sentence; the latter "integral." In
nearly all Homeric cases of integral enjambment the verse-end
intervenes at a point of natural articulation in the sentence,
even though not at a point where pause or punctuation would
occur. Very rarely it intervenes more drastically, between words
which belong closely together: for example, between a preposition or preceding epithet and its noun. Such rare cases I
shall term "violent." This terminology is summarized in the
table on p. 108, which also gives the crude "pragmatic" test, in
terms of possible or conceivable punctuation, for each kind of
enjambment.

The *numbers* shown in the table have some relevance, since
they are used to indicate kinds of enjambment in the schematic
analysis of xvi (appendix, pp. 141 ff.). I shall also use them at

Number	Term used here	M. Parry's term	Possible punctuation
0	(no enjambment)	(no enjambment)	strong stop (actual)
1	progressive	unperiodic	strong stop (conceivable), comma (actual)
2	periodic	necessary (type 1)	comma
3	integral	necessary (type 2)	none
4	violent		none

times, for brevity, in the main text. They have the advantage of symbolizing the *degree* of enjambment—of involvement of one verse with the next—from none (0) to violent (4). It will be seen later that the concept of degree can be misleading, or rather that it needs to be controlled by the concept of kind. I emphasize that the main divisions are into "unenjambed" and "enjambed" on the one hand (0 contrasted with 1, 2, 3, 4); and into "progressive" and stronger types (Parry's "necessary"; 1 contrasted with 2, 3, 4) on the other.

Some examples will illustrate the distinctions and uncover further problems of differentiation.

> Ὣς οἱ μὲν περὶ νηὸς ἐϋσσέλμοιο μάχοντο·
> Πάτροκλος δ᾽ Ἀχιλῆϊ παρίστατο, ποιμένι λαῶν,
> δάκρυα θερμὰ χέων ὥς τε κρήνη μελάνυδρος,
> ἥ τε κατ᾽ αἰγίλιπος πέτρης δνοφερὸν χέει ὕδωρ.   (XVI.1–4)

0: *no enjambment.* (The symbol actually used in the analysis is 0̲, underlined, since underlining marks all strong stops—see the explanation of symbols used in Table A, p. 141. Thus 0̄ means a whole-sentence verse, since there is a strong stop at the end of the preceding verse also.) XVI.4 above is unenjambed, an example of 0; it completes a (longer) sentence which ends with the verse. It is in a sense enjambed with its predecessor, but the term "enjambed" is normally restricted to verse-end qualities only. On the other hand XVI.1 is a possible example of a whole-sentence, independent verse, 0̲. It is not the strongest example, since its μὲν leads on to the δ᾽ of the next verse; it could be punctuated by a comma, not a strong stop as in e.g. T. W. Allen's Oxford Classical Text. Parry would have counted it as in "unperiodic" enjambment with its successor, which adds a "clause of the same grammatical structure as in the foregoing verse." This definition, with its exclusion of clauses of different structure, also means that Parry counted as whole-sentence verses many which in most printed texts are separated from their predecessor only by a comma. There is a real ambiguity here, which fortunately is limited in its effects. Although Parry's definition is grammatically sound and easier than many to apply objectively, it often appears unrealistic in practice. I have been guided by how a reasonable editor might punctuate the text: if a strong stop seems just, I have taken that as indicating no enjambment. At the same time one must agree with Parry in distrusting the "varying punctuation of our texts" (*op. cit.* p. 203); the instincts of literates, too, about the length and quality of verse-end pauses are likely to be an erratic guide to oral tendencies. The ambiguity has one important implication: it draws attention to a dichotomy, to be discussed later, between *grammatical* continuity and *oral* continuity (the latter in terms of rhythm, pause, emphasis). I have tried to identify in the first instance the oral effects.

1: *progressive enjambment.* For example xvi.2 and 3 quoted above: each could terminate the sentence, which actually continues by the addition first of a participial clause describing the main subject, then of a relative clause expanding a simile applied to the main subject.

2: *periodic enjambment.* For example xvi.36, εἰ δέ τινα φρεσὶ σῇσι θεοπροπίην ἀλεείνεις, or xvi.21, ὦ Ἀχιλεῦ, Πηλῆος υἱέ, μέγα φέρτατ' Ἀχαιῶν, must clearly be continued in the succeeding verse by a main clause to which they are preliminary. Nevertheless each verse ends with a pause, which marks the conclusion of a subordinate (or in other cases correlative or antithetical) clause or phrase; the pause could always be indicated by a comma.

3: *integral enjambment.* For example xvi.81,

ἔμπεσ' ἐπικρατέως, μὴ δὴ πυρὸς αἰθομένοιο
νῆας ἐνιπρήσωσι. . . .

Here the end of 81 does not coincide with the end of a separate phrase or clause, and no comma is possible; the semantic impulse continues more or less uninterrupted into the next verse. Of course the end of the verse-unit itself probably implies, here and everywhere, *some* interruption by pause or emphasis, and this interruption might be accentuated by the normal sentence-end associations of a verse-end formula like πυρὸς αἰθομένοιο. In xvi.46, for example, this second factor is lacking:

ὣς φάτο λισσόμενος μέγα νήπιος· ἦ γὰρ ἔμελλεν
οἷ αὐτῷ θάνατόν τε κακὸν καὶ κῆρα λιτέσθαι.

4: *violent enjambment*. There are three plausible cases in xvi:

ἀλλ' ὁπότ' ἂν δὴ
νῆας ἐμὰς ἀφίκηται ἀϋτή   (62f.)
δεινὴν δὲ περὶ κροτάφοισι φαεινὴ
πήληξ βαλλομένη καναχὴν ἔχε   (104f.)
ἀλλὰ μεσηγὺ
νηῶν καὶ ποταμοῦ   (396f.)

Of these 62 f. is the least striking. 104 f. is odd since normal formular usage (probably as in xiii.805, ἀμφὶ δέ οἱ κροτάφοισι φαεινὴ σείετο πήληξ) has been disrupted. This might reflect literate intervention: see pp. 171 ff., on Archilochus' drastic re-modeling of Homeric formulas. In the third case 397 might be an afterthought, which converts μεσηγύ from adverb to pre-position and so creates the excess.

Clearly the distinction of 4-type from 3-type enjambment is to some extent subjective, and in the totals in Table B (appendix) I have counted them together. In any case 4 is so rare as to be statistically unimportant. Another difficulty arises from the distinction, in one type of sentence, between 3 and 2. For example xvi.433 f.:

ὤ μοι ἐγών, ὅ τέ μοι Σαρπηδόνα, φίλτατον ἀνδρῶν,
μοῖρ' ὑπὸ Πατρόκλοιο Μενοιτιάδαο δαμῆναι.

On the one hand there is a distinct pause (marked here by a comma) at the end of 433, produced by the parenthetical description φίλτατον ἀνδρῶν. On the other the main sentence continues straight over the verse-end (ὅ τέ...Σαρπηδόνα... | μοῖρ'...δαμῆναι); that is, the verse-end does not coincide with a major structural break in the sentence, and if it were not for the structurally unimportant parenthesis the sentence would run across the verse-end without syntactical interruption or possible punctuation. In grammatical terms the enjambment is integral, type 3; in phonetic or auditory terms it is akin to periodic, type 2 enjambment. In the analysis it is counted as 2 but distinguished as 2–. Such cases are not numerous, but they call attention once more to an important duality in the concept of enjambment as a whole.

This duality is that of continuity of sense and continuity of sound. The term "enjambment" implies, primarily, the first of these; and, since a grammatical definition of the sentence (for example) is more accurate than any possible definition of the pause at the end of different types of verse, there is much to be said for restricting the classification, like Parry, to what can be assessed grammatically. And yet Parry *was* concerned with the effects of pause—more so, in fact (apart from the obvious distinction of Homeric practice from that of Apollonius and Vergil) than with the semantic continuity implied by enjambment. It is arguable that one cannot have it both ways, by clinging to a purely grammatical classification and using that classification as the basis for judgments on stylistic effects seen in terms of pause. It is in this belief that I have departed in some respects from the stricter method of classification, even at the cost of a loss in precision. Now as Parry recognized (*op. cit.* p. 205 top), the kind of break caused by different types of verse-end can vary both in time and in intensity (emphasis, intonation). We shall never know the exact mixture of these elements in the case of any individual enjambment, nor shall we ever reconstruct in detail the oral habits of ancient Greek singers. At the same time our own reading of a Homeric sentence may well give an approximate but valuable indication of the *total* interruption, as a compound of pause and emphasis, between one verse and the next; and this because our (Indo-European) language and many of our speech-habits are not basically distinct from those of the Greeks. This total interruption has its own range of stylistic implications.

The effects of enjambment on style can, indeed, be divided into two main classes corresponding with the distinction between sense-enjambment and sound-enjambment: (*a*) the effects of continuing sense beyond a certain range of words or syllables (i.e. beyond the verse considered as a unit of length merely); and (*b*) the effects of varying the rhythmical structure of the poetry by differences of interval and intonation at the ends of verses. Class (*b*) is parallel to the effects of rhythmical variation, and the interactions of rhythm and sense, *within* the verse, as discussed by Fränkel and Porter and in the preceding study. That parallel reminds us that the interplay between rhythmical and semantic units is relevant outside the verse-unit (that is, in the relations of one verse to another) as well as inside it, and that the dichotomy between the sound aspects of enjambment and its sense aspects is potentially misleading as well as possibly useful. The actual stylistic effects of enjambment are the product both of the continuation of sense in various ways and of particular phonetic effects at the intervals between verses; that should not be forgotten.

Now (*a*) raises the question of complexity; style is affected by the length and complexity of propositions, whether in verse or in prose. The oral style in its simpler manifestations avoids long and complex sentences, for obvious reasons. Sense-enjambment entails a departure, in the direction of greater complexity, from that simple style: either deliberately (so as to produce a particular effect, or to encompass a thought which could not easily be reduced to a short sentence or a series of such) or accidentally. Enjambment-complexity needs to be treated together with other types: complex sentence-structure within the verse, special rhythmical complexity within the verse, complex uses of formular phraseology, or sheer length of sentence. Long sentences of four verses or more are indicated in the analysis of xvi in the appendix, and these instances of sheer length—in which both the singer and his audience have to retain an uncompleted thought for an unusually long period—have their own stylistic implications for the technique of oral poetry. Again, class (*b*)—the phonetic effects of enjambment—can be either accidental or deliberate (or rather, instinctive). They may be byproducts of (*a*), length and complexity, or they may be consciously or unconsciously sought by singers as appropriate to their subject-matter of the moment. The analysis of xvi suggests that sound-enjambment is sometimes unrelated to subject; and we must remind ourselves that certain rhythmical or phonetic effects may be preferred, in poetry, for their own sake, without reference to the special content and supposedly appropriate style of a particular verse or passage. Singers may have liked the variety of enjambment, and more or less unconsciously introduced it on many occasions for that reason alone. Yet there are certainly many passages of xvi, as will be shown on pp. 125 ff., in which enjambment has a special relation to the subject-matter, and there can be little doubt that it was an important element in the *choice* of styles within the embracing category of the oral hexameter style in general.

Thus enjambment is conspicuous, for instance, in the rapid description of battle, as in xvi.306–50. Yet this passage reminds us that integral enjambment, at least, is often associated with internal stop. Many of these verses have a major stop at the bucolic caesura; one sentence ends there, another begins—and can obviously only rarely be completed by the verse-end. Therefore it runs on, in integral enjambment, into the next verse. But here the enjambment is the effect, rather than the cause, of the internal stop; or rather it is impossible to dissociate the two phenomena in this kind of verse. Let us say that the stylistic effect (of rapid, urgent, interrupted, and disorganized action) is produced *both* by a sequence of short, complete sentences *and* by the consistent devaluation of the verse as the natural rhythmical and semantic unit. The short sentences are displaced so that they overrun the verse-end, and the strong stops occur within the verse instead of at its end, as in the simplest form of oral narrative. Thus the positioning of internal stops, both strong and weak, is a relevant factor which is shown in the analysis.

A further difficulty in the classification of enjambment can be caused by what I term "cumulation," a special aspect of the adding style. It will be necessary, before describing the difficulty, to give a provisional indication of what cumulation entails. A kind of cumulation occurs whenever progressive enjambment takes place: the singer sings a verse potentially complete in itself, then he qualifies or adds to it in a succeeding verse connected by progressive enjambment. In the broadest sense, indeed, any simple and paratactic narrative is cumulative; each new piece of information, as the story proceeds, can be envisaged as being heaped upon its predecessor. It is important to remember, then, that in its narrower and most typically Homeric aspects cumulation is simply a special application of a general principle of linear narrative.

In this narrower aspect cumulation can be regarded in the first instance as a means of elaboration. The elaboration can be purely *decorative*, in that it enriches a concept already outlined and semantically adequate in itself; or it can be *explanatory*, in that it adds a qualification necessary in the whole context to a statement which in itself is formally complete. Clearly it is sometimes impossible to draw a sharp line between these two uses. Now a further theoretical distinction can be made between purely *supplementary* cumulation, whose purpose is solely to supplement (either by decoration or by explanation) what has already been stated in a preceding verse, and *transitional* or *prospective* cumulation, which provides some further description of what has preceded but whose main purpose seems to be to lead into a new thought and a fresh accession of meaning. Furthermore cumulation can either take place in a whole verse (in which case it is one aspect of progressive enjambment) or in the first part of a verse: either by the addition of a single cumulative word at the beginning of the succeeding verse (this I call

"runover-word cumulation," abbreviated in the analysis as rc),
or by the addition of a clause or phrase which continues to the
main caesura (this I call "half-verse cumulation," abbreviated
as hc).

These distinctions may be illustrated from two similes in the
sample:

Πάτροκλος δ' Ἀχιλῆϊ παρίστατο, ποιμένι λαῶν,
δάκρυα θερμὰ χέων ὥς τε κρήνη μελάνυδρος,
ἥ τε κατ' αἰγίλιπος πέτρης δνοφερὸν χέει ὕδωρ.   (xvi.2–4)

αὐτίκα δὲ σφήκεσσιν ἐοικότες ἐξεχέοντο,
εἰνοδίοις, οὓς παῖδες ἐριδμαίνουσιν ἔθοντες,
αἰεὶ κερτομέοντες, ὁδῷ ἔπι οἰκί' ἔχοντας,
νηπίαχοι· ξυνὸν δὲ κακὸν πολέεσσι τιθεῖσι.   (xvi.259–62)

Here xvi.3 is an elaboration, explanatory rather than decorative: it is germane to the whole scene that Patroclus is weeping,
is deeply moved. The next verse, on the other hand, is purely
decorative—it enriches the picture of the spring, but is not
essential to it. It is a good example of whole-verse cumulation;
while part-verse cumulation is well exemplified in the second
passage. εἰνοδίοις in 260 is an instance of runover-word cumulation, and it is transitional or prospective as well as supplementary: it introduces a new description of the wasps directly
related to, and leading on to, the information that boys annoy
them, and that they then retaliate on the public. 261 is an
example of half-verse cumulation which is elaborative in an
explanatory sense: the boys make the wasps angry *because they
repeatedly provoke them.* Here the cumulation is supplementary
and not prospective; the further progress of the narrative is
achieved by a further runover-word cumulation, νηπίαχοι in 262.
This is an elaborative word, supplementary in a sense, but its
main function is to lead into the new information contained in
the rest of the verse: that as a consequence of the boys' folly
many people suffer. In this case the material introduced by a
prospective cumulation, while it is fresh, merely completes a
particular scene. Sometimes a cumulation will lead on, directly

or indirectly, to an important new accession of meaning: so, for example, in the well-known runover-word cumulation (the participle being a common type) of *Iliad* 1.2, οὐλομένην, ἣ μυρί'. . . .

Clearly cumulation is an important factor in the relation of verse-structure to sentence-structure; and its assessment, which cannot be reduced to precise rules, affects the interpretation of certain cases of enjambment. Cumulation at the beginning of a verse presupposes a special pause or interruption at the end of the preceding verse; the enjambment at that point is not integral, and, even if a cumulative runover-word is an epithet qualifying a noun at the end of the preceding verse, it is natural to regard it as a kind of afterthought, an attribute dropped into place once the main idea is outlined in its essentials. On occasion, however, one cannot be sure how a singer would have treated the semantic—and therefore rhythmical—flow from verse to verse; in other words, whether the sequence is cumulative or not. In xvi.17 f.

ἦε σύ γ' 'Αργείων ὀλοφύρεαι ὡς ὀλέκονται
νηυσὶν ἔπι γλαφυρῇσιν ὑπερβασίης ἕνεκα σφῆς;

it is impossible to be sure that 18 should be treated as an instance of half-verse cumulation. It consists of two elaborative and inorganic phrases, each filling about half the verse. But supposing, like Allen in OCT, we print a comma after ὀλοφύρεαι. Then the sentence runs on more smoothly, the enjambment becomes integral not progressive, and "by the hollow ships" becomes a more pointed qualification of "they are being destroyed." In my analysis I have counted such ambiguous cases as being, indeed, cumulations; and that entails assessing the enjambment of the preceding verse as progressive and not integral. Thus, in concentrating attention on the cumulative nature of the style as a whole, I have probably understated the total number of integral enjambments—a total which can never be precisely determined, since the singers themselves might vary from performance to performance in the treatment of such ambiguous sequences. Yet the number of ambiguous cases in book xvi hardly exceeds fifteen; which is less than 10 % of all firm occurrences of integral enjambment. The enjambment-status of the sample will not, then, be too seriously distorted.[1]

THE NATURE OF XVI AS A SAMPLE

xvi, the fourth longest book in either Homeric poem, contains a crucial sequence of the monumental plot in the intervention and death of Patroclus, and many different types of description: arming and preparation for battle, divine scenes, speeches both calm and excited, exhortations and taunts, fighting scenes of all kinds (generic scenes, rapid incidents, major duels, fighting round a corpse), many developed similes. The book does not contain any long section untypical of the *Iliad* as a whole—like the Prologue in I, the Embassy in IX, the Dolon episode in X, the Beguiling of Zeus in XIV and XV, the Funeral Games in XXIII, Priam's visit to Achilles in XXIV. Its one unusual aspect, indeed, is its very lack of action off the battlefield and outside Troy and the Achaean camp; it is untypical of the style of the *Iliad* only in that it is too typical of it. Yet in sum it is no worse as a sample, and probably better, than most other complete

---

1. Another example of ambiguity: it is impossible to say whether "out of hostile head" at the beginning of xvi.77 is a necessary continuation of "nor yet have I heard the voice of Agamemnon sounding" in 76. If it is, then 76 is in integral enjambment with 77, and therefore 77 should not be classified in the analysis as hc. But "out of hostile head" may be a cumulated attempt to refine the meaning of the previous verse—the statement is so odd in either case that one cannot be sure. On the other hand Ἀργεῖοι at the beginning of 69 looks like a cumulative elaboration (since it is clear from the preceding verse that οἱ δέ in 67 cannot refer to the Trojans), and presupposes a preceding verse-end interruption greater than that of integral enjambment; while Τρῶες at the beginning of 42, on the contrary, is probably a simple runover word, not cumulative, with the preceding verse running on in integral enjambment—since Τρῶες is a necessary subject for the verb in 41, which might otherwise seem to be Δαναοί or Μυρμιδόνες from 39. But even here the singer might pause at the end of 41 and add the specification Τρῶες almost as an afterthought, albeit a necessary one.

books. It is somewhat more extensive, with its 867 verses, than Milman Parry's 600-verse sample, composed of the first hundred verses each of I, V, IX, XIII, XVII, XXI (i.e. every fourth book after the first).

METHODOLOGY

It is an advantage in any stylistic analysis to set out all the results, not simply to summarize them. Parry's main concern was to present broad distinctions between oral and literate epic, and for this purpose his table of summarized enjambment characteristics (*TAPA*, 60 (1929), 204) was adequate. Yet it would have been useful to have his detailed workings. Even using Parry's own criteria for the sentence, I cannot arrive in my sample very close to the total for unenjambed verses in his column I. This may be partly due to the difference of sample, but to some extent it is certainly caused by the blurred limits of categories even by Parry's formal and grammatical definitions. It is difficult, without a full analysis, to see precisely where such a divergence comes. Furthermore, the summarization of results and the use of short passages of only 100 verses do undoubtedly obscure the *irregular* occurrence of enjambment and kindred phenomena. This is one important lesson of the tabulation of totals (appendix, Table B) for *Iliad* XVI: occurrences of integral (type 3) enjambment, for instance, vary significantly from one 50-verse sequence to the next—from 3 occurrences to 17 to 12 to 9 to 8 to 16 to 22 and so on. The frequency of integral enjambment depends to an important degree on the type of passage and its subject-matter (it is not sure that Parry when he wrote his article would have accepted this), and 100-verse samples can prove seriously misleading in this respect. Thus if a random choice had picked on lines 701–800 of book XVI, the results in terms of integral enjambment would be very distorted, the number of occurrences being only 12 against an average for the whole book of 21. This kind of variation makes it dangerous to say, for example, on the basis of our excessively exiguous samples, that "the *Odyssey*...has a slightly higher percentage [*sc.* than the *Iliad*] of instances of necessary enjambement" (A. B. Lord, *TAPA*, 79 (1948), 122).

The differences between Parry's summarized conclusions and mine, based on different samples, are not alarming. Using his more stringent definition of the complete sentence, he finds 48·5 % of unenjambed verses, against my 38·3 % by a looser criterion (which is close to, but not identical with, that implied by the punctuation of xvi in OCT). He finds 24·8 % of unperiodic enjambment, against my 28·6 % for my (almost identical) progressive enjambment; and 26·6 % of necessary enjambment of all types, against my 33·1 % for my types 2, 3, 4.[2]

The difference of 6·5 % in the averages for necessary enjambment (his class III, my 2's and 3's) is more surprising than the greater difference over unenjambed verses, since in the former case there is no overt difference in criteria. But in fact a test comparison of part of Parry's sample, xiii.1–100, shows that my count of this passage gives a minimum of 23 % and a maximum of 25 % (i.e. from 23 to 25 instances) of necessary enjambment, while his figure was 21 %—and this, of course, over the same sample. Further examination suggests that the discrepancy almost certainly does arise, after all, out of different methods of treating certain equivocal cases. In cases like xiii.21, 29, 55 I tend to count the enjambment as "necessary," in Parry's term, rather than "unperiodic." In other words, Parry was even *more* tolerant than I in accepting what I have termed cumulation, which implies an interruption in terms of pause or emphasis (which could be marked by a comma) at the end of the preceding verse, and so entails "unperiodic" or "progressive" enjambment.

2. My percentages are derived from the totals of 332, 248, and 287, respectively, out of the 867 verses of the sample. The first total is that of col. O in Table B, showing all verse-end major stops; the second is that of col. D, the third that of col. G, showing the sum of type 2 and type 3 instances (the last including the three verses counted as type 4).

THE LIMITS OF PRECISION IN STRUCTURAL ANALYSIS

It has been seen that classification difficulties arise in the analysis of enjambment and cumulation. The very fact that the inquiry involves style as well as syntax shows that high precision should not be expected. Moreover the present investigation concerns not literary but oral style, in which additional intangibles like the rhythmical and declamatory habits of ancient singers enter the discussion. Obviously the estimation of oral style, founded as it must be solely on the evidence of later written texts, on the comparative study of oral poets of other cultures, and on a precarious use of *a priori* suppositions, cannot be reduced to fully precise terms.

One of the dangers of presenting any kind of detailed analysis in this kind of inquiry is that of giving a misleading impression of precision, either achieved or at least intended. Thus the analysis in Table A and the list of totals in Table B look complicated and vaguely scientific. The effort to reduce a set of observations on 867 different units to concise form is apt to produce these effects, and numerals and abbreviations can hardly be avoided. But enough has been said here about the difficulty of establishing precise criteria, and about the irreducible remainder of equivocal instances, to counteract that merely superficial impression. The important question arises whether, if subjective interpretations cannot be excluded, one should attempt a detailed analysis at all. The dangers of trying to subject general phenomena to specific analysis have been known since Aristotle; are we trying to be too specific here?

Obviously I believe not; the phenomena under investigation are among the most concrete aspects of style and are to a large extent, at least, determined and categorized by precise criteria like the length of a hexameter verse. More debatable questions like "What constitutes a sentence?" or "When is an addition an afterthought?" affect our judgment of only a relatively small minority of verses. It seems to me beyond dispute that there are differences of sentence- and verse-structure in different passages of the *Iliad* and the *Odyssey*, and that the establishment of these differences, in as accurate terms as are possible, is a worthwhile critical activity. That means, not only presenting broad totals in the form of percentages for random samples, as Parry did, but also undertaking the detailed analysis, with full presentation of workings, of major continuous sections of the poems. If the indefinite limits of certain categories call attention to the ambiguous structure of certain types of Homeric sentence, and the ambiguous effects of different emphases and pauses, that is all to the good. There are bound to be differences of opinion over the classification, in certain respects, of a small minority of verses. These differences scarcely affect the preliminary and general stylistic observations which follow; and they do not concern at all those parts of the analysis, like the occurrence of the simple runover word or the positioning of many internal stops, which are hardly subject to variety of interpretation.

THE DISTRIBUTION OF STRUCTURAL CHARACTERISTICS IN THE SAMPLE

A. Whole-sentence verses

i. *Actually complete, independent verses ($\bar{0}$'s in the analysis)*

In the first instance unusual occurrence of this and other characteristics will be deduced from the totals for each sequence of 50 verses, as given in Table B. These 50-verse sections possess no more than an arbitrary statistical unity, and provide a mere initial indication which must be checked against the analysis and then against the text. The analysis may show, for example, that occurrences in a section are in fact concentrated in its latter part, and spread into the beginning of the following section. Needless to say the constitution of the section in terms of subject-matter is important, and can be initially checked from Table C.

$\bar{0}$'s vary considerably in the course of the 50-verse sections: two sections have 10 instances each, while another has one and a third none at all. The high frequencies come in 601–50, or more particularly (as reference to the analysis shows) in 608–32;

and in 701–50 (particularly 720–50, with 9 occurrences). In the
first of these passages Aineias attacks Meriones and taunts are
exchanged, then Patroclus exhorts Meriones to action not words.
There are three concise speeches, each with a whole-sentence
introduction like 616, Αἰνείας δ' ἄρα θυμὸν ἐχώσατο φώνησέν τε.
Such introductory verses are a relatively common source of $\bar{0}$'s,
and sometimes there is also a whole-verse resumption of the
"thus he spoke" type. Patroclus' speech ends with two *gnomai*,
each of which fills a verse; this again is apt to occur in some
types of battlefield speech, and we may note the tendency of
moralisms to fill a complete verse. There is also a series of three
$\bar{0}$'s at 608–10, in battle-narrative. The action at this point is
fairly rapid, but the sequence appears accidental, except in so
far as singers seem to have had a tendency to create short
sequences of verses of similar type (p. 133 below). Turning to
720–50, we find Apollo urging on Hector and Cebriones and
panicking the Achaeans; Patroclus and Hector meet, and the
former kills Cebriones and exults over him. Eleven of these
thirty-one verses are speech; there is a sequence of four $\bar{0}$'s at
720–3, composed of an introductory "Apollo spoke" verse and
an abrupt series of question, wish, and comment. Similarly
three other whole-verse sentences are accounted for by the
introduction (744) to a short boast by Patroclus and by the
laconic first and last verses (745, 750) of the speech itself, which
are carefully interrelated and enclose a more leisurely simile-
like conceit. The other two $\bar{0}$'s occur together in a concise
description of Hector's movements at 731 f.

The sections low in $\bar{0}$'s are 51–100 (only one instance) and
151–200, or rather, as the analysis shows, 140–208; in these
69 verses there is no single whole-sentence verse. The former
span consists entirely of Achilles' long and impassioned speech
to Patroclus (which begins at 49 with a whole-verse exclamation
immediately after a "thus spoke" verse). Column G of Table B
shows that this speech has a very high proportion—26 instances
—of periodically and integrally enjambed verses; this naturally
reduces the possible number of whole-sentence verses, which

are in any case out of place in this kind of disordered utterance. Yet it will be seen that the heavy use of whole-sentence verses can convey a comparable effect by quite different means (p. 124). The second long run of $\bar{0}$-less verses, 140–208, begins in the course of the arming of Patroclus; then come the preparation of horses for him, the marshaling of the Myrmidons and catalogue of their leaders, and Achilles' exhortation. $\bar{0}$'s re-establish themselves with the last verse of that speech, a concise closing instruction, and the "thus speaking" verse (210) which follows. Yet only nine verses of the 69-verse sequence are speech; this scotches any feeling that excesses or deficiencies of whole-verse sentences tend to occur in speeches. In fact the passage, unlike the previous one, is not high in periodic or integral enjambment; rather, whole-sentence verses are pre-judiced by a high degree of progressive enjambment, and that is associated with heavy cumulation. No less than 18 of the 69 verses are probable part-verse cumulations, and the frequency of whole-verse cumulation is suggested by the large number of 1's or ·1's (p. 141) not first verse in their sentence. 145–54 strike the eye in this respect in the analysis, and in the text the description of the horses and of Automedon is heavy with whole-verse cumulation, the leisurely adding of one detail after another: "And he bade Automedon swiftly to yoke the horses / — him whom he honored most after Achilles breaker of men / — and was most faithful to await his call in battle" (145–7). This kind of description of a minor figure is closely paralleled in the list of Myrmidon leaders, where again there is a heavy concentration of cumulation, this time part-verse cumulation (170 ff.). The explicit catalogue tends to be more condensed, to have more half-verse cumulation, with the occasional interjection of more complicated and heavily-enjambed details (as in the involuted description of Eudorus, 179–92), than the shorter list, in which the singer tends to expand rather casually in verses not very full of content. At all events, arming scenes and those describing minor figures are ripe for elaboration and tend to be strongly cumulative, and this excludes whole-sentence verses; such scenes

compose the bulk of our passage. Achilles' short exhortation at
its end is neither impassioned nor particularly hurried; again
it is leisurely, somewhat cumulated, and devoid of *gnomai* or
concise statements until its final verse.

Finally, the analysis shows up a remarkable sequence of five
Ō's outside the sections dealt with: 126–30 consists of four
urgent verses of instruction from Achilles to Patroclus, followed
by a brief "thus spoke" and a concise statement of Patroclus'
reaction:

> "ὄρσεο, διογενὲς Πατρόκλεες, ἱπποκέλευθε·
> λεύσσω δὴ παρὰ νηυσὶ πυρὸς δηΐοιο ἰωήν·
> μὴ δὴ νῆας ἕλωσι καὶ οὐκέτι φυκτὰ πέλωνται·
> δύσεο τεύχεα θᾶσσον, ἐγὼ δέ κε λαὸν ἀγείρω."
> ὣς φάτο, Πάτροκλος δὲ κορύσσετο νώροπι χαλκῷ.

We may contrast this urgent style with that which makes use of
heavy enjambment and broken verses (pp. 129 f.); it gives an
impression of businesslike and urgent conciseness, rather than
disordered thought or action or ideas too complex for the
ordinary bounds of speech. It may be noticed that the urgency
does not deprive Patroclus of his epithets, though the verses
which follow are spare enough.

ii. *Potentially complete verses* (·Ō's, ·1's)

Column B in Table B gives the total of verses which could
formally be regarded as complete in themselves but in their
extant use are connected with a neighboring verse, usually in
progressive enjambment. The total is 129, about one verse in
seven; of these only eight are ·0's (for the exact reference of this
and other symbols see pp. 141 f.). The distribution varies from 15
instances in section 1–50 (actually 1–40) to only one instance
each in 301–50 (actually 300–71) and 601–50.

To take the high rate first: 1–50 is high in verse-end, low in
internal strong stops, and also low in integral enjambment
(cols. O, N, F). This implies, in plain language, that in this
conversation between Achilles and Patroclus the sentences are
fairly numerous and tend to begin with the verse; progressive

enjambment and whole-verse cumulation are fairly common. The result conveys much information in a moderate and un-hurried style. In the low sections, on the other hand, progressive cumulation is rare; in 301–50 most of the sentences begin with a verse in integral enjambment with its successor: some 3 out of 4, indeed, a remarkable proportion. That is incompatible with potential whole-sentence verses, and the numerous internal stops and integral enjambments, too, are quite out of keeping with whole-verse cumulation or potential or actual whole-sentence verses. What, then, is this passage about? It is almost entirely a rapid and impetuous description of fighting of the "man took man" variety (306, ἔνθα δ᾿ ἀνὴρ ἕλεν ἄνδρα), in which the effect of disordered or complex action is quite different from the systematic and somewhat leisurely impression conveyed by many potentially whole-sentence verses. The total of 225 actually and potentially self-contained verses, over the whole sample of 867, is suggestive: more than a quarter of the verses in this book consist of statements (usually simple, but with a few instances of strong internal stop) which exactly match the verse in length.[3]

B. Enjambed verses

i. *Progressive enjambment (type 1)*

The totals of 1's (col. D) vary considerably, between 22 instances to a mere six or seven. The highest incidence is in 151–200; but if this section is widened to 131–206 the propor-tion rises to 37 occurrences in 76 verses, or 48·7 %. (Perhaps this is a good place to emphasize once again that these apparently precise totals and percentages are misleading, in that the number of occurrences could vary somewhat according to how, for example, one defines the sentence.) Verse 131 comes exactly at the beginning of the arming of Patroclus, and the passage

3. This proportion must be kept distinct from the 38·3 % of unenjambed or potentially unenjambed verses, which could or do end with the sentence but do not necessarily begin with it, i.e. are not necessarily complete in themselves.

then covers the list of horses and of Myrmidons and Achilles' exhortation; comment has already been made on the lack of $\bar{0}$'s in all this (pp. 122 f.). There is a leisurely but systematic advance of the narrative, with a loving development of details. Cumulation, and especially whole-verse cumulation, is part of this style, especially in lists of minor figures (p. 123); and that relies on progressive enjambment too.

Other concentrations of 1's or ·1's stand out from the analysis: e.g. 2–10, Patroclus weeps and Achilles questions him (straightforward narrative with some internal pause; but the last $3\frac{1}{2}$ verses are a simile, heavily cumulative as similes tend to be); 530–7, Glaucus exhorts the Trojans (leisurely, no marked character; two or perhaps three cumulative verses); 733–9, Patroclus kills Cebriones (inevitability, not urgency or leisureliness, is the main impression conveyed by this straightforward narrative, with all its verses in progressive enjambment).

Of sections low in progressive enjambment, 301–50, with but seven instances, consists (except for the first five verses) of the confused fighting discussed on p. 125 above. The passage is notable for its frequent integral enjambment and internal stops, especially at the bucolic caesura; and is correspondingly low in whole-sentence verses. Progressive enjambment, cumulation, leisureliness, system and inevitability are quite out of place in this deliberately disordered and hurried style. 601–50 is again low in progressive enjambment with only seven instances, of which three come in similes. The rest, mainly fighting and taunts, is in a moderate style with no marked formal characteristics.

ii. Periodic and integral enjambment (types 2 and 3)

Integral enjambment is more common than periodic, by my criteria, in the proportion of 181 to 106 occurrences over the whole sample. There is an important distinction between the two types from the point of view of the history and development of oral poetry. Integral enjambment is exceedingly rare in the Yugoslav singers: of 2,400 lines of poetry examined by A. B.

Lord less than one per cent had this type of strong enjambment, and all except one instance came in the songs of a single unusually sophisticated singer, Avdo Međedović (*TAPA*, 79 (1948), 119; cf. *The Singer of Tales* (Harvard 1960), p. 54 and n. 17 on p. 284). On the other hand it is extremely frequent—much more so than in Homer—in the literary epics of Vergil and Apollonius. According to Parry (*TAPA*, 60 (1929), 217) it occurs in every second or third verse in Vergil and Apollonius, against about every fifth verse in Homer. Moreover Parry observed that the literary epic is addicted to what I have classed as violent (type 4) enjambment.[4] There is no doubt that in the post-oral period the integrity of the essential rhythmical unit, the verse, was infringed more and more; and in the oral period the Yugoslav comparison suggests that, the simpler and less sophisticated singers were, the more conscious they were of the verse-end as a limit of meaning. Unfortunately the development of the Greek oral epic is too obscure for us to conclude that heavily or integrally enjambed verses are relatively late in the tradition. Integral enjambment may have occurred even in the formative stages of stories about Troy, although we may feel that the earliest narrative poetry of all consisted largely of independent and unenjambed verses. It may be significant that the most conspicuous typical passages in Homer (the preparation of a meal, the beaching or departure of a ship; cf. e.g. II.421–31, IX.206–21; I.432–7, 475–87) are relatively low in integral enjambment, though internal stops and part-verse cumulation do occur. Indeed, if the hexameter verse developed as a unit, and not as an agglomeration of shorter units, then it is possible that integral enjambment and strong internal stops

4. Apollonius has a preceding adjective at the verse-end of about every twentieth, Vergil about every tenth, verse (Parry, *op. cit.* p. 219). In some circumstances, of course (for example where the following noun is at the end, not the beginning, of the next verse; e.g. *Argonautica* I. 686), the enjambment is much less violent than in cases like φαεινὴ | πήληξ (*Il.* XVI.104) or ἀρίστην | βουλὴν (*Il.* IX.74). Parry also noted that πᾶς, πολύς, ἄλλος are more commonly separated from their noun in this way in Homer and seem to form a special case.

entered the poetical tradition at a comparatively early stage;
for A. B. Lord has well pointed out that the longer dactylic
hexameter has greater opportunities for the completion of a
thought before the verse-end than has, for example, the shorter
decasyllable of the Southslavic tradition (e.g. *TAPA*, 79 (1948),
123).

Periodic (type 2) enjambment is prominent in the sample in
401–50 (11 instances), or rather 415–65 (15 instances in 51
verses). The passage begins with a list of Trojan victims of
Patroclus, then Sarpedon rallies the Lycians and faces him.
Zeus wonders whether to save his son and is dissuaded by Hera;
he sends bloody rain, and the fighting continues. Seven of the
2's occur in the exchange of speeches between Zeus and Hera.
Like many of the shorter Iliadic speeches, these debate alternative courses of action, different contingencies, and therefore
contain disjunctions and conditional clauses; and whole-verse
protases and alternatives tend to give rise to 2's.[5] Similarly there
is a notable concentration of periodic enjambment in verses
10–40, again mainly owing to alternatives, conditions and the
like. That is mainly why, in 1–50, periodic enjambment is,
exceptionally, commoner than integral. On the other hand 2's
are low in 501–50 (only two instances), a passage full of incident:
Sarpedon dies, Glaucus is wounded, relieved by Apollo after a
prayer, and rallies Hector. There are two speeches, but the first
is a prayer and the second an exhortation; in neither type are
conditions or alternatives to be expected, and periodic enjambment is absent. In the remainder of the passage a rapid but
simple style with many verse-end stops inhibits the stronger
forms of enjambment in general.

5. "Tend to," because this depends on whether the protasis, for example,
precedes or follows the apodosis. If the former, the enjambment is periodic;
if the latter, it is progressive. The distinction is not so arbitrary and
mechanical as it looks: in the former case the singer has formed a complex
and periodic sentence in his mind before he starts the first verse; in the
second the condition is framed as an afterthought, and the mode of conception may well be different.

Integral enjambment is a more conspicuous stylistic charac-
teristic than periodic enjambment, both in its number of occurrences and in its whole effect on the sound and rhythm of the
poetry. The two sections highest in 3's are 301–50, the man-
took-man fighting, and 51–100, Achilles' impassioned speech to
Patroclus; both are rapid, urgent, and heavily broken up by
internal stops (cols. M and N). Strong overrunning of the verse-
end is often caused by stops at the bucolic caesura (which
account for no less than 70 of the total of 182 instances of
integral enjambment in xvi): this is so in the former passage,
which is high in s·'s, though not in the latter (col. T). There
is, however, a conspicuous sequence of such enjambments
at 60–3:

> ἀλλὰ τὰ μὲν προτετύχθαι ἐάσομεν· οὐδ' ἄρα πως ἦν
> ἀσπερχὲς κεχολῶσθαι ἐνὶ φρεσίν· ἤτοι ἔφην γε
> οὐ πρὶν μηνιθμὸν καταπαυσέμεν, ἀλλ' ὁπότ' ἂν δὴ
> νῆας ἐμὰς ἀφίκηται ἀϋτή τε πτόλεμός τε.

Here it is as though whole-sentence verses were being systematically displaced so as to straddle the verse-end; the sequence
of displacements causes a mounting tension which is relieved,
with a sense of completion, in the undistorted whole verse at the
end. This is an effective piece of rhetoric, in which the trans-
gressing of the verse-units helps to reproduce Achilles' indignation
and excitement, his spilling over of thought after thought, until
the closing verse, with its inevitable restoration of the rhythmical
norm, reinforces the simple basic idea "not until the fighting
reaches my ships."

A less regular sequence, making a more disordered and less
rhetorical effect, is seen a little later in the same speech at 70–3;
and a similar irregularity in the placing of the internal stop
makes an analogous impression in the description of chaotic
battle at 373–5:

> Τρωσὶ κακὰ φρονέων· οἱ δὲ ἰαχῇ τε φόβῳ τε
> πάσας πλῆσαν ὁδούς, ἐπεὶ ἄρ τμάγεν· ὕψι δ' ἀέλλη
> σκίδναθ' ὑπὸ νεφέων, τανύοντο δὲ μώνυχες ἵπποι
> ἄψορρον προτὶ ἄστυ νεῶν ἀπὸ καὶ κλισιάων.

Again the closing verse, uninterrupted by internal stop in contrast with its predecessors, has a marked effect, and seems to embody in its smoother rhythmical flow the idea of the long and swift retreat of the chariots once they had extricated themselves from the rout. Yet often these effects are purely rhythmical and can have no intended relation to the meaning. A distinction in the flow of a concluding verse, in a long sentence or stylistically unified passage, seems often to have been sought by singers; either as in this type or in its converse, an interrupted verse after a sequence of uninterrupted ones, such as 389–92, 462–5, 487–91. Other sequences of integral enjambment occur at 727–9, 833–5; the former conveys a salutary warning, because it seems to have no special motive and produces no special effect, being part of a description of fighting and divine intervention which, although full of incident, is not particularly wild or hurried. The latter comes in Hector's boast over the dying Patroclus; he seems to become excited, flushed with arrogance, at this point, after a quiet beginning in 830–2. Among concentrations (not sequences) of 3's which show up in the analysis but not in the 50-verse totals, the most conspicuous is 103–25, which contains 11 cases of integral enjambment (including one violent) in 23 verses, six of them after a stop at the bucolic caesura. This passage, generally high in internal stops, describes the rapid and critical fighting during which fire is set to one of the Achaean ships; it is as urgent and broken-up as the man-took-man section at 306–50, but is disguised in Table B because it is immediately followed by the arming of Patroclus, with little strong enjambment and a marked change in style.

Sections notably low in integral enjambment are 1–50, 551–600, 751–800; in each of these periodic enjambment is relatively high. The first passage (Achilles and Patroclus) has already been discussed; the others are almost entirely narrative, not speeches, and describe mixed fighting. 551 ff. is interesting, since a large part of it (especially 569–607) describes violent fighting with a fairly swift transition from one encounter to another. Yet the effect is subtly different from that of the other notable confused-

fighting passage at 306–50; here there is a good deal of cumulation and a number of pauses at the main caesura, but (from
562 on) almost no stop at the bucolic caesura with its usual
consequence of obtrusive enjambment. The effect is of steady,
almost interminable fighting rather than of great passion and
confusion. On 751–800 see below, and p. 137.

C. Internal stops, short sentences

Internal stops, since they diminish the unity of the verse as a
rhythmical continuum, are more obtrusive and often have a
more marked stylistic effect than verse-end stops. The man-
took-man fighting of 306 ff. has already been remarked on
several counts; it is notably high in internal stops both weak and
strong (cols. M, N); the broken effect suits the broken fighting,
but it is wise to remember that a similar effect might be due
simply to a singer's concentrating a great deal of incident in a
small space. Incidentally this section does not have many double
internal stops (ss's); these give the most staccato effect of all,
but are uncommon. They are most prominent, and then only
five in total, in 1–50. Four of the five instances occur in the
interchange between Patroclus and Achilles at 7–21, since they
are most frequently caused by the use of a simple vocative
within the verse. The repeated use of the vocative does, of
course, have a distinctly emotional effect.[6]

No 50-verse section is outstandingly low in total internal stops
(which include, of course, those produced by part-verse cumulation and simple runover words); but it may be useful to consider 751–800, which is lowest with 21 instances. As it happens,
half-verse cumulative stops are high within this total, other
types exceptionally low (cols. J, Q–T). This, with the high
frequency of progressive enjambment, suggests a strongly
cumulative passage. It describes the fight for Cebriones' body,
then the stunning of Patroclus by Apollo, and it includes three

---

6. Sometimes the vocative may not cause a very marked break in the
stream of sound; e.g. verse 29 is not counted as having double internal stop:

ἕλκε' ἀκειόμενοι· σὺ δ' ἀμήχανος ἔπλευ, 'Αχιλλεῦ.

similes (which tend to be cumulative) accounting, without their "apodoses," for ten verses. It is revealing that at this dramatically crucial point the poet avoids a staccato style; rather the deliberate, cumulative effect (which is notable, as often with armor, in the verses on the helmet as it falls to the ground, 793–800) conveys a certain sense of inevitability. Some critics might feel that the cumulative description of the helmet is almost too leisurely in style, and might suggest a degree of post-Homeric elaboration.

In many other places, however, the more obvious device of using short sentences is chosen for the representation of violent action. The following passages stand out from the analysis as being particularly high in all stops, especially strong ones, and the brief description of their content tells its own tale:

19–22	urgent conversation
67–73	part of Achilles' impassioned speech
102–107	missiles rain on Ajax
122–129	ship fired, Achilles excited
289–296	Patroclus routs Trojans
315–325	man-took-man fighting
330–341	man-took-man fighting
400–406	Patroclus kills Thestor
550–555	Trojans react strongly to Sarpedon's death
625–632	Patroclus rebukes Meriones
656–662	Trojans panic
787–792	Apollo strikes Patroclus
833–846	mostly Hector's angry boast over Patroclus.

Only the last two of these passages need further comment. The former is part of a description which has already been assessed as generally deliberate and not staccato; but these few verses describe the actual blow. In the latter Hector's angry speech is succeeded by a more fluid reply from the dying Patroclus (844–54), which reflects, intentionally or not, his weakness and resignation as death approaches.

Finally, we may observe from the analysis certain sequences

of stops in the same position in the verse, which exemplify the sporadic tendency of singers to repeat a rhythmical pattern—perhaps because they just stuck in a rhythmical groove, as it were, perhaps because they liked the repetition (as they certainly liked anaphora and alliteration, for example) from time to time.[7] A sequence of four weak stops at the main caesura illustrates the tendency:

πᾶν πεδίον κατέχουσι, μάχῃ νικῶντες Ἀχαιούς.
ἀλλὰ καὶ ὧς, Πάτροκλε, νεῶν ἀπὸ λοιγὸν ἀμύνων
ἔμπεσ' ἐπικρατέως, μὴ δὴ πυρὸς αἰθομένοιο
νῆας ἐνιπρήσωσι, φίλον δ' ἀπὸ νόστον ἕλωνται. (XVI.79–82)

The masculine caesura of 81, in contrast with the feminine caesuras of the other verses, slightly reduces the effect, which is more marked in 743–5 with a sequence of hephthemimeral stops (ṣ's), partly because of the comparative rarity of this position anyway (col. S):

κάππεσ' ἀπ' εὐεργέος δίφρου, λίπε δ' ὀστέα θυμός.
τὸν δ' ἐπικερτομέων προσέφης, Πατρόκλεες ἱππεῦ·
"ὦ πόποι, ἦ μάλ' ἐλαφρὸς ἀνήρ, ὡς ῥεῖα κυβιστᾷ."[8]

D. Cumulation

i. General remarks

Much has already been said about cumulation, which implies a state of mind and a whole technique of poetical assimilation rather than a particular structural device leading to a particular stylistic effect. For this reason I shall not attempt to detect concentrations of whole-verse cumulation, except where they may be suggested by the more specific indications

7. On this point see also J. A. Russo on p. 230 below.
8. For other examples see 71–3, 347–9, 584–7, 626–8. Particularly noticeable are the sequences of stops at the bucolic caesura followed by integral enjambment; in addition to 60–3, quoted earlier, cf. 109f., 168f., 353f., 395f., 517f., 552f., 834f. More complex patterns, too, can be traced through the analysis; one example is 330–4, a brief episode of fighting which both begins and ends with an uninterrupted verse, in contrast with the symmetrically broken verses between.

provided by runover words and, to a lesser extent, half-verse cumulations. The criteria for determining whole-verse cumulation (for example, among ·1 verses not first verses in their sentence) are far too vague, and it may prove difficult to sharpen the criteria even after the much fuller investigation that cumulation and the adding style, in general, deserve.

In its more "decorative" uses (p. 114) cumulation probably varied from performance to performance, in response to the energy and imaginativeness of the singer and the reaction of his audience. Some cumulations will appear particularly successful, and will gradually be worked into the permanent texture of an individual song, to be assimilated, perhaps, by younger singers. Others will be discarded, reverting to the singer's general repertory or to the context from which he originally acquired them. The fact that cumulation is often inorganic means that it may sometimes be due to post-Homeric efforts at elaboration, whether by subsequent oral singers, reciters, or copyists and glossators. Yet, because of the essentially cumulative nature of the oral style as a whole, it is almost always impossible to be sure that a doubtful-looking cumulation is non-Homeric; in a sense the poems were always in a process of elaboration, from the formation of Homer's shorter prototypes to the gradual making of the monumental poems, and probably, also, during the period of subsequent oral performances of those poems, whether by Homer or by his successors.

ii. *Cumulation within the sentence*

The particular problem presents itself whether, if the adding style is a fundamental mode of oral composition and re-creation, passages which are not overtly in the adding style can have been oral. There is a particularly good test-case in book xvi, namely the man-took-man fighting from 306 to 350. This passage, in which internal stops and integral enjambments and the overrunning of the verse-end are rife, in which the simplicity of the verse as the primary rhythmical unit is suppressed or transcended (however one happens to look at it), lies at the opposite extreme from heavily cumulative passages in which one verse leads to the next either with a new sentence or with progressive enjambment. Was it not very difficult, perhaps impossible, for an oral and illiterate poet to develop or to assimilate such a long and complex sequence, in which there is little opportunity for leisurely aggregation and in which many of the verses are strongly interwoven with their successor, so as to confront the singer with a confusing tension between units of rhythm and of meaning?

First, I think it must be admitted that this exceedingly complicated kind of passage is likely to have been within the grasp only of the most proficient singers. If there is a serious case for supposing some help from writing in the composition of our *Iliad*, then in relation to the detailed deployment of language it must rest largely on passages like the one under consideration. Yet the complexity of this passage *from the point of view of the singer* should neither be exaggerated nor exactly equated with the undoubted complexity of its effect on the reader or, probably, the hearer. In fact closer examination shows that the cumulative principle *is* at work, within the sentence rather than in the accretion of verse on verse. Consider the first eleven verses, 306–16:

306   Ἔνθα δ' ἀνὴρ ἕλεν ἄνδρα κεδασθείσης ὑσμίνης
     ἡγεμόνων. πρῶτος δὲ Μενοιτίου ἄλκιμος υἱὸς
     αὐτίκ' ἄρα στρεφθέντος Ἀρηϊλύκου βάλε μηρὸν
     ἔγχεϊ ὀξυόεντι, διαπρὸ δὲ χαλκὸν ἔλασσε·
310   ῥῆξεν δ' ὀστέον ἔγχος, ὁ δὲ πρηνὴς ἐπὶ γαίῃ
     κάππεσ'. ἀτὰρ Μενέλαος ἀρήϊος οὖτα Θόαντα
     στέρνον γυμνωθέντα παρ' ἀσπίδα, λῦσε δὲ γυῖα.
     Φυλεΐδης δ' Ἄμφικλον ἐφορμηθέντα δοκεύσας
     ἔφθη ὀρεξάμενος πρυμνὸν σκέλος, ἔνθα πάχιστος
315   μυὼν ἀνθρώπου πέλεται· περὶ δ' ἔγχεος αἰχμῇ
     νεῦρα διεσχίσθη· τὸν δὲ σκότος ὄσσε κάλυψε.

There is obvious cumulation, in part-verse form, only at 307 and 309; 312 is cumulative, too, in a form which happens not to be recorded in our limited analysis. There is, then, a certain amount of ordinary progressive composition even in this apparently uncumulative passage. Moreover the five integral enjambments do not give rise to long or complex sentences in themselves: less than three verses in the longest instances. We notice once more the important function of the four positions in the verse where internal pause occurs; they are in fact the caesuras which mark off the "cola" identified by Fränkel and discussed in the preceding study, but here they are used as the limits of sentences—secondary limits, admittedly, but not purely random ones once the verse-end is abandoned as primary limit. Often it can be seen that short sentences which cross the verse-end in integral enjambment are composed of brief phrase-units dropped successively, as it were, into these "colon" slots. That process is itself cumulative in a valid sense, as can be seen in 314 f., where ἔφθη ὀρεξάμενος provides a possible completion of sense but is supplemented by a more detailed specification which fills the next slot, and so on. Now these phrases are often standardized units or adaptations of them—formulas, in fact. Here metrical, structural, and formular analyses coincide; and here we see most clearly how the proficient singer could have handled a passage as apparently complex and irregular as the present one, by oral means alone. Whether such a passage could have been easily passed down for long in the tradition is more doubtful; it is probable that passages like these were the work of Homer or a close predecessor; but that is another question.

iii. *Runover-word cumulation*

This is not very frequent over the whole sample, with some 48 occurrences in 867 verses (col. K). The cumulated runover word is a conspicuous element in the Homeric style, but its scope tends to be exaggerated. So does that of the simple, uncumulated, strongly enjambed runover word, which occurs only 27 times in the book. These 27 instances are not afterthoughts,[9]

9. Except, possibly, in a limited sense and in a small minority of instances: see n. 1 on p. 117, *ad fin*. See also Bassett, *TAPA*, 57 (1926), 116 ff.

they are an integral and necessary completion of the sentence. At the same time the singer could undoubtedly have fitted his meaning into a complete verse, and that he did not do so suggests that he favored the runover word as a stylistic device for its own sake. It follows that runover-word cumulation, also, may sometimes have been practiced for the sake of the runover effect as much as for the cumulative effect. Neither rc's nor r's are common enough to have a significant distribution over the 50-verse sections; but, taking the totals for both together, 151–200 (actually 157–94) has a relatively high frequency with nine instances. Three of these occur in a single simile, 156–63, and a fourth in its "apodosis"; the rest (4 rc's, 1 r) come in catalogue-summaries of minor characters (Myrmidon leaders in this case), which are, as has been shown before, notably cumulative. Might this provide a significant connection between the style of these brief sketches and that of the developed similes?

iv. Half-verse cumulation

This is high in 751–800, with nine instances; the passage is also noticeable for its dearth of other internal stops and integral enjambment. Only four verses in it can be regarded as whole-verse cumulations, and it only has a single runover-word cumulation. The half-verse cumulations are most concentrated in the descriptions of Patroclus' last rushes at the enemy and of his stunning by Apollo (781–800); I have already remarked that the impression given is of inevitability or inexorability rather than of urgency and rapidity.[10] It is worth noting that three of the nine instances are organic to the general context in that the latter half of their verse leads into the next verse in integral enjambment; the other six verses are complete in sense by their close, and are inorganic. Thus only a minority,

10. On the other hand 551–600 (actually 575–600, an equal concentration with seven instances) is a scene of mixed fighting where the narrative is rather leisurely, devoid equally of great urgency and of any special sense of inevitability.

over this section, fulfill the function which runover-word cumulation often performs, of leading into a fresh topic, of providing
a transition, more subtle and variegated than that of ordinary
progressive enjambment, between one chain of thought and the
next. The total of 83 instances of half-verse cumulation (against
e.g. 48 of runover-word cumulation), in the 867 verses of the
sample, shows that this is an important structural type which
deserves special categorization. Other part-verse cumulations—
for example, those extending to the bucolic caesura—are rare,
and negligible by comparison.

v. Other cumulative passages

Other passages which stand out from the analysis as cumulative are as follows:

131–154	arming of Patroclus
172–186	catalogue of Myrmidons
190–195	(ditto)
260–262	simile
479–481	fatal wound
482–491	simile
520–527	Glaucus' prayer to Apollo
570–576	description of a minor victim
733–739	Patroclus kills Cebriones

Arming scenes, descriptions of pieces of armor, developed
similes, the description of minor figures and their genealogy,
whether or not in a catalogue—these are the typical *loci* for
cumulation; but it is a mode of composition which can make
itself felt even in some passages of fighting. In the last of the
passages listed above there is very obtrusive half-verse cumulation, which is not simply decorative but is made to perform a
function in the progress of the narrative. The result in this
case is in my own view fluent enough, but mechanical and a little
tame.

CONCLUSION

One danger of this kind of stylistic analysis is tautology. The mere identification, totaling and setting down of characteristics like enjambment and cumulation—if done with reasonable *general* accuracy, which is difficult in itself—do not of themselves reveal much more about the style of a passage than that it is, precisely, cumulative or not, heavy or light in enjambment. Sometimes the listing of formal, structural characteristics simply reproduces the obverse side of other listed characteristics, and it is important not to be misled here. Nevertheless certain general conclusions *have* emerged—far fewer, I am sure, than could be elicited by a fuller study, based upon more sophisticated criteria, by someone with the classificatory genius of a Milman Parry. The total usage and detailed distribution of whole-sentence verses, both actual and potential, of progressively, periodically, and integrally enjambed verses, of probably cumulated beginnings of verses, of verses interrupted by internal pause in various positions, reveal something important about the complexity and variety of the Homeric style in its structural aspects. Moreover the relation between structure and meaning becomes clearer. Certain structural properties tend to be accompanied by certain stylistic effects and to be associated with certain sorts of subject-matter; but there is no rigid correspondence between structure and style, and in many cases a quite different effect can be produced, according to context, by similar structural means, or conversely different structural means can produce a closely similar effect. There is nothing remarkable in the conclusion that short sentences with broken verses and heavy enjambment give an effect of rapidity and urgency in speech or action. That is obvious enough, though it helps to have a degree of quantitative documentation. But the observation that an apparently similar effect is sometimes attained by quite distinct means (as far as rhythm is concerned, at least)—namely by a sequence of whole-sentence verses— may not be so obvious, and raises a series of possibly fruitful questions: Are the effects really similar? Is sentence-length more important, for this sort of effect, than rhythm? Is the choice of means fortuitous? Could it depend in any respect on the period of composition?

Obviously such investigations must be carried beyond the range of a single part of the *Iliad*. I would like to see them extended to sizable portions, not less than about 250 verses in length, of other books of both poems; for test purposes, indeed, to particular passages with an apparently individual style as well as to passages apparently composed relatively late in the tradition—to Nestor's reminiscences and the Phaeacian scenes as well as to the Doloneia, Priam and Achilles, and Odysseus' false tales. Much of Homer, in any case, is probably in a style that does not exceed in any one direction, but contains a more or less harmonious mixture of the various structural, rhythmical, and formular elements. Even in book XVI it is noticeable that many stretches have lain low during our analysis; yet 201–300, 651–700 and 801–50 (which contains, indeed, the wounding and death of Patroclus) are stylistically as effective, to use general terms, as the passages which show an obvious excess or deficiency in certain characteristics. Yet the study of those characteristics in their more extreme uses can help to illuminate their less dramatic function in the frequent stretches of more "normal" poetry. That is part of the justification of the present type of investigation.

Appendix

The schematic analysis, in terms of enjambment, stops, sentence-length, cumulation, of *Iliad* xvi.

Explanation of symbols used in Table A, the verse-by-verse analysis*

Strong stops

Underlining of a symbol marks a strong stop (colon or full stop), either at the verse-end (when an enjambment-number is underlined) or internally (when s, r, hc or rc is underlined).

Enjambment

0̲   indicates no enjambment (and, of course, a strong stop at the verse-end).

·0̲   (see ·1)

0̄   indicates a whole-sentence unenjambed verse.

1   indicates *progressive* enjambment.

·1   indicates 1-type verses which either do or could begin a sentence; that is, they are potentially complete in sense. Similarly with ·0.

2   indicates *periodic* enjambment.

2–   indicates verses in which the main sentence is interrupted by verse-end as in 3, but a weak stop at the verse-end is induced by e.g. a parenthetical phrase (see pp. 110f.).

3   indicates *integral* enjambment.

3–   indicates integrally enjambed verses in which the overrunning sentence or clause begins at the bucolic caesura.

4   indicates *violent* enjambment (counted with 3 in Table B).

* The analysis sometimes presupposes a punctuation different from that of e.g. OCT.

Internal stops

s marks an internal weak stop (possible comma)
s̲ marks an internal strong stop

⎫
⎪
⎬ position in verse in-dicated by dot, as below.
⎪
⎭

·s = stop at position 3, 2 or $1\frac{1}{2}$, rarely 1.

ṡ = stop at main caesura, position 5 or $5\frac{1}{2}$.

s̩ = stop at position 7.

s· = stop at bucolic caesura, position 8.

ss marks two internal stops in the verse, position and strength as
    further indicated: e.g. ·s̲s·.

Cumulation

hc   indicates the special cases of cumulated clauses or phrases
     ending with a stop (h̲c̲ if strong) at the main caesura,
     position 5 or $5\frac{1}{2}$.

rc   indicates runover-word cumulation: a single word is cumu-
     lated at the beginning of the verse, followed by a weak or
     strong stop and a fresh impulse of meaning.

Runover word

r   indicates the simple (uncumulated) runover-word, com-
     pleting the meaning of the preceding verse (which is in
     integral enjambment).

Sentence-length

| marks sentences of 4 verses or more.

Table A

A verse-by-verse analysis of *Iliad* xvi in terms of enjambment
and other structural features

#			#			#		
1		0̄	40		·1		ṡ	0
	s·	·1			3	80	ṡ	2–
		1		r	1		ṡ	3
		·0		rc	0		ṡ	0
5		·1			3			·1
		·0	45		0			1
	ṡs·	·1		s·	3–	85	hc	3
	rc	1			0		ṡ	0
	hc	1			0		s·	3–
10		·0		·ss·	0			2
	·sṡ	0	50	s·	2			3
	s·	2			0	90	ṡ	0
		0			2			2–
	s·	·1			1		ṡ	1
15		·1		hc	0			3
		0	55	ṡ	0		r	0
		·1			2	95	ṡ	3
	hc	0		hc	2–		r	0
	·sṣ	0			1		·s	2–
20	ṣ	0		rc	0		s·	2
	·sṣ	2	60	s·	3–		ṡ	2
	·ṣ	·0		s·	3–	100		0
	ṡ	2–		s·	4–			0
		0			0		ṡ	0
25		2			·1			·1
		·1	65		·1	rc		4
		·0			3	105	s·	3–
		·1		ṡ	3		ṡ	1
	hc	0		r	1		s·	3–
30	s·	·1		rc	1			0
	rc	2	70	rc	3		s·	3–
		0		ṡ	3	110	s·	3–
	·s	·1		ṡ	3		·s	0
	ṡ	1		ṡ	0			2
35	hc	0			3			0
		2	75		0			3
		2			·1	115	ṡ	1
	ṡ	1		hc	3		ṡ	3
	rc	0		s·	3–		s·	3–

TABLE A (*cont.*)

		0			1		rc	0
	s·	2–		rc s·	3–	205		·1
120	·s	3		ṣ	0		rc	0
	ṣ	0			3		s·	3–
	ṣ	3	165		2		ṡ	0
	·s	0		r	1			0
	s·	3–			0	210		0
125		0		s·	3–			0
		0		s·	3–			2
		0	170		0		hc	2
		0			·1			0
	ṡ	0		rc	0	215	ṡs·	0
130	·s	0			·1			·1
		·1		hc	0		rc	0
	rc	0	175		·1			·1
		·1		hc	1		ṣ	1
		0		ṣ	1	220	s·	3–
135		·1		hc	0		ṣ	1
	rc	0			·1		hc	3
		·1	180	rc	1		ṡ	1
	rc	0		hc	3			0
		0		r	1	225	s·	3–
140		·1			0			2
	hc	3			·1			0
	r	1	185	hc	1			·1
	hc	1		rc	0		rc	1
	hc	0			3	230	ṡ	·0
145		·1			2		s·	·1
		1			3		hc	0
		0	190	ṡ	1		ṡs·	2
		·1			·1		s·	3–
	hc	1			0	235		0
150		1			·1			2
		0		rc	1		hc	2
		·1	195		0			0
		1			·1			2
		0		ṡ	0	240		1
155		·1			3		rc s·	1
	s·	2		ṡ	0		s·	3–
	rc	2	200	·s	·1			3
		3			1		ṡ	3
	r	0		hc	0	245	r	0
160		·1		ṡ	·1			2

TABLE A (cont.)

Line			Value
			1
			0̲
		ṡ	0̲
250		ṣ	0̲
			3
	r		0̲
			3
		ṡ	1
255		ṣ	3
			0̲
			3
	r		0̲
			·1
260	rc		1
	hc		1
	rc̲		0̲
			3
		ṡ	3
265			0̲
			3
		ṡ̲	0̲
			0̲
			2
270		ṡ	·1
		s·	3–
			1
			3
		·s	0̲
275			0̲
		s·	3–
			0̲
			2
	hc		2
280		ṡ	1
			3
		ṣ	0̲
			0̲
			·1
285	hc		1
			1
		ṡ	3
			0̲
		ṣ̲	3

Line			Value
290		ṡ	1
	rc̲		1
	hc̲		0̲
		ṡ	0̲
		s·	3–
295		ṣ̲	3
	hc̲		0̲
			3
			2
			·1
300	rc		1
			2–
		ṡ	0̲
			2–
			1
305		ṡ	0̲
			·1
	rc̲		3
			1
	hc		0̲
310		ṡ	3
	r̲		1
		s·	0̲
			3
		s·	3–
315		ṣ	3
		ṣ̲ ś̲	0̲
			2
	rc		0̲
		ṡ̲	3
320			1
	hc̲		3
		s·	2–
		·s̲ ś̲	3
		ṡ	0̲
325		ṡ	0̲
			3
		ṡ	1
		s·	3–
		ṡ	0̲
330			3
		s·	3–
			0̲

Line			Value
		s·	3–
			0̲
335		s·	3–
		ṡ̲	0̲
		s·	3–
		s·	3–
		ṡ̲	1
340	rc	s·	3
	r	ṣ	0̲
			3
			0̲
		ṡ	0̲
345			3
	r̲		3
	hc̲		0̲
		ṡ	3
		ṡ̲	3
350		·s̲	0̲
			0̲
			2
	rc	s·	3–
		s·	3–
355			0̲
		s·	3–
		ṡ	0̲
			3
		ṡ̲	2
360			2
			0̲
			0̲
		ṡ	0̲
			2
365	hc		1
			1
		s·̲	3–
		s·	1
	rc		0̲
370			3
			1
			·1
	hc̲		3
		ṡṡ·	3–
375		ṡ	3

Table A (cont.)

		0			3			2
		2	420		2			2–
	ṣ	1			0			2
	hc	0		ṡs·	0	465	s·	0
380		·1		s·	3–			·1
	rc	1			1		hc	1
	ṣ	0	425	rc	0		hc	1
	ṣ	0			0		ṣ	0
		2		ṡs·	0	470	ṡs·	3–
385	hc	3			3		r	0
	r	2			2			0
		1	430		0			2
		·0			·1			0
		·1			·0	475	ṡ	0
390		·1		s·	2–			0
		1			0			·1
	ṡ	0	435		·1			·1
		0			3		rc ṡ	1
		2–			2	480	rc	1
395	s·	3–			0			0
	s·	4–			0			·1
		3	440	ṡ	0		hc	3
	ṡ	0		ṡ	2–			0
		·1			0	485		·1
400	s·	0		·ṡ / ṡ	0		rc	0
	ṡs·	2–			0			2
	ṣ	3	445		2		hc	2
	·ss·	3–			3			·1
	ṣ	1			0	490		3
405	hc	1			3		ṡ	0
	s·	3–		ṡ	0		·ss·	3–
		1	450	ṡ	2			0
		0			2–		s·	0
		·1			0	495		2–
410	ṣ	0			2		ṡ	0
		·1			·1			0
	hc	1	455		1			3
	hc	3			1		s·	3–
	r	0		hc	0	500		0
415		2		·s	0			0
		2			·1			·1
		2	460	hc	3		hc	3
		0		s·	0		ṡ	0

TABLE A (*cont.*)

505		0			·s	·1	590		2
		·1		rc	ṡ	3			2
	hc	0	550		ṣ̲	3		ṡ	2
		0			·s	0		ṣ	0
		0			s·̲	3–		ṡ	2–
510	s·̲	3–			s·̲	3–		r	1
	r	1				0	595	hc	3
	hc	0	555			0			0
		0			·s	·1			·1
	·s	3				0		hc	0
515	ṣ	1				·1		ṡ	·1
	hc	0	560		·s̲	1	600	hc	1
	s·	3–			s·	3–		s·̲	3–
	s·	3–				0		ṣ̲	0
	ṣ	0			·s	0			·1
520		·1				2–		·ss·	3–
	hc	1	565			2	605		0
	hc	0		hc		1		s·	3–
	ṣ	·1				0		ṣ̲	0
	ṣs·	3–				·1			0
525		1				0			0
		0	570			2	610		0
	ṣ	0			s·	1		ṡ	3
	ṣ	3				1		ṡ	1
	ṣ	0		rc		2		rc	0
530		·1				0			3
		0	575			·1	615	r	0
		2		hc		0			0
	ṣ	0				·1		·s	3
		·1		hc		1		s·	0
535		1		hc		3			0
		·1	580	r		0	620	·s	3
		0				·1		s·	3–
	·s	·1				·1		ṣ̲	0
		2–		rc		0			2
540	ṣ̲	0			ṣ	2–			2–
	ṣ	·1	585		ṣ	0	625		0
		0			ṣ	·1		·s	0
		0		hc		0		·s	0
	ṣ	·1				0		·s	3
545		1						ṡ	0
	rc	1					630	ṣ	0
		0							0

Table A (cont.)

		ṡ	0			·s	0	720			0
			2-				·1			·ss·	0
	hc		2				2-			ṡ	0
635			1				1				0
			1	680		ṡ	0			·s	·1
			0				·1	725		ṡ	0
			3			s·	3-				·1
	r		3				0				3
640			0				2-			s·	3-
		s·	3-	685		s·	1			ṡ	3
			1		rc		2	730		·s	0
	hc		0				0				0
		s·	3-|				0				0
645			1				·1				·1
			2	690	rc		0		hc		1
			2				0	735	hc		1
			3			ṡ	2			ṡ	1
			3			·s	0			ṡ	·1
650			1				·1		rc		1
			0	695			1		hc		0
			·1				0	740		s·	3-
			3			·s̲	0		r		1
			3				·1		hc		3
655		ṡ	0		hc		1			ṣ	0
			0	700			3			ṣ	0
		s·	3-		r	ṣ	0	745		·ss·	0
		ṡ̲	0				3				2
		s·	·1		r		1				1
660	rc		1				0		hc		1
		ṣ	3	705			2				0
	r		0				0	750			0
			·1		·ss·		3-				·1
	hc		3				1				3
665			0		hc		0		hc	ṡ	0
			0	710		·s	·1			ṡs·	0
		ṡ	3				0	755			0
		s·	3-				0				·1
			1				2				2-
670		ṡ	0				0			ṡ	0
			·1	715			·1				2
		s·	3-				1	760			2
			1		rc		1				0
			1				1				0
675	hc		0				0			s·	3-

TABLE A (*cont.*)

#			#			#		
		0			1	850	hc	0
765		2–		hc	3		ṡ	0
		1			0		s·	3–
		1	810		·1			1
		·1		hc	0			0
	hc	1		ṣ	·1	855		0
770		2–		·s	1			·1
	r	0		s·	3–		hc	0
		·1	815		0			0
		1			2–		·s	0
		·1			0	860	ṡ	2
775	hc	3			3			0
		0		ṡ	2			3
		2	820		1		ṡ	0
	s·	0		hc	0			·1
		2		ṡ	0	865		0
780		0			2		ṡ	·1
		·1			·1		rc	0
	hc	1	825	hc	1			
		0			0			
		·1			3			
785	hc	0			1			
		2			·0			
	·sṡ	0	830	·s	·1			
		·1			2–			
	rc	0			0			
790		0		·s	3			
	·s	·1		s·	3–			
	hc	0	835	s·	3–			
		0		ṡ	0			
		·1		·s	·1			
795	hc	1			0			
	hc	3		ṡ	2			
		1	840	ṡ	3			
		3			0			
	ṡ	1		ṡ	0			
800	hc	0		ṣ	0			
		·1		ṡs·	3–			
	s·	3–	845	s·	1			
		0		rc	0			
		0			2			
805	ṡ	·1			0			
	·s	3			·1			

Table B

Tabulation of the phenomena listed in Table A, by 50-verse sections, with totals
(For key to symbols see pp. 141f.)

Verses	0̄	·0̄+·1	0̄+·0̄+·1	1 (inc. ·1)	2	3	2+3	s (inc. ṣ)	ss (inc. ṣs etc.)	hc	rc	r	All internal stops (i.e. H, J, K, L, +2×I)	Internal strong stops	Verse-end strong stops	All strong stops	·s, ·s[s] (inc. r, rc)	ṡ, ṡ[s] (inc. hc)	ş	s·
1–50	6	15	21	17	8	3	11	12	5	4	4	1	31	5	22	27	11	8	2	8
51–100	1	4	5	10	9	17	26	21	0	4	2	3	30	10	14	24	7	19	0	6
101–150	8	8	16	15	2	12	14	18	0	4	4	1	27	10	21	31	9	11	0	7
151–200	0	12	12	22	4	9	13	10	2	5	6	3	24	7	15	22	10	9	1	4
201–250	6	7	13	14	8	8	16	16	2	5	5	1	31	4	20	24	6	14	2	9
251–300	4	4	8	14	4	16	20	17	0	5	4	2	28	8	16	24	7	14	3	3
301–350	2	1	3	7	4	22	26	27	0	3	3	3	36	15	17	32	8	17	2	10
351–400	5	6	11	13	8	13	21	18	1	4	3	1	28	7	16	23	4	13	0	10
401–450	7	5	12	9	11	10	21	12	4	3	1	1	25	9	20	29	4	14	0	7
451–500	6	8	14	14	9	7	16	10	2	6	3	1	24	4	20	24	6	11	1	4
501–550	7	11	18	18	2	9	11	20	1	6	2	2	31	7	21	28	6	19	1	4
551–600	4	10	14	17	9	5	14	15	0	8	2	2	27	9	19	28	8	14	1	4
601–650	10	1	11	7	6	15	21	19	0	2	1	1	26	5	22	27	9	9	1	7
651–700	5	9	14	17	4	10	14	16	3	3	3	3	23	5	19	24	7	9	1	6
701–750	10	6	16	18	3	7	10	13	2	6	2	1	30	5	22	27	11	11	1	4
751–800	6	10	16	20	8	5	13	6	1	9	1	1	21	5	19	24	2	13	4	3
801–850	5	9	14	14	6	11	17	19	0	5	1	0	27	9	19	28	6	13	0	6
851–867	4	3	7	4	1	2	3	6	0	1	1	0	8	1	10	9	2	5	0	1
Column	A	B	C	D	E	F	G	H	I	J	K	L	M	N	O	P	Q	R	S	T
Totals	96	129	225	248	106	181	287	275	22	83	48	27	477	125	332	455	125	222	21	103

TABLE C

Summary of episodes in *Iliad* XVI, with lists of speeches and similes

Episode	Description	Speech	Narrative
1–47	Dialogue of Patroclus and Achilles		
48–100	Achilles' impassioned speech		
101–124	Ajax forced back, Achaean ship fired		
124–129	Achilles urges Patroclus to hurry		
130–144	Arming of Patroclus		
145–154	Preparation of horses for him		
155–167	Marshaling of Myrmidons		1–6
168–197	Catalogue of Myrmidon leaders	7–19	20
198–210	Achilles exhorts them	21–45	46–48
211–220	Myrmidons in close array	49–100	101–125
220–248	Achilles' libation and prayer to Zeus	126–129	130–199
249–256	Zeus' response; Achilles watches	200–209	210–232
257–267	Myrmidons advance	233–248	249–268
268–275	Patroclus exhorts them	269–274	275–421
276–305	They attack, led by Patroclus	422–425	426–432
306–350	"Man-took-man" fighting	433–438	439
351–357	Generic description of fighting	440–457	458–491
358–376	Hector gradually forced back	492–501	502–513
377–418	Patroclus triumphs over retreating Trojans	514–526	527–537
419–430	Sarpedon rallies Lycians, faces Patroclus	538–547	548–555
431–438	Zeus wonders whether to save Sarpedon	556–561	562–614
439–458	Hera dissuades him	615–618	619
459–461	He honors Sarpedon with a portent	620–625	626
462–491	Duel of Sarpedon and Patroclus	627–631	632–666
492–501	The dying Sarpedon exhorts Glaucus	667–675	676–706
502–512	Sarpedon dies, Glaucus, wounded, is dismayed	707–709	710–720
513–526	He prays to Apollo for help	721–725	726–744
527–536	Inspired by Apollo he rallies the Trojans	745–750	751–829
537–547	He urges on Hector	830–842	843
548–553	Trojans rally	844–854	855–858
553–562	Patroclus exhorts the Ajaxes	859–861	862–867
563–568	General summary of fighting		
569–607	Mixed fighting, Trojans dominant		
608–625	Aineas attacks Meriones, taunts exchanged		

Table C (cont.)

		Developed similes
626–631	Patroclus exhorts Meriones to action not words	
632–643	General fighting round Sarpedon's body	3–4
644–655	Zeus wonders how Patroclus shall die	7–10
656–665	Zeus panics Trojans, Achaeans strip Sarpedon	156–163
		212–213
		259–265
		297–300
666–683	He bids Apollo to rescue the body	352–355
684–697	Patroclus, deluded, advances, routs Trojans	364–365
		384–392
698–711	Apollo hurls him back from wall of Troy	406–408
		428–429
712–730	Apollo urges on Hector and Cebriones, panics Achaeans	482–484
		487–489
731–750	Patroclus and Hector meet; Patroclus kills Cebriones, exults	582–583
		589–591
751–782	Fight for body of Cebriones, won by Achaeans	633–634
		641–643
783–806	Patroclus advances, is stunned and stripped by Apollo	752–753
		756–758
806–817	Patroclus wounded by Euphorbus	765–769
818–861	Hector kills him; taunts and counter-taunts as he dies	823–826
862–867	Hector chases Automedon	

These references do not include "apodoses." Total number of verses, about 73.

Formular Language and Oral Quality

G. S. KIRK

Formular Language and Oral Quality

J. A. NOTOPOULOS has maintained at length that the practice of oral poetry in Greece extended beyond the bounds of the Homeric tradition in Ionia. In *Hesperia*, 29 (1960), 177 ff., he argued in favor of the probability that there was a long-standing mainland tradition, exemplified in the Hesiodic poetry and also, no doubt, in some of the north-mainland subject-matter of the *Iliad*. Subsequently, Notopoulos extended his examination to the Homeric Hymns (*AJP*, 83 (1962), 337–68) and the fragments of the Cyclic epics (*HSCP*, 68 (1964), esp. 18–45). In these contributions there gradually becomes obtrusive an underlying assumption which requires detailed reconsideration both for its own sake and because of its crucial position in Notopoulos' general argument.

The assumption can be put very briefly: it is that any hexameter poetry which contains a high proportion of Homeric (or Hesiodic) formular phraseology (both in verbatim repetitions and in the use of so-called formula-patterns) must be, like the *Iliad* and the *Odyssey*, oral. In other words, the heavy employment of the traditional phraseology of the Ionian epic— without regard, I think it would be fair to add, to possible differences of skill in the articulation of that phraseology—is in itself a total and adequate proof of oral composition.[1]

This is, of course, a very remarkable contention, of which the effect would be to demonstrate that virtually the whole corpus of the Homeric Hymns—to take the most conspicuous case— was orally composed by singers of pure Homeric type. That would indeed be, as Notopoulos himself claims, a "sudden,

---

1. Thus "solidly formulaic character" is described by Notopoulos as constituting the "*sine qua non* test" of the oral character of early epics (*HSCP*, 68 (1964), 30f.). Indeed the presence of *one* key phrase is implied (*op. cit.* pp. 33f.) to reveal the oral character of fr. 1 of the *Cypria*.

major breakthrough" (*HSCP*, 68 (1964), 62). Now there are
notable stylistic differences, detectable through and in spite of
the plethora of Homeric phraseology, between different hymns
of the "Homeric" collection: between the long hymns and the
shorter ones, between different parts of the long hymns themselves, and between various shorter hymns. Notopoulos is not
concerned with such differences: because both the Delian and
the Delphic part of the composite Hymn to Apollo contain a
high proportion of formular language, they are according to him
both fully oral.[2] He allows, of course, that there are likely to be
differences in date of composition for different parts of the
corpus, within the range of the period extending from the
eighth century B.C. down to the sixth (*AJP*, 83 (1962), 353).
The situation with regard to the Cyclic poems is similar, and so
too with the whole Hesiodic corpus including the *Scutum*: they
are all seen as fully oral (and so, almost by definition, the work
of illiterate singers), and all come from within this period.

Before this viewpoint becomes widely accepted it should be
examined more closely.[3] There is little point in holding back
my own judgment that the viewpoint is wrong: not necessarily
wrong in effect (for little is objectively demonstrable in the field
of oral poetry) but certainly wrong—or at least imperfect and
misleading—in method. In short, Notopoulos has attacked a
subtle and complex problem with an excessively blunt instru-

2. Roughly 87% of the verses of the Delian part contain one or more
formulas, roughly 93% of the verses of the Delphic part do so, according to
the analysis given by Notopoulos at *AJP*, 83 (1962), 358. The corresponding
figures for the *Iliad* and the *Odyssey* are 88% and 93% (*op. cit.* p. 359). This
is, if fact, a very rough-and-ready kind of analysis even when regarded as a
merely quantitative type: Homeric verses containing only one formula
(especially by Notopoulos' wide definition of "formula," including formula-
types) are in fact rare. Some method of indicating the amount of formular
material within the verse is necessary if even this very limited quantitative
comparison is to have much value.

3. Surprisingly little comment appears to have been made; but see now
A. Hoekstra, *Homeric Modifications of Formulaic Prototypes* (Amsterdam 1965),
esp. p. 17.

ment—the idea that, because all oral poetry is formular, all formular poetry must be oral.

There is, of course, more to it than that; Notopoulos is too skilled to be deceived by a mere false conversion; but his real reasons for making that kind of assumption (in whatever logical form one likes to put it) seem tenuous and indeed unexamined. In essence he poses an extreme disjunction: either this post-Homeric hexameter poetry is the product of conscious and deliberate literary imitation, or it must be oral poetry similar in method to the poetry of the *Iliad* and *Odyssey*. In fact, as I shall show later, there are intermediary stages which also deserve serious consideration.

First, however, let us consider what Notopoulos terms literary *mimesis*. In the nineteenth century, at least, it was widely supposed that the Homeric Hymns, for example, were due to precisely that kind of imitation—they are school works, as it were, and the result of a conscious effort on the part of literate composers to imitate, with some adaptation to the special requirements of a hymn, the language and style of Homer. Now this is a one-sided view, certainly; but Notopoulos rejects it as a totally impossible one. He consigns it to the limbo of obsolete absurdities by a single broad contention: that the "oral theory" developed by Parry and further elaborated by Lord proves that "literary mimesis" with this degree of formular content is impossible. I do not believe that in the articles cited, or anywhere else, Notopoulos ever says substantially more on this subject than he does at *AJP*, 83 (1962), 360: "Lord's decisive chapter on the way formulae work in oral composition should bury the ghost of literary mimesis for ever" (the reference is to chapter 3, "The Formula," of *The Singer of Tales* (Cambridge, Mass. 1960), pp. 30–67). As a preliminary I should like to suggest that the implied argument is formally defective, since *no* description of "the way formulae work in oral composition" can of itself rigorously define the way in which formulae might be used in literate composition. Second, the truth is that Lord's chapter, valuable as it is, has nothing whatever to say about literary mimesis.

What Notopoulos has in mind, presumably, is that the extreme functionalism of a formular system such as we find in Homer (or rather, of *the* system we find in Homer; for that system, *pace* Lord, is unique in its degree of functionalism) entails that the system was developed for oral use. As Lord puts it (*op. cit.* p. 65), "Without this usefulness the style, and, more important, the whole practice [*sc.* of formular composition] would collapse or would never have been born." That was argued by Milman Parry and is certainly true. But is it a corollary that literary imitation can never achieve the same degree of usefulness or functionalism *or anything resembling it*?

The answer to this question surely depends on the *kind* of imitation. Imitation so slavish as to consist in simply rearranging whole verses and passages from the Homeric tradition might, as it happens, retain close to 100% of the potential and apparent functionalism of the formular vocabulary of those particular verses and passages. Now the literate imitation of oral poetry is without doubt an impure form of literature, but it can happen (and has happened, certainly, in more recent times and with other traditions); and, if it were to be slavish in the sense above, that would not in itself destroy the natural qualities of the original oral poetry—or at least those qualities which pertain to its formular phraseology. In practice the mere rearrangement of Homeric verses and verse-sequences was not carried on, or, if it was, examples have not survived. But consider a somewhat less slavish and less exact degree of imitation, in which half-lines derived from the *Iliad* or the *Odyssey* are recombined, or other formulas which fill substantial and useful portions of the verse are deployed in fresh combinations. This would be a sort of mechanical reproduction of the instinctive oral process of composition; we know it can be done, since most of us who are interested in Homer as oral poetry have probably done it, at some time or another, for our own amusement. This is literate pastiche; we operate from our exact knowledge of the text and assemble our formulas from the printed page. A low activity, indeed; and in fact nearly all literary imitation of oral epic produces results greatly inferior to the model. Yet that does not of itself prove Notopoulos' point. On the contrary, most of the Homeric Hymns, like the pseudo-Hesiodic *Scutum* or the exiguous fragments of the Cyclic poems, are vastly inferior to the Homeric exemplar. They are inferior precisely in this respect, that they take the Homeric language of formulas and redeploy it mechanically, woodenly, and with faulty or obtrusive articulation; and, where they attempt to develop or elaborate it, they often overstep the traditional boundaries of interest, taste, factual realism, or linguistic naturalness.[4]

The last sentence concedes what is obviously true, that the post-Homeric hexameter poetry with which we are concerned is both less and more than the slavish imitation that was posited to prove that literate imitation and full formular structure are not necessarily incompatible in theory. Even the lesser Hymns do more than merely rearrange established formular phrases. There is some new vocabulary,[5] a few new themes and ideas. These could certainly be the result of literate intervention, but they could also be due to regional variation or other special developments in an oral tradition. We know that adaptation and extension of the traditional language go on constantly within any living oral tradition: new words, for example, are not necessarily a sign of non-oral origin, provided that they serve some useful purpose. But, if it is true that not all formular extension is non-oral, it is equally true that not all of it need be oral. There are indeed two kinds of formular extension, and some sort of criterion is needed by which they may be dis-

4. Against the possible objection (e.g. by Lord, *AJP*, 85 (1964), 85) that we cannot tell clearly what was "traditional" since "we have two poems from ancient Greece and nothing more," I reply that these two immensely long poems present a corpus of oral style and oral elaboration from which, with care, we can learn a great deal about the probable progress of the tradition and the probable limitations of its capacity for extension and development. Naturally we would like to have evidence which was more explicit and more complete.

5. Some of it is curiously Attic: see O. Zumbach, *Neuerungen in der Sprache der homerischen Hymnen* (Winterthur 1955), pp. 57–63.

tinguished. I do not mean to imply that it necessarily exists or is available. But my own view is that a loose and tenuous criterion *is* available, and that it is associated with ease of handling, consonance with the general lines of the previous tradition, preservation at least of oral economy. In other words, and not to put too grand an appearance on a simple thought, oral extensions of the oral tradition are likely to maintain the main qualities of that tradition. If fluent handling of the formular vocabulary was a characteristic of the preceding tradition (as it presumably was with the Homeric singers), then we should expect that fluency to be continued with, at most, a steady but slight decline. Only if the practice of oral poetry suffered some significant interruption would that cease to be probable. Nothing in the known history of the seventh or sixth centuries B.C. is likely to have caused such an interruption—except, of course, the spread of literacy itself. The intervention of literate techniques of composition and literate tastes and ambitions would certainly reduce the clarity, ease, and simplicity of the old use of formulas. It is my belief that they *are* reduced, in part at least of the poetry we are considering, and that literate intervention, in one form or another, is the probable cause.

No one can doubt that literate imitation of the *Iliad* and *Odyssey* was possible in the sixth century as in the fifth and fourth. By literate imitation in this context I mean an imitation, with some degree of extension, which is committed to writing, which owes some of its detailed working-out to the aid of writing, but which might be founded upon a close *memorization* of the Homeric poems. These were known by heart by many Greeks of the fifth and fourth centuries and, presumably, of the sixth as well. Their vocabulary influenced all the nondactylic poets who were the successors of the *aoidoi*, some of them profoundly. Many Greeks, whether or not they were poets by profession, would have found it easy enough to write more or less in the Homeric style, using the Homeric formular vocabulary in a way which would be artificial—since they were not working as true oral singers—and would show many signs of strain, but which would achieve that merely quantitative resemblance which Notopoulos has roughly distinguished.

They could have so composed—but did they in fact do so? Were some of the Hymns, some parts of the Hesiodea, some of the Cyclic epics actually due to this kind of imitative technique? Unfortunately we have no direct evidence on this subject, and are unlikely to be able to find even indirect evidence which would be compelling one way or the other. There is no simple answer to this kind of question, and certainly no simple criterion like the greater or lesser incidence of formulas derived from the Ionic tradition. But at least one piece of later evidence proves absolutely, despite Notopoulos' insistence to the contrary, that literate pastiche was sometimes practiced. When one considers the learning, ingenuity, and love of *paegnia* manifested by poets of the Hellenistic age, it is not surprising that the Homeric poems became the models for pastiche; and it is to that intellectual and poetical milieu (rather than to the full classical period to which Pigres is assigned in parts of our tradition) that the *Batrachomyomachia*, the Battle of the Frogs and Mice, must probably be assigned.[6] This labored jest, consciously mock-heroic, naturally makes much use of Iliadic language and Iliadic formulas. Many of these formulas are adapted or extended to fit the circumstances of pond life, and that is part of the joke. No one could seriously suggest that this is an oral poem, or indeed that it closely resembles the Hymns, the Hesiodea, or the Cyclic fragments. Its literacy, declared in the opening verses with their mention of the poet composing with his tablets on his knee, is manifest and undeniable; but so, in patches at least, is its formular quality—if "formular" here can be taken to include a purely artificial and superficial use. This quality deserves a brief survey.

Apart from the repetition of complete Homeric verses (like 152 τοίγαρ ἐγὼν ἐρέω ὥς μοι δοκεῖ εἶναι ἄριστα or 205 δούπησεν

6. Hoekstra, *loc. cit.*, observes that the *Posthomerica* of Quintus of Smyrna is a good example of close literary imitation, formular style and all. Its lateness is irrelevant.

δὲ πεσών, ἀράβησε δὲ τεύχε' ἐπ' αὐτῷ) and many half-line or other
formulas (like 168 εἰς οὐρανὸν ἀστερόεντα or 170 ἔγχεα μακρὰ
∪ – ∪ |), there are many instances of formular adaptation. For
example the first half of 168, Ζεὺς δὲ θεοὺς καλέσας: this is not
taken directly from the *Iliad* or the *Odyssey* or any other known
source, but | Ζεὺς δὲ (e.g. *Il.* VIII.2), | νεῦσ' ἐπὶ οἷ καλέσας (*Od.*
17.330), and θεοὺς ἀγορήνδε καλέσσας | (e.g. *Il.* XX.16), show
clearly enough how the wording of the later poem is compounded.
Two verses later, at 170, ἔγχεα μακρά is Homeric enough, as
already noted, but the whole verse is, strictly speaking, "new":
πολλοὺς καὶ μεγάλους ἠδ' ἔγχεα μακρὰ φέροντας. Yet its parts are
all Homeric: compare e.g. XII.57, | πυκνοὺς καὶ μεγάλους, while
φέρονται -εσ -ας comes frequently at the verse-end, as does
ἠδ', -έ as a connective after the main caesura. This whole verse
could conceivably have occurred in some lost part of the epic
tradition, though the total effect is not very happy; so it is not
proved that the literate poet of the *Batrachomyomachia* could
achieve this degree of formular recombination. Yet his powers
can be proved by referring to his replacement of Iliadic proper
names by the comic names of frogs and mice, or by his adaptation of the formulas of Homeric battle-scenes to the mock-heroic
warfare of his animals: for example 17 f.,

> εἰμὶ δ' ἐγὼ βασιλεὺς Φυσίγναθος, ὃς κατὰ λίμνην
> τιμῶμαι βατράχων ἡγούμενος ἤματα πάντα,

or 226 ff.,

> Λιτραῖον δ' ἄρ' ἔπεφνεν ἀμύμων Βορβοροκοίτης
> χερμαδίῳ πλήξας κατὰ βρέγματος· ἐγκέφαλος δὲ
> ἐκ ῥινῶν ἔσταξε, παλάσσετο δ' αἵματι γαῖα.

The sharp and experienced observer (or, more to the point,
perhaps, the careful and assiduous concordance-user) easily
detects in this sort of thing much that is foreign to the Homeric
tradition, even apart from the mock-heroic conversions. Yet
there is a good deal, too, which *is* traditional, and which has
been deployed in a manner other than utterly slavish. The fact
is that this poet, whom we tend to regard as a mere hack and

whose popularity in later antiquity and in the later middle ages is no tribute to the literary judgment of those periods, can imitate Homer quite well when he wishes, not only by verbatim repetition but also by the recombination and adaptation of formulas:

ὣς ἄρ' ἔφη· καὶ τῇ γε θεοὶ ἐπεπείθοντ' ἄλλοι,
πάντες δ' αὖτ' εἰσῆλθον ἀολλέες εἰς ἕνα χῶρον.
καὶ τότε κώνωπες μεγάλας σάλπιγγας ἔχοντες
δεινὸν ἐσάλπιγξαν πολέμου κτύπον· οὐρανόθεν δὲ
Ζεὺς Κρονίδης βρόντησε, τέρας πολέμοιο κακοῖο. (197 ff.)

All this from a professedly literate poet of mean ability and a period when the oral tradition was utterly dead.

If we started marking up the last passage, for example, with those solid or broken underlinings which Notopoulos (following Parry and Lord) uses to distinguish formula-repetitions or formula-patterns respectively, we should end up with just as impressive-looking a network as anything he produces. And on his principles we ought therefore to claim that this passage must be oral poetry. We know in fact that it is not, and in addition we can recognize by careful (and not just superficial) examination that it has certain characteristics which reveal that its composer is not a natural oral singer. Of course this is in part an unfair argument: the *Batrachomyomachia* as a whole would not possess the quantity of formular language that occurs in the passages I have selected, and thus would not share the total formular characteristics of many of the Hymns, for example. But it does suffice to invalidate, utterly and completely as I believe, the contention that "literary mimesis of the *Iliad* and *Odyssey*" is impossible; and the Homeric pastiche of Quintus of Smyrna, several centuries later, does the same.

Formular *quantity*, then, proves to be an imperfect test of orality. It raises the possibility, certainly; but the *Batrachomyo-machia* proves, if proof be needed, that literary imitation can result in as heavy a concentration of formulas as can be found in the oral exemplar. It does not achieve this degree of

concentration consistently, in more than patches, but that may
be due to its author's special intention of parodying, rather than
more or less exactly reproducing, a style. The Hymns, Hesiodea,
and Cyclic fragments are for the most part consistent in their
predominant employment of formular language; that difference
may be due to earlier date, greater reverence for the Homeric
model, and so on, rather than to a similarly oral kind of
composition.[7]

If a poem on the Homeric model is oral, then it will certainly
possess formular *quantity*, but it will also possess a natural style
(and of course a traditional economy in vocabulary) of which an
important part is concerned with the deployment, adaptation,
and articulation of formulas and may be crudely termed
formular *quality*. Literate imitations will be unlikely to achieve
this natural quality, which is a more subtle, less tangible, and
less easily imitable aspect of oral style. It is to this, then, that
one will look for a criterion which is theoretically more reliable
but also, unfortunately, more subjective in practice than the
merely quantitative assessment of formular characteristics.

Thus a short Hymn like xxvii, to Artemis, is stuffed with
Homeric phraseology, but gives a forced, redundant or
plethoric, and artificial impression. When one examines the
poem closely one notices that a verse like 12, εὐφρήνῃ δὲ νόον
χαλάσασ᾽ εὐκαμπέα τόξα, contributes to this impression of strain
by some new uses of what at first sight appears to be traditional
formular language. Phrases like εὐφρήνῃ δὲ νόον are reserved in
Homer for the idea of pleasing another person (e.g. *Od.* 20.82,
μηδέ τι χείρονος ἀνδρὸς ἐϋφραίνοιμι νόημα); the part of oneself
that one gives pleasure or pain to is the φρήν, in phrases like

7. I do not of course mean to suggest that the Hymns and the other
works are necessarily *not* oral; rather that Notopoulos' quantitative criterion
is indecisive, and must be supplemented by other criteria. Even then a
definite decision may be impossible for the bulk of this poetry. My own
impression is that the longer Hymns are for the most part oral, but that
many of the shorter ones are literate; that the Cyclic fragments are in part
literate; that much of the poetry associated with Hesiod is oral, but that the
Scutum shows signs of skilled literary intervention.

φρένα τερπόμενον (ix.186). As it happens, τερφθῇ has already occurred in the preceding verse, of which 12 is an expansion or repetition. Perhaps that accounts for the apparently new adaptation; though it is worth noting that, whereas the repetition of an idea in a separate verse is not uncommon in the oral tradition, it does not normally entail the use of unfamiliar or untraditional language; the singer is prepared to create, but presumably not often in this kind of small-scale, normally automatic elaboration. εὐκαμπέα, too, is not otherwise applied to the bow (it is not found in the *Iliad*, but appears twice in the *Odyssey*, once of a key and once of a sickle). A frequent formula is καμπύλα τόξα; I suppose there is no reason why εὐκαμπέα τόξα should not also be an oral formula, used when the extra syllable was required, since the space from the hephthemimeral word-break to the end of the verse was one which sometimes needed to be filled by a single formula. Yet it remains curious that no such formula occurs in the *Iliad* or the *Odyssey*, where τόξον or τόξα recur nearly 80 times and where καμπύλα, ἀγκύλα, and παλίντονον, -α in various positions in the verse seem to form an adequately flexible mainstay of the system. But the really odd word in our verse is χαλάσασ'. This verb does not occur in the Homeric poems; that does not of itself worry me—what does worry (or at least puzzle) me is that its uses in post-Homeric literature show that when applied to a bow it regularly means "loose" in the sense of "unstring", while the context here suggests that it means "loose" in the sense of "discharge, release, shoot."[8] The former meaning is clear in the only other occurrence of the verb in the Hymns (*Hy. Ap.* 6). Here a non-Homeric verb is used in a sense which is surprising even by the standards of its post-Homeric application. That in itself may not argue decisively against its oral quality; what aggravates the situation is that it is an uneconomical variant for a well-

---

8. That is, the participle χαλάσασ' must surely depend on εὐφρήνῃ δὲ νόον. The only alternative would be to attach it to l. 13: "having unstrung her bow she comes into the hall..."; but that leaves εὐφρήνῃ δὲ νόον intolerably in the air.

developed and traditional formular expression of this kind of
concept, namely that of stringing, unstringing, or, more
specifically, discharging a bow: τιταίνουσ᾽ ἀγκύλα τόξα is an
obvious and fully traditional phrase which would have avoided
some of the strains of the verse with which we are presented.
That it is a (short) syllable shorter presents no real problem.

Four verses later in the same Hymn another verse, also
concerned with the bow, points in the same direction. Here the
language seems more exactly Homeric: ἔνθα κατακρεμάσασα
παλίντονα τόξα καὶ ἰούς (16). Yet παλίντονα τόξα καὶ ἰούς gives a
weak and anticlimactic effect, mainly because of the last two
words (contrast xv.472); moreover hanging up *arrows* is a
slightly odd idea in itself. It makes sense only if the arrows were
in a quiver, which must have been the case; but the traditional
formular language has a perfectly good word for that, namely
φαρέτρη: τόξον δ᾽ ἀγκρεμάσασα παλίντονον ἠδὲ φαρέτρην (cf.
i.440, xv.443) would have been a far more satisfactory, and
fully traditional, way of expressing the poet's thought.[9]

Verse-sequences like these may look very Homeric by the
crude criterion of vocabulary or sheer quantity of formulas;
they look very un-Homeric, very untraditional, in certain other
important respects. It is not my purpose here to argue that they
must therefore be non-oral; that certainly could not be proved.
But they do raise a distinct possibility—perhaps more—of non-
oral, imitative composition, and that should not be disguised by

---

9. ἀγκρεμάσασ᾽ is vastly preferable to κατακρεμάσασα, which stresses
hanging *down* (from a peg in its only Homeric use, *Od.* 8.67) and is
inappropriate here—unless the extraordinary suggestion in LSJ *s.v.* κατα-
κρέμαμαι is correct, that the meaning in this passage is "having hung the
bow on herself." I take it that she hangs the bow and quiver on a wall or
pillar, as normally in Homer with bows, quivers and lyres.
   There is another difficulty at the beginning of the following verse, 17,
where καλὸν χορόν from 15 has to be understood, with some strain, as
object of ἡγεῖται, with ἐξάρχουσα χορούς in 18 as resumptive and elaborative. Alternatively, χορούς in 18 is intended to be the object of ἡγεῖται,
with the rest of 17 strictly parenthetical—but in that case ἐξάρχουσα is
strange. Whichever is correct, the sentence-structure is clumsy and unnatural.

sweeping generalizations or excessive enthusiasm for the idea of oral poetry as such.

I have already noted that, as a whole, the short Hymns present more untraditional characteristics of style than the longer ones. In contrast with Hymn xxvii, the Hymn to Delian Apollo, for example, seems fluent and traditional in its handling of the oral language. All of it, that is, except for its first eighteen verses, a prologue which has been generally recognized as a later attachment to the hymn. Unfortunately it is just this passage that is chosen by Notopoulos as typical, and subjected to a detailed examination (*AJP*, 83 (1962), 354 ff.). Those who wish to analyze sample passages of hexameter poetry might do well to avoid prologues and opening passages altogether, as they are particularly prone to reworking. Yet Notopoulos' use of this passage helps my case, though not his own, by emphasizing once again the contrast between the quantitative occurrence of Homeric formulas and the qualitative use and articulation of those formulas. Notopoulos' underlinings, whether broken or continuous, make an impressive ocular demonstration of "Homeric" style; but, once the subtler criterion of articulation and use is brought to bear, the "Homeric" style becomes much less certain—in fact a careful reading of the passage reveals that beneath the surface it is strikingly untraditional. Consider what this prologue tells us: that the gods in Zeus' house tremble and leap to their feet when Apollo approaches, stretching his bow (1–4); that Leto looses his bow (i.e. unstrings it, ἐχάλασσε; compare what was said on this verb on p. 165 above) and closes his quiver, takes his bow from his shoulders, and hangs it up "against the pillar of his father," πρὸς κίονα πατρὸς ἑοῖο (8), where one would expect— and the formular language of the tradition would most naturally supply—"of his father's *house*" or some similar phrase; then Zeus himself offers Apollo nectar (10), and finally the birth of Apollo in Delos is referred to, with Leto "leaning against tall mountain and Cynthian hill," κεκλιμένη πρὸς μακρὸν ὄρος καὶ Κύνθιον ὄχθον (17), a clause in which the linking of generic and then more specific description is only superficially similar to Homeric repetitions of the κατὰ φρένα καὶ κατὰ θυμόν kind (and in which ὄχθος, for what it is worth, is unknown to the hexameter tradition). The last line, 18, of this prologue further describes Leto as leaning "closest to the palm-tree, under the streams of Inopus," ἀγχοτάτω φοίνικος ὑπ᾽ ᾽Ινωποῖο ῥεέθροις, in which ἀγχοτάτω is an *Atticism* (and a grossly uneconomical departure from the tradition, in place of the traditional and metrically equivalent ἄγχιστον) and ὑπ᾽ with the dative, of water, is bizarre.[10]

There are three particular peculiarities in this passage: the ethos of the description of Apollo—his fierce arrival and the respect shown him by the other gods, including Zeus; the description of his bow and quiver and what happens to them (here we may fruitfully compare the uncertain language of the bow-passage in Hymn xxvii, considered above); and the description of the birth of Apollo in Delos. In the two last cases it is the manner of using and varying formular language, as much as the underlying thought, which seems strikingly un-traditional. (There are, of course, other points at which this prologue diverges from Homeric practice or belief, but they can be paralleled from other Hymns and are a perfectly possible development carrying no implications for the treatment of the traditional epic language.) The peculiarities raise a legitimate doubt about the method and date of composition of this prologue: a doubt which will be felt more or less strongly by different judges, but which there is no advantage in concealing by the misleadingly one-sided quantitative type of analysis. That analysis does, of course, have its positive lesson: that even poetry very dissimilar from the Homeric in ethos and idiom

10. Reiz's ἐπ᾽ for ὑπ᾽ looks an obvious improvement; but why should the tradition have stuck so firmly to the *lectio difficilior*? Moreover ἀγχοτάτω φοίνικος might suggest that the sense "close to the river" was also aimed at; and this suggests an (impermissible) extension of e.g. ὑπὸ Τμώλῳ, *Il.* ii.866, rather than the vaguer location of ἐπί ᾱs in e.g. ἐπ᾽ ὠκυρόῳ Κελάδοντι, vii.133. But I do not press this point.

may contain a high proportion of Homeric vocabulary and phraseology. The same lesson was learned from the consideration of certain passages of the *Batrachomyomachia*.

The dangers of the *qualitative* criterion, on the other hand, are obvious enough. Its application involves a personal opinion about what may or may not be acceptable oral practice in the way of analogy and oral extension. Not all singers were in the class of a Homer—perhaps none other than he. Even a good singer would have his less adept days. Normally the process of tradition would eradicate the weaker songs, but some might survive. The examples from the Hymns considered above may be violent enough and concentrated enough to cause serious doubt about a completely oral origin. In the fragments of the Cyclic poems, by contrast, which Notopoulos considers at *HSCP*, 68 (1964), 28 ff., the departures from a smooth and traditional application of the formular language are rarer and more ambiguous. Fr. II (Allen, 2 Kinkel) of the *Thebais*, for example, contains in its ten verses one conspicuous departure from the economy of an epithet-system and one rather strained combination of two uses of a traditional phrase. In l. 3, ἀργυρέην Κάδμοιο θεόφρονος· αὐτὰρ ἔπειτα, the choice of θεόφρονος—a compound unique in the epic tradition—is a clear departure from the thrift of the oral epic. The standard laudatory epithet for this position in the verse is δαΐφρονος (28 × in Homer, 2 × in *Hy. Dem.*); compare for example *Il.* XI.197 (cf. IX.647), εὗρ' υἱὸν Πριάμοιο δαΐφρονος, Ἕκτορα δῖον.[11] There may be some reason for emphasizing Cadmus' piety or godlike qualities at this point, but it is hardly enough to justify, by the normal standards of the oral tradition, the obtrusive departure from accepted phraseology. This sort of thing smacks of the literate poet.

Then at line 6, when Oedipus perceived his father's valuable gifts set beside him, "great evil fell upon his spirit," μέγα οἱ κακὸν ἔμπεσε θυμῷ, and he cursed his two sons. Notopoulos simply underlines these words as a Homeric formula, and

11. On the use of δαΐφρονος see M. Parry, *L'Épithète traditionnelle dans Homère* (Paris 1928), pp. 159ff.

refers in a note to xvii.625 and 12.266. Yet neither these verses
nor others which he might have cited explain the oddness of the
Thebais phrase. ἔμπεσε θυμῷ is evidently a well-established
formula; it is used five times in the *Iliad*, once in the *Odyssey*.
What "falls upon the spirit" is a kind of emotion: usually
anger, χόλος ἔμπεσε θυμῷ, once fear. In the Odyssean occurrence
an extension takes place, and a word or saying falls upon
Telemachus' spirit (12.266), meaning that Telemachus remembered that saying. In the *Thebais* fragment the application
is different again; and the author is probably now thinking of
another kind of formula involving ἔμπεσε, represented by *Od.*
2.45 and 15.375, ∪ – κακὸν ἔμπεσεν οἴκῳ. An evil can come upon
a household; can it come upon the spirit? And if so, in what
sense? The exact sense is surely ambiguous in the fragment:
what falls upon Oedipus' spirit might be an evil emotion,
namely rage, or a bad (undesirable) emotion, namely grief, or
it might be a great evil for the future. Yet in the first and second
case the exact emotion should and would be named in normal
traditional language: for example by the words δριμὺς χόλος
ἔμπεσε θυμῷ (cf. xvi.206, xviii.322; δριμύς here rather than
κακός, to establish a metrically equivalent phrase). The verse
would probably have been cast somewhat differently if ἄχος,
grief, had been involved—had been clearly in the composer's
mind, that is; but any true oral poet could have expressed the
idea "grief came upon him," after the masculine caesura, in
several different ways, all clear, unambiguous, and fluent. In
the third case, if μέγα οἱ κακόν in the *Thebais* fragment implies
"great evil" in more general terms, as in the μέγα...κακόν (in
a similar rhythmical context) of xi.404 and 9.423, then its
application to Oedipus' spirit is strained indeed; to avoid an
almost meaningless vagueness we should have to understand
κακόν to mean ἄτη. No precise reconstruction of the author's
state of mind at this moment of composition is possible; but it
looks as though he is simply conflating two distinct formular
applications of ἔμπεσε: an emotion "falls upon" the spirit, an
evil "falls upon" a house. Our author, for no apparent reason,

has made an evil "fall upon" the spirit of Oedipus, with consequent detriment to clarity and sense.

The question is whether a fully oral poet, completely and instinctively familiar with the traditional language of formulas, would have committed this kind of mild *gaffe*. Again, obviously, no certain answer is possible: I merely observe that a difficulty of this kind is relevant to the oral or literate status of this passage, and that unfamiliarity with the traditional uses and possible extensions of a traditional phrase must be balanced against sheer quantity of formular phraseology. In the present case, I confess, my own feeling at present is that the superficial combination of formular uses, with an underlying semantic confusion, is more appropriate to the literate *pasticheur* than to the illiterate, instinctive, usually logical singer.

The use of epic phraseology in the post-Homeric era extended, of course, beyond hexameter poetry. Callinus, Tyrtaeus, Solon, Alcman, and Alcaeus all use epic words and phrases to a noticeable degree. Recently D. L. Page has shown that the surviving fragments of Archilochus are replete with epic language—much more so than had been suspected.[12] This language occurs not only in the dactylic poems, but even in the iambic elements of the mixed poems and also in the purely iambic or trochaic poems. In these nondactylic, epodic poems the dactylic formulas of the epic have to undergo some rearrangement or adaptation. Page argues that cretic types of verse may be quite old, and certainly go back beyond the introduction of alphabetic writing into Greece *ca.* 800/750 B.C. He thinks, too, that the adaptation of dactylic formulas into cretic shapes may be a traditional occupation, carried out orally, and that in the majority of his poems Archilochus too was composing as an oral poet. Now the argument for the antiquity of epodic poetry is interesting, but it seems to me that no more than a possibility can be regarded as established. Moreover Page seems to accept the essence of that other argument, presented in its clearest

12. *Entretiens Hardt* (Vandœuvres-Genève 1965), x, pp. 119 ff.

form by Notopoulos, which I have been trying to question: that the frequent use of Homeric (or at least Ionic-epic) phraseology is a sure sign that the poetry in which it occurs was composed orally, that is, in the way in which the *Iliad* and the *Odyssey* were composed. He adduces as supporting evidence the relative newness of alphabetic writing even around the middle of the seventh century, when much of Archilochus' composition was probably done. This particular point seems to me (as it seemed to some of the members of the *Entretien*) to be uncompelling: the written composition of an *Iliad* before 700 B.C. may well be difficult to envisage, but the writing of short poems some two generations later is a very different matter.

Archilochus is, of course, in a different category from that of the composers of the Hymns and the Cyclic poems: the amount of exact verbal repetition of epic phraseology is not so large (surprisingly large though it may be) even in the purely dactylic poems. What is chiefly of interest is the conversion of dactylic formulas into cretic variants. Here, in my opinion, probability is against Page's hypothesis of oral composition, since oral poetry is by its nature conservative and functional. Semantic and rhythmical needs overlap to produce a system of language whose units are only rarely susceptible of variation. A formular phrase has a particular association for the singer, a single function which it, and it alone, performs whenever the semantic and rhythmical needs conspire to demand it. That any true oral singer would take such formulas and deliberately apply them to different rhythmical functions, in a different type of verse, seems *a priori* unlikely (though here we must remember that rare singers in the modern Balkans have been, or become, bilingual, and have succeeded—though usually, it seems, under difficulties—in converting songs from one language to another).

Using Page's analysis, one can see that there are two degrees of formular adaptation in Archilochus:

(1) Simple alterations of word order, number, or case: e.g. fr. 25 D., l. 4, ὤμους κατεσκίαζε καὶ μετάφρενα. Compare (as Page observes, *op. cit.* p. 150) *Il.* II.265, *Od.* 8.528, μετάφρενον ἠδὲ καὶ

ὤμους; similarly fr. 22 D., ll. 2–3, οὐδ᾽ ἀγαίομαι | θεῶν ἔργα, on which Page (*ibid.*) cites *Od.* 20.16, ἀγαιομένου κακὰ ἔργα, and *Il.* xvi.120, ἔργα θεῶν.

(2) The reworking of a complex formula, with changes not only in word order and word form but also in some terms (this occurs especially in the trochaic tetrameters): e.g. fr. 65 D., οὐ γὰρ ἐσθλὰ κατθανοῦσι κερτομέειν ἐπ᾽ ἀνδράσιν—"an adaptation, with the least possible change, of *Od.* 22.412, οὐχ ὁσίη κταμένοισιν ἐπ᾽ ἀνδράσιν εὐχετάασθαι" (Page, p. 155).

To take the last example, it seems unlikely that an oral poet would deliberately convert οὐχ ὁσίη into οὐ γὰρ ἐσθλά, and so on, if he were operating as a "true" oral poet, by which I mean instinctively and with unconscious reliance on the formular arsenal of his particular tradition. On the other hand *any* poet who was steeped in the *Iliad* and the *Odyssey*, who knew the whole of them by heart in the way in which many Greeks did, even in the fifth and fourth centuries B.C., might choose to reproduce an aphorism of the "rejoicing over dead men" kind in a different verse-form; and in so doing he might naturally reuse, with some adaptation, as much of the familiar phraseology of the well-known Homeric form of the idea as was feasible. Whether he might do so with stylus continuously in hand, or just mentally, is not very important; the point is that, even if he did the latter, he would not really be acting as an oral poet in the sense in which we use that term. That Archilochus probably worked from his remembered knowledge of Homer, and not from a written text; that he might have composed his poems in his head, and even recited them before ever they were set down on papyrus—these things we may concede, without thereby saying or implying that he was therefore an oral poet.

I believe that at the present stage of Homeric studies, at the present stage of theorizing about oral poetry in general, there is a serious danger of getting our categories mixed. Indeed I believe they already *are* mixed; that the contrast between "oral" and "literate" has already caused confusion—and I do not refer to the confusion in the minds of those who use the excesses of the comparative method as an excuse for rejecting it altogether. Even for more sophisticated minds than these, *literate composition* has come to stand as the only alternative to *oral poetry*. Yet "oral poetry" itself is far too imprecise an expression, as we have seen; primarily it has come to refer to the mode of composition of *aoidoi* and *guslari*, but it can also be applied to recitations by rhapsodes, for example. A truer and less confusing antithesis, I suggest, is between *natural composition in a formular tradition* (that is, "oral poetry" in its primary sense) and *deliberate, self-conscious composition in a formular style*, whether with the aid of writing or not. The natural type of composition *depends on* a system of traditional verbal and rhythmical patterns, irrespective of whether it is significantly creative or almost completely reproductive. The self-conscious type is deliberately imitative; it *uses* but does not depend on formulas, just as it may use but does not necessarily depend on writing.

Archilochus certainly belongs to the second type, not the first. How far and at what stages he used the art of writing in the process of composition and standardization is of secondary importance, and is a matter for conjecture. Certainly his case does nothing to support the Notopoulos theory that all poetry heavily infected by the terminology of the Ionic epic was necessarily "oral" in the full sense. On the contrary, it demonstrates that an intimate knowledge of the poems of Homer enabled people who were not true oral poets to make remarkable use of the old formular vocabulary. Let us keep it absolutely clear in our minds that the use—even the heavy use—of formular phraseology derived from true oral poetry is not a certain sign of similarly true oral procedures, unless other signs are also present; signs such as the observation of formular economy, the naturalness of formular extension and articulation, and the preservation of traditional details of rhythm and enjambment.

Have We Homer's *Iliad*?

ADAM PARRY

Have We Homer's *Iliad*?

THE GREAT HISTORIAN of Greek literature, Albin Lesky, singles out as the Homeric Question of our time, the relation of the orally composed song to our texts of the *Iliad* and the *Odyssey*.[1] Since the original assertion of Milman Parry, in the early 1930s, that modern improvised narrative poetry (such as that of Yugoslavia) is in fundamental respects similar to Homer, almost every Homeric scholar has discussed the validity of the analogy, and taken up a position in regard to it. The names of Sir Maurice Bowra, T. B. L. Webster, Cedric H. Whitman, Denys Page, A. B. Lord, and G. S. Kirk come immediately to mind. The last-named scholar in particular has directly confronted the question, first in two articles, "Homer and Modern Oral Poetry: Some Confusions" (*CQ*, NS 10 (1960), 271–81) and "Dark Age and Oral Poet" (*Proceedings of the Cambridge Philological Society*, NS 7 (1961), 34–48) and then in his comprehensive book on Homer, *The Songs of Homer* (Cambridge 1962), esp. pp. 55–101.

It is with the arguments and the conclusions of Kirk's first article, and their amplifications in his book, that we shall be concerned here.[2] These arguments open the widest perspectives upon the traditional questions of the origin and the transmission of the Homeric poems. And they involve a more fundamental question: what are the *Iliad* and the *Odyssey*?

1. In his *Geschichte der griechischen Literatur* (2nd ed. Bern 1963), p. 34, henceforward referred to as *Lesky*. The whole section on oral composition has been added since the first edition of 1957/8.

2. The book will henceforth be referred to as *Songs*, the first article as *Poetry*. The second article deals primarily with the question of oral poetry in the post-Mycenaean Age, and does not often enter this discussion. If the first article is referred to nearly as often as the book, it is because it states in explicit and argumentative form some relevant ideas which then become the theoretical basis of what is said in the book.

177

By modern or living oral poetry, any student of Homer will now mean that of Yugoslavia, as it is known to us by the at once scholarly and romantic field work of Milman Parry, carried on between 1933 and 1935, and then by its continuation under M. Parry's assistant and successor in this endeavor, A. B. Lord of Harvard University. This work is so far available in the form of (*a*) articles by Milman Parry himself after the Yugoslav work was begun, especially "Whole Formulaic Verses in Greek and Southslavic Heroic Song," *TAPA*, 64 (1933), 179–97; (*b*) articles by A. B. Lord;[3] (*c*) in Lord's publication of the songs from Novi Pazar (English translations appear in vol. I), first of a projected series of volumes of Yugoslav heroic narrative verse collected by Parry and Lord and now in the Milman Parry Collection at Harvard University;[3] and (*d*) in Lord's recent book, *The Singer of Tales* (Cambridge, Mass. 1960).

It cannot be said that the discovery and publication of this Yugoslav material put the whole question of Homer in a new light: Parry had already done that several years earlier by the elaborate and precise examination of the text of Homer in his French *thèses, L'Épithète traditionnelle dans Homère* and *Les Formules et la Métrique d'Homère* (Paris 1928), which showed that our *Iliad* and *Odyssey* are composed in a traditional style designed to enable illiterate singers to improvise heroic song.[4]

3. Articles: *TAPA*, 67 (1936), 106–13; 69 (1938), 439–45; 82 (1951), 71–80; 84 (1953), 124–34; *AJA*, 52 (1948), 34–44. The initial volumes of *Serbocroatian Heroic Songs* (vol. 1, subtitled *Novi Pazar: English Translations*, vol. 2, subtitled *Novi Pazar: Srpskohrvatski Tekstovi*) were published in Cambridge, Mass., and Belgrade in 1954 and 1953 respectively. I have not dealt here through lack of space with the important work of J. A. Notopoulos in modern Greek oral poetry.

4. That the style is traditional and therefore *oral* (for composition in performance and not dependent on the use of the written word) may be taken as proved: it is not necessarily proved that our *Iliad* and *Odyssey* were composed orally. See below, pp. 210 ff., and my forthcoming introduction to *The Making of Homeric Verse, the Collected Papers of Milman Parry* (Oxford: Clarendon Press).

But the exposition of the living tradition in Yugoslavia, which Parry conceived as an external confirmation of his analytic conclusions, following as it does Parry's demonstration of the nature of Homeric diction, has made a powerful impression of its own. It has seemed to some that we can now observe living bards who are, to be sure, less great than Homer and work in a less great tradition, but who, apart from the differences in aesthetic quality, of which little need be said after one has recognized that they exist, are in all essentials like Homer himself. It is, against all hope, our dream come true: we can see and hear Homer sing! There is no doubt that such a dream animated the ardent though precise mind of Parry himself; and I hope it is not wrong to say that almost all of what Lord says in his fascinating book assumes this essential equivalence of the Yugoslav bard with the author of the *Iliad*.

With this belief Kirk disagrees. He is not alone in doing so: there are those who have objected on general grounds, e.g. Wade-Gery in *The Poet of the Iliad* (Cambridge 1952); and there are others who ignore the whole question, speaking of Homer in terms which any validity at all of Parry's and Lord's work would show to be wholly inapplicable to Homer.[5] And Lesky himself in his careful and magisterial survey (*op. cit.* pp. 53–8) seems to bring up the analogy, only finally to reject it in favor of a Homer who wrote and cross-checked in writing, and was far more like a literary poet than like the minstrel in the Serbian coffee-house.[6]

It is Kirk, however, who confronts the matter directly. In his key article he is debating with Lord and to some extent with S. Dow, who has accepted and generalized some of Lord's conclusions. The purpose of this article is to continue the fruitful

5. E.g., S. Benardete's study of Homeric epithets, "Achilles in the *Iliad*," *Hermes*, 91 (1963), 1–16.

6. This does not mean that Lesky rejects Parry's proof of the traditional nature of Homeric diction and much that the study of Yugoslav epic can tell us. He is only aware of the limitation of the proof as I stated it above (n. 4).

debate. For we have here not merely a scholarly argument: what is in question is our whole conception of the *Iliad* and the *Odyssey*.

Parry avoided the old Homeric Question: was the *Iliad* (to concentrate for the sake of convenience on the greater poem), substantially as we now have it, the product of a single designer, or is our text some sort of composite to which many hands contributed?[7] The proof of the traditional character of Homeric diction seemed to Parry to make this question almost otiose: even if one singer did put together our *Iliad*, his debt to the tradition was so great that the song could still be said to be a direct manifestation of the tradition and the work of the generations of bards who made and preserved that tradition. The important thing was the style, and above that, the mood, of heroic poetry. This belonged to all bards when the tradition was in its vigor. The particular responsibility for our *Iliad* was incidental. Such seem to have been Parry's feelings on the question. At any rate, the revelation of how thoroughly the language of the *Iliad* is controlled by a formulary system which it took generations of bards to form, was, as Parry clearly saw, one more hopeless impediment to any analytic solution of the old Homeric Question: the style of both *Iliad* and *Odyssey* was so uniform in respect of formula and meter that chronological layers or different hands could not conceivably be detected. Parry therefore contented himself with defining *Homer* for practical purposes as "either the text of the *Iliad* and *Odyssey* or the poet or poets of these poems,"[8] and never entering into the question further, except to state that old-fashioned analysis was impossible and to imply that it was irrelevant.

Absolute dating interested him little more. He regarded the Homeric poems as historical documents only in so far as they attested and embodied an heroic world where bards kept alive the tradition of heroic narrative. The only *date* he was concerned

7. Cf. Paul Shorey's review of M. Parry's *thèses*, *CP*, 23 (1928), 305–6.
8. *L'Épithète*, p. 3 n. 1.

with was the point at which the traditional style loses its hold on the singers of tales.[9]

Lord has been less austere in relation to these points. Dating has not engaged his efforts, but he has generally, though without argument, assumed that the *Iliad* and the *Odyssey* have each one author or have the same author.[10] And on the matter of the formation of the written text and the date of composition he takes a clear, and original, stand. Two principles determine the answer to these problems: (1) an orally composed poem cannot be handed on by the tradition of oral song without fundamental change;[11] and (2) "the [oral] poet's powers are destroyed if he learns to read and write."[12]

Kirk rejects the first of these principles and accepts the second. It may be, as we shall consider later, that he has made the wrong choice. But first we must look at the consequences of

9. E.g., Parry's discussion (*L'Épithète*, pp. 163–4) of the Hesiodic line fr. 94, 21 Rzach, where he argues, from the oddity and possible particularity of the phrase, that the epic tradition no longer "possédait toute sa vigueur." The argument there depends on the assumption that the Hesiodic poet disposed of the same stock of formulae as Homer.

10. Cf. *Singer*, ch. 7, "Homer," pp. 141 ff., where he constantly refers to, e.g., "the composer of the Homeric poems."

11. Kirk quotes Dow's formulation of the principle (*CW*, 49 (1956), 117) as an example of the extreme view he wishes to combat: "*Verbatim* oral transmission of a poem composed orally and not written down is unknown."

12. The formulation is Dow's, from a mimeographed sheet accompanying his recent Sather Lectures. Cf. Lord, *Homer's Originality*, pp. 129 ff., and *Singer*, pp. 124 ff. Actually, Lord is rather more cautious: there are oral poets who can read and write (*Singer*, p. 129). He insists only that they cannot *use* their knowledge of writing to help them compose a song. The song itself is either a product of the unlettered tradition (though conceivably the singer might be able on another occasion to write something), or it is a literary poem, which, whatever its merits, will have lost the qualities of heroic song. On this last point cf. the quotations from Kačić, *Singer*, 132, and Lord's comments.

Parry could not make a statement on this point in his pre-Yugoslavian work, since there was no evidence. But his firm distinction between poets of traditional, and poets of individual, style (esp. *L'Épithète*, pp. 146 ff.) favors such a conclusion on logical grounds.

Lord's principles; for it is disagreement with what follows from them that leads Kirk to his criticisms of detail.

If an improvised heroic poem is, as Lord is convinced, a Protean thing which can never be reproduced unless it is somehow recorded then and there, at the moment of its performance,[13] then our text of the *Iliad* can only have come into being at the point when it was first put into writing. Even if what Kirk calls the "monumental" composition took place earlier, still that large-scale song would have so changed with each singing that "Homer" must have been the man who performed it when it became fixed with the help of the alphabet. This will necessarily give to the composition of the *Iliad* a *terminus post quem* in the later part of the eighth century, depending on when it is believed that the use of the alphabet achieved some sort of currency.[14]

More important to our concept of what we have in the text of the *Iliad*, the application of Lord's first principle gives us the comforting sense that our *Iliad* is in its essentials a faithful transcript of the song the great poet sang. Admittedly there may be scribal errors and interpolations; but the thing must have been put into writing at the moment of composition, and there is good hope—though neither Lord nor Bowra nor Whitman enters much into this phase of the problem—that the written text survived at least two centuries or so until the

13. Cf. Bowra, *Homer and his Forerunners* (Edinburgh 1955), p. 9; and *Lesky*, p. 33.

14. On the date of the introduction of the alphabet, and the uses to which it was first put, cf. H. L. Lorimer, "Homer and the Art of Writing," *AJA*, 52 (1948), 11–23; Bowra, *Forerunners*, pp. 5 ff.; Kirk, *Songs*, pp. 68 ff.; L. H. Jeffery, "Writing" in *A Companion to Homer* (London 1962), pp. 545–59.

On the question which concerns many writers—were writing materials in sufficient quantity available to Homer—L. H. Jeffery in *A Companion to Homer* is cautious, saying we know nothing except that the Greeks knew what papyrus was by the time of Homer, that they learned it from Phoenicia (Βύβλος), and that it may or may not have been *writing* papyrus. She thinks on the whole that if the poems were written down before the sixth century, they were probably written on leather. H. L. Lorimer, dating the *Iliad* to 750 or earlier, sees no difficulty at all in there being an adequate supply of papyrus in the later part of the eighth century.

Panathenaic Recension (if such existed[15]), and thence down through antiquity and at last to our own day. It almost seems, by one of the many paradoxes that greet us as the problem unravels itself, that the very fluidity of oral transmission is what guarantees us the *ipsissima verba* of Homer.

Lord's second principle enables him to explain how the unique transcription from improvised song to established text took place. The oral poet—and this was Parry's great principle, long before the empirical evidence of Yugoslavia, a principle in which he was hardly anticipated except by the genial speculations of Robert Wood[16]—is fundamentally a different kind of artist from the literary poet. The two kinds cannot mix, and when they seem to,[17] the apparent exception proves the rule. Homer, then, cannot have used the newly introduced alphabet to record his own poem, so someone else—a genius in his way, but one who had no oral style to lose—must have done so. Hence Homer dictated his text to a scribe, as the Yugoslav bards dictated theirs to Parry and Lord and their assistants twenty-eight centuries later. Again we note the romantic—but not necessarily for that reason less scholarly—strain: not only, as Lord would have it, can we see and hear Homer sing; we can even be his scribe, we can do what the first man who put the *Iliad* into writing once did.[18]

It is fairly obvious that this theory of the creation of our text involves some difficulties, although Lord presents it as what we are left with after the elimination of all impossible alternatives. Some of these difficulties have not been stated either by Lord, who champions the theory, or by Kirk, who doubts it. But we must now look at Kirk's own position.

He is unimpressed by the dictation theory (*Songs*, pp. 98 ff.) but, as we indicated, he is "prepared to accept absolutely" the

15. Cf. J. A. Davison in *Companion to Homer*, pp. 237 ff.
16. *On the Original Genius of Homer* (4th ed. London 1824), esp. pp. 157 ff.
17. See n. 12 above.
18. Cf. Lord, "Homer's Originality: Oral Dictated Texts," *TAPA*, 84 (1953), 124–34, esp. 132.

premise on which it is based: that literacy destroys the heroic singer's craft. Kirk can accept the premise but deny the conclusion because he holds that the other premise, Lord's first principle, "that the poems must have been written down as soon as they were composed because otherwise they could not have been transmitted, is fallacious and must be absolutely rejected as it stands" (*Poetry*, p. 279).

Kirk in fact does want the "monumental composition" of the *Iliad* to be a completely oral process, in accordance with Lord's second principle. But he does not want the work as a whole put into writing for at least 100 years after composition. His reasons for this assertion are negative, and he would evidently argue that they must necessarily be so. They are the difficulty of imagining the process of making a very large book at the probable time of composition, and the alleged interpolations such as the Doloneia and the end of the *Odyssey*, which presumably could have been added more easily to a written text than to one handed down by repeated singing. To these he would now add (in conversation with me) the argument that the written recording of a poem as long as the *Iliad* or the *Odyssey* in the late eighth century would have been an event of too great magnitude not to have left a memory of its own.

None of these reasons appears to be unambiguous or decisive. There is no evidence whatever that the act of writing on so large a scale would not have been possible at that date. It would, of course, have been a remarkable event. But the introduction of the alphabet was itself a remarkable event. And so was the composition of the *Iliad*. The interpolations are themselves questionable. The end of the *Odyssey* will seem to many an essential, if in some respects unsatisfactory, portion of that poem. And there will always be some who feel that the tenth book is not extraneous to the *Iliad*. But if they, or other passages, were added to the Homeric poems after the main composition, this really tells us nothing of the state in which the main compositions were transmitted. Interpolations, particularly if singing on a smaller scale continued, could always be made in a written text. As for the lack of any record of the epoch-making (epic-making?) act of putting such long poems into writing—is this any stranger than our virtually complete lack of any record of the person Homer himself, on any theory?

Denys Page, whose *History and the Homeric Iliad* has exerted a strong influence on Homeric scholars, wanted an extraordinarily early date for Homer—around the end of the ninth century. Since this would place the date of composition well before the introduction of writing, it would make Kirk's notion of *reasonably accurate oral reproduction* a necessity. But Kirk himself, although he raises the possibility that Page's date may be right,[19] is much more inclined to the now commonly accepted late eighth-century date; and Page's own reasons appear curiously casual in the texture of his brilliantly argued book.[20]

Given the forcefulness with which Kirk argues the point, the lack of genuinely strong arguments for an illiterate Homer who once sang a song then reproduced accurately by word of mouth for six generations (or three or four or five) is disappointing. On the face of it, the idea seems hard to accept, harder indeed than Lord's notion of a prototypical Parry or Lord sitting down with Homer and a batch of appropriate writing materials over a period of several weeks *ca.* 725 B.C. Had Homer, Kirk can be asked, often sung the *Iliad* all the way through? Given the experience of Avdo Međedović, the one bard Parry and Lord found who sang a song comparable in length to our *Iliad*, it was not a thing to be undertaken lightly.[21] Did he say on some occasion: "I'll never do it better than that: reproduce *that* version!"? Or were his versions so alike that his apprentices began to reproduce the whole song (each reproduction taking at

19. *Songs*, p. 287.

20. *History and the Homeric Iliad* (Berkeley 1959), p. 158. One wishes one knew who all these "less famous and interesting" persons flourishing *ca.* 725 and well remembered by later generations were.

21. Lord, "Homer, Parry, and Huso," *AJA*, 52 (1948), 34–44, esp. 42. Avdo's song may seem to an outsider a case of the effect of the observer on an experiment.

least a week), having learned it by repeated hearing? And were *their* successors so struck with this one version that they too reproduced it for all intents and purposes accurately, being willing to spend months or years working it into their repertories? The whole process by which a poem of that length (to say nothing of the *Odyssey* as well) becomes frozen into what anybody must admit was a fluid tradition before Homer, and then retains the stamp of its first singer over many generations of men, is very obscure; and I think the truth is that Kirk has not been able to imagine just how it did happen. Perhaps it is commendable that he has not tried to do so; but the difficulty may lead us to suspect the value of the theory itself.

In addition to the negative and uncertain reasons I have discussed above, Kirk seems to have been led to his theory by impatience with the arguments of Lord, or at least with the certainty with which these arguments were advanced by Lord and accepted by others. In *Songs* (p. 99) he states: "It is of itself improbable that writing and bookmaking techniques could cope with anything on this scale in this period," and continues "and, as I think, no evidence...exists that such dictation was necessary for the composition of the monumental poems."

We must at this point first realize that Kirk's hypothesis is unnecessary, even if we grant it possible; for it does not explain any facts which cannot be explained otherwise. But it may then be objected that any theory accounting for the transition of the Homeric poems from oral song to written text is conjectural, so that it becomes a matter of choosing according to our taste and our intuitive calculus of probabilities. This might be so if Kirk's theory of adequately accurate oral reproduction were not ruled out by what we know and can legitimately conclude of the processes of oral poetry. We must therefore consider those arguments which Kirk offers to show that his theory is not so ruled out.

We find at the outset a general difficulty. Kirk argues simultaneously that (*a*) the Yugoslav poetry itself shows the possibility of reasonably accurate oral transmission, and (*b*) accurate oral transmission of Homer was possible because Homeric poetry was significantly different from the Yugoslav. To be sure, (*a*) and (*b*) are not absolutely contradictory, but there is clearly some arbitrariness of choice here. Kirk selects certain material from the Yugoslav analogy, and rejects the rest, without setting forth clear and valid criteria of selection.

But the particular arguments will tell us most. Kirk has studied the Novi Pazar songs with sensitivity and care, and his fair report of the relevant data in this volume is one of the many valuable things in his own presentation. His interpretation is not, however, everywhere indisputable. He states a number of times that accuracy of reproduction is the aim of the Yugoslav bard (we shall see that this helps him to form his distinction of *reproductive* and *creative* bards, to be discussed below): "...we see clearly that it is the aim of the best singers in the Novi Pazar region to reproduce exactly each song that they hear" (*Poetry*, p. 275); "It is their professed ideal to achieve *verbatim* precision" (p. 276); "Complete verbal accuracy is even now the ideal" (p. 277); and so on.

Kirk leans heavily on these assertions of the Yugoslav poet's purpose. We must comment first that there is here a confusion of language: "reproduce exactly," "professed ideal," "*verbatim* precision" are not the terms in which bards speak. Nothing in what they say can be legitimately translated by such expressions; nor is it even possible to translate them back into language which they would understand. The following extract from an interview between Nikola Vujnović, Parry's assistant, and the singer Đemo Zogić of Stolać will make this most clear. Đemo was describing his success in singing in the place of another singer, Suljo Makić, the song that Makić was to sing.

N: Was it the same song, word for word, and line for line?
Đ: The same song, word for word, and line for line. I didn't add a single line, and I didn't make a single mistake....
N: Tell me this, if two good singers listen to a third singer

who is even better, and they both boast that they can learn
a song if they hear it only once, do you think that there
would be any difference between the two versions?....
Đ: There would.... It couldn't be otherwise. I told you
before that two singers won't sing the same song alike.
N: Then what are the differences? *Đ:* They add, or they
make mistakes, and they forget. They don't sing every
word, or they add words. Two singers can't recite a song
which they heard from a third singer and have the two
songs exactly the same as the third. *N:* Does a singer sing a
song which he knows well (not with rhymes, but one of these
old Border songs), will he sing it twice the same and sing
every line? *Đ:* That is possible. If I were to live for twenty
years, I would sing the song which I sang for you here
today just the same twenty years from now, word for word.[22]

I have quoted this at length because it shows so strikingly
how far the bard is from any understanding of verbal accuracy
in our sense. (Kirk, by quoting only part of the above passage,
unwittingly gives a misleading impression, *Poetry*, p. 275.) The
fact is that a member of an illiterate culture not only does not
conceive of verbatim accuracy as we know it, but is also psycho-
logically incapable of grasping the abstract concepts implied
by such terms. The Serbo-Croat expression "word for word"
(*riječ za riječ*) may seem at first sight to be equivalent to Kirk's
phrases: an examination of how the bard uses such a phrase
reveals that this is not the case.

Let us turn from what bards say to what they do. By far the
best example of accurate reproduction we have from the
Yugoslav material is Zogić's two versions of "Alija Rescues
Alibey's Children": in other cases we find much greater variation. Between Zogić's versions, sung at an interval of seventeen
years, we find, in Kirk's words, "comparatively minor differences, involving the occasional substitution of one formula
or line for another and the addition or subtraction of a number

22. Lord, *Singer*, p. 27.

of incidental themes. Lord lists twenty-three alterations of various degrees of importance in a song of which the later version was something over 1,430 lines long and some sixty lines longer than the earlier version" (p. 275). Let us try to assess as objectively as we can the *rate of change* here. A song of 1,370 lines becomes one of 1,430 lines, with changes in theme and formula amounting to twenty-three distinct alterations. The quantitative difference is sixty lines out of 1,370, which is about 4·4%. This is a change taking place in one singer's performance in less than a generation. Over six generations, this would give us a quantitative difference of $6 \times 4·4\% = 26\%$. But this of course is far too simple a measure. Within the song there were twenty-three alterations. 6×23 (assuming but one minimal unit of change a generation) will give us 138 alterations in a song of about 1,400 lines. But this implies that a singer's successor will reproduce his song as accurately as the singer himself, which can hardly be the case. It also assumes that a song the length of the *Iliad* can be as accurately reproduced as a song the length of Zogić's song of Alija, which is again unlikely in the extreme. It is surely evident that an "Iliad" transmitted in a series of oral performances over six generations would end up as something vastly different: so different that it is surely the singer at the end of this process whom we should think of as the author of our text, rather than the hypothetical singer at the beginning who first put together the story of the *Iliad*.

This brings us to the vital question which no one has yet confronted clearly: what is the essence of the *Iliad*? How much would our vulgate text have to be changed before a reasonable student would have to say: "This is no longer the *Iliad*, it is a song sung in much the same style, treating of similar themes"? To this question no precise answer can be given. But until we are ready to give it some kind of answer, we have no right, I submit, to talk about *accuracy of reproduction*; for to talk about such matters at all, we must have some clear and rational notion of what is, or is not, being reproduced.

The whole Homeric Question,[23] from its beginnings with writers like d'Aubignac and Robert Wood to the present day, is, after all, a function of one thing: the overwhelming and universally acknowledged greatness of the Homeric poems *as we have them*. It is because these poems, and particularly the *Iliad*, are manifestly among the supreme creations of the human mind, that d'Aubignac wrote his attack on the concept of a single author, that Wolf wrote his *Prolegomena*, that Schliemann dug at Mycenae and Troy, that Parry carried through his examination of Homeric diction, and that today still the problem of Homer exerts so powerful a fascination over the minds of scholars and all educated men.

The point hardly needs laboring; but it must be made here. For the question, How elastic is our concept of the *Iliad*?, is not other than the question, In what does the greatness of the *Iliad* lie? Neither of these questions can be answered categorically here. But some answers are clearly wrong, or insufficient. The greatness of the *Iliad* cannot be that of any poem composed in the formulary style examined and described by M. Parry. The *Odyssey* for all its excellence is evidently a less great poem than the *Iliad*. The Homeric Hymns are composed in a style sufficiently like that of the *Iliad* and the *Odyssey* to demonstrate that the formulary style can be used to create poems unquestionably inferior to them both. And within the *Iliad*, some passages are so much more powerful and moving than others that we must agree without hesitation that the Homeric style can be employed with as much final variety of quality and effect as, say, the individual styles of Elizabethan blank verse.

But it is also not true that the story of the *Iliad*, that is, its succession of themes,[24] is what makes it great. Its excellence is

23. For the history of the Homeric Question, see Nilsson, *Homer and Mycenae* (London 1933), pp. 1–55; H. L. Lorimer, "Homer and the Art of Writing," *AJA*, 52 (1948), 11–23; J. A. Davison, "The Homeric Question" in *Companion to Homer*, pp. 234–66; *Lesky*, 49 ff.

24. Using *themes* more or less as Lord uses the term, *Singer*, 68 ff.

no more mere μῦθος than is that of Sophocles' *Oedipus*.[25] For in that case a translation, and even a paraphrase or extended summary, would have the same greatness.

Nor is the greatness the negative one of the consistent avoidance of inept or obscure expressions over a considerable number of lines. We may or may not agree with Longinus' contention that negligence is a mark of artistic genius as it is of great wealth,[26] but we must surely agree with him that purity from definable faults, even if the *Iliad* showed this quality, cannot confer greatness.

If these qualities, the proper use of the formulary style, the plot, and freedom from awkwardness of expression, cannot account for the greatness of the *Iliad*, can their combination do so? Kirk declares (*Songs*, p. 82): "[Homer's] originality did not lie in the choice of specially appropriate epithets or phrases, but on the one hand in the whole conception and scale of the poem, on the other in the consistently fluid and adept handling of traditional phraseology. Not every singer of his time would be capable of systematic creation, of constructing such lines as his, of extruding clumsy locutions, as effectively as the main composer of the *Iliad*...." "Constructing such lines as his" and "systematic creation" seem to be all we have in definition of "fluid and adept handling," and this seems to amount to keeping clumsy expressions out of the traditional diction. We have then a statement of the three criteria we discussed above: plan of the poem, adherence to the heroic style, and avoidance of awkwardness. But if no one of these criteria can take us far toward grasping the peculiar excellence of the *Iliad*, it may be that the three of them together will not do so. So far we have a long poem with a good plot—though not exactly a tightly constructed one: Kirk is the first to admit that there are long developments of doubtful relevance and structural difficulties to boot—composed in the heroic style, and free *most of the time* from blunders. Does this make an *Iliad*?

25. Cf. R. A. Brower, "The Heresy of Plot," *English Institute Essays, 1951* (New York 1952), 44 ff.   26. Περὶ Ὕψους 33.2.

The answer of course is *no*. To say what does would require an extended work of rigorous criticism, and that is not possible here. But perhaps we can see the direction of such criticism. If we should try to define the *Iliad* in a general way, we might think of a long poem dealing critically with the heroic conception of life.[27] The values of a heroic society are everywhere presented to us in the *Iliad*, and they are constantly presented to us in different aspects. Distinct figures—Agamemnon, Achilles, Odysseus, Paris, Hector—are dramatized for us in crucial situations, and their *attitudes* as they speak and act in conflict with each other constitute the real force of the poem.[28] For these conflicts to be expressed, there must be a plot to occasion them. The fierce and immediate resentment of Achilles in book i,[29] his meditated disillusionment in ix, his reconciliation with his own society, with the gods and with his enemy Priam in xxiv—these are some of the things that make up the *Iliad*, and they require the plot of the poem to work themselves out. But these key attitudes and these great dramatic moments involving the chief characters of the poem could not have their value if we did not see them in the perspective of the whole heroic universe. Book xxii would be an admirable piece of poetry if it were all we had. But the encounter between Achilles and Hector gains immeasurably from other encounters elsewhere in the poem, for example from the chivalrous encounter of Glaucus and Diomede in vi, which presents a different and strongly contrasting view of the heroic code and heroic feelings. And this scene itself has its significance partly determined by the ἀριστεία of Diomede which im-

27. Cf. W. Sale, "Literary Values and the Homeric Question," *Arion* (Autumn 1963), pp. 86–100. The values of the warrior as such are not the only values in the *Iliad*: there are hedonistic values (Paris), patriotic values (Hector), domestic values (Andromache), and so on. But they are all seen in relation to heroic values, expressing themselves in a world where heroic values are dominant.

28. "Attitudes" as in I. A. Richards, *Principles of Literary Criticism*.

29. Some good remarks on the moods of Achilles in *Songs*, p. 353.

mediately precedes it.[30] Sarpedon's sense of the obligations of
the warrior-prince in xii enlarges our understanding of Achilles'
rejection of the Embassy earlier in ix. And again, the scenes on
Olympus—and Ida—define the lot of man by contrast as they
do that of the gods directly.[31] There are very few "incidental"
themes in the *Iliad*. The term implies an ornamental view of
poetry, an inadequate understanding of the interrelation of the
parts of the dramatic structure.

To offer a succession of scenes so comprehensively evaluating
the human situation, to present them in a dramatic trajectory
which reaches a climax in xxii and ends in the resolution of
xxiv, requires an artistic construct of the highest order. It will
seem evident to many (Kirk and Lord on the whole among
them)[32] that such a construct could only be the design of a
single mind. But that point need not be made here. The fact is

30. The differences between Diomede's temporary exaltation in battle
with the gods (*aut ope Palladis | Tydiden superis parem*) in v and his humanity
in the encounter with Glaucus in vi have been taken by some as symptomatic
of multiple authorship. It is true that if we are looking for large sections of
the *Iliad* which could be removed with the least disturbance to the whole, v
would (in my opinion) be as good a candidate as x. But that does not mean
that its function in the whole structure is unclear. The extravagant heighten-
ing of Diomede's powers in v, with Athene by his side, until the encounter
with Apollo (which anticipates xvi), serves to delimit human potentiality.
(And the almost puppetish godlikeness of Diomede in v contrasts with
Achilles' deliberate and self-sufficient sense of his powers and limitations in
battle later, e.g., xix.420ff., xxi.99ff., xxii.15ff.)
Diomede has his moment of brittle greatness when the gods are with him
(or, if you will, he outdoes himself as he is caught up, like a *berserker*, in the
fury of battle); once the gods (or his battle mania) leave him, he becomes
very human again, even a little ordinary. vi.141ff., where he states this
himself, far from being out of harmony with v, is a clear reference to it.
And the return to humanity which the Glaucus–Diomedes scene represents
is a transition from the battle to the latter domestic scenes of vi.
31. The similarities and the differences between the quarrels of men and
of gods in i is an obvious example.
32. The carefully qualified discussion in *Songs*, chs. 10 and 11, "Structural Anomalies in the *Iliad*," and "Structural Anomalies in the *Odyssey*,"
gives us a "main composer" for each poem.

that the construct exists, and to describe it is to begin to describe what the *Iliad* is.

This construct is in the first place a certain proper order of scenes. The scenes must be of the right length, and they must follow each other in the right sequence. To use Homer's own critical term here, the poet must sing κατὰ κόσμον.[33] But a scene is not a given block of material, as some critics seem to assume. It is itself made up of parts, and will be more or less effective, and more or less able to fulfill its function in the economy of the whole, as those parts are more or less well arranged. The κόσμος of Homeric poetry, then, involves the quality of language as well as the construction of the plot.

Of this language there are two essential things to be said. First, we must throughout the poem have persons (and the poet himself) speaking the same language and expressing the same assumptions. For the unity lies, as we said, in a constant critical presentation of heroic values. The homogeneous formulary language is necessary to accomplish this. Everyone, from Zeus to Thersites—who echoes, as we know,[34] the speech and attitudes of Achilles—must in some way talk the same. And the Homeric descriptions and similes, which are also dramatic scenes, must continually evoke and further define this heroic world. Herein lies the "golden light" which Homer sheds over the world, and herein is the nobility and strangeness of the language, which must be everywhere "holy and sweet and wonderful."[35] The heroic diction, which the poet uses because he is in a tradition that knows no other, enforces the concentration on heroic values which is the ultimate subject of the poem.

But, and this is the second point, this language must vary with his speakers. We must be aware, from everything that they say, and that Homer says about them, that Achilles and

33. 8.489. The art of the bard resembles that of the general.

34. E.g., Whitman, *Homer and the Heroic Tradition* (Cambridge, Mass. 1958), p. 161.

35. M. Parry, "The Traditional Metaphor in Homer," *CP*, 28 (1933), 30–43.

Odysseus are in the same world, but we must also be aware that they occupy distinct and different positions in that world. The irreducible character and attitude of each man must show through. The analysis of formulary diction shows us that there can be no or very little individual vocabulary and individual combination of single words.[36] Therefore the individuality which is so obviously there, and so much a part of the poem's greatness, must lie in the *juxtaposition* of formulae. Achilles and Odysseus must use the same phrases: but they combine them into speech in separate ways.[37] This process can work between one half-line and the next, or even between smaller parts of lines, but it is easiest for us to see it in the case of whole lines. For example: Achilles' words in 1.155–7 are not compelled by grammar or connection of formulae. The way they move from indignation ("The Trojans never wronged *me*!") to the nostalgic sense of his distance from home, culminating in the over-powering line 157, is peculiar to Achilles. No one else in the poem speaks in this way.[38]

36. The idea that *all* of Homer is formulary, commonly attributed to M. Parry, was already held and stated by A. Meillet (see *Ep. Trad.* pp. 9–10). Parry himself was rather cautious about this, although as early as his University of California M.A. thesis he clearly felt that virtually all of Homer was somehow *traditional*, and in his later articles (e.g., "About Winged Words," *CP*, 32 (1937), 59–63) he all but stated that formulae filled the whole of the text. Recently debate has centered on the exact definition of "formula," e.g., Hainsworth in *CQ*, 58 (1964), 155–64, answered by J. A. Russo on pp. 221 ff. below. But the points to bear in mind are that (1) a very large amount of Homer is demonstrably formulary, (2) if we had more ancient Greek heroic poetry, this amount would increase, and (3) the attempt to distinguish parts of Homer which are not formulary is bound to fail, because we do not have enough evidence. What we are beginning to be able to do is to see how the poet combined his formulae in effective ways. This will be one important future direction of Homeric criticism.

37. See A. Parry, "The Language of Achilles," *TAPA*, 87 (1956), 1–7, now reprinted in G. S. Kirk, *Language and Background of Homer* (Cambridge 1964).

38. 157 is not *evidently* formulary: we do not find it elsewhere (or its parts) in the *Iliad* or the *Odyssey*. But to argue that its effectiveness derives from the poet's having transcended the tradition to invent a special phrase here is wrong: first, because elsewhere equally effective lines do turn out to

No one else in our *Iliad* speaks in this way; but it is evident that in the heroic tradition others could. It is easy to imagine an epic poem (by Homer or someone else) in which Odysseus quarreled with Agamemnon and expressed regrets over his distance from home in the same way.[39] But if Odysseus were allowed such emotional and imaginative developments of his thoughts in the *Iliad*, we should have lost something fundamental. No longer would these two characters be symbolic for us of something like the passionate and practical attitudes to life. The argument between the two men in xix, for example, would lose much of its force. No one else in the *Iliad* questions the heroic code—that is, the value of leaving one's home to fight and win possessions—so profoundly as Achilles, although in the legend, we note, it is Odysseus who is marked as the man originally reluctant to leave his home, not Achilles. To express this questioning, Achilles, here and throughout, has his own use of the formulary language.[40]

The lines discussed are an essential part of one scene, the third in the rapid succession of scenes that brings us into the poem in i. Now a reader—like Homer's audience—will not normally isolate them for attention as we have done here. But they will be for him nonetheless an essential part of that scene. Granted, that if they were not in our text we should not constate a lacuna.[41] But the scene would be poorer without

be formulary, but more important, second, because a criticism is poor which could be undone by a chance discovery, such as that of another poem containing a regular use of the line.

39. Odysseus does quarrel with Agamemnon in xiv.82 ff., and the motive for his anger has something to do with the necessity of staying away from home. Then there is the statement in his rhetorically masterful speech in ii (esp. 291 ff.) of the hardship of separation from one's wife. The difference of the grim resignation of the speech in xiv and the sincere, but objective and policy-conscious, concession in ii from anything Achilles says or could be imagined as saying, is as good an illustration as any of my point.

40. See note 37 above.

41. The famous statement of Aristotle (*Poetics*, 1451 a 31 ff.) on what constitutes the wholeness of a work of art has been interpreted too literally to mean that all the parts of a work of art are essential in the same way as the moving parts of a machine. But art is not like that.

them. Take them away or replace them by something else, and we have a weaker conception of Achilles and hence a weaker conception of the crucial conflict between him and Agamemnon.

This is a small example of how each scene, like the work as a whole, must be "systematically constructed," i.e. how the value of each scene depends on a particular economy of treatment within it. Now here is a larger example. The τειχοσκοπία and with it our introduction to Helen, ends with the famous lines about Helen's brothers, for whom she has looked in vain in the Achaean army:

> So she spoke; but the fruitful earth already possessed them
> Back in Lacedaemon, in their own native land.

Then the poem turns abruptly to the battlefield and the preparations for the duel: κήρυκες δ' ἀνὰ ἄστυ.... To the whole scene, marked by the surprising affection between Priam and Helen and Helen's rueful memories of her homeland and those she knew there, the poignant brevity of these lines forms a perfect close. A popular modern translator, however, replaces them by the following: "The truth was that both her brothers were long since dead and buried in their native country, after they had ambushed a pair of rival twins from Messene: Idas and Lynceus. None of the four survived that fight."

The addition is altogether out of harmony with the scene. The legendary information about the death of Helen's brothers, so like what we actually find elsewhere in the *Iliad*,[42] here destroys the effect of the closing lines of the scene. It is essential that we not think of how or why Castor and Pollux died, but only of the fact that they are dead, and dead back in Lacedaemon, and that Helen is so far from the life she bitterly regrets (εἴ ποτ' ἔην γε) that she does not know it. Certainly the scene is *recognizable* if we read it in the translation with the translator's appendage; but the effect of the ending is no longer

---

42. I mean the filling in of genealogical or other background, usually by means of *ringkompositie* (see *Lesky*, p. 84), e.g., ix.555 ff., where it helps to create Phoenix's particular type of garrulity.

of the *Iliad*. If a number of similar changes were made in the body of the scene, it would indeed no longer be the scene we know in the *Iliad* at all.

We must consider further that the ostensible purpose (or so it has been said) of the scene is to introduce us to the captains of the Greek army. But it fulfills in fact the much more important purpose, here in the third book, of introducing us to Helen herself. This second purpose is woven into the first, after the dialogue between Priam and Helen begins, by a succession of carefully placed touches throughout the scene. Helen does not merely declare her feelings at the beginning of the dialogue (172–6). She intersperses her description of the Greek leaders with delicate references to herself.[43] Thus in 230–3, she varies the pattern of the dialogue by singling out Idomeneus on her own, instead of answering Priam's questions as she has done before. The strongly formulary responses[44] οὗτός γ᾽ Ἀτρείδης (178), οὗτος δ᾽ αὖ Λαερτιάδης (200), οὗτος δ᾽ Αἴας ἐστί (229) here give way to the more abrupt Ἰδομενεὺς δ᾽ ἑτέρωθεν (230). This shows us the poet's skill in varying a pattern at the right moment, and it indicates as well that Idomeneus is a less outstanding leader (physically and otherwise) than Agamemnon, Odysseus, and Ajax. But more important, the spontaneity of the response makes it more natural for Helen to touch on her own past:

> πολλάκι μὲν ξείνισσεν ἀρηΐφιλος Μενέλαος
> οἴκῳ ἐν ἡμετέρῳ ὁπότε Κρήτηθεν ἵκοιτο.   (232–3)

The four lines about Idomeneus could have been left out without disturbing the "fluidity and adeptness" of the formulary

---

43. Cf. K. J. Reckford, "Helen in the *Iliad*," *Greek, Roman, and Byzantine Studies* (Spring 1964), p. 13.

44. The formulary language of the *Iliad* and the *Odyssey* gives a kind of ritual quality to all the poetry, although this quality obviously does not inhibit spontaneity and dramatic force. But within the world created by this language, some passages are more ritual, emphasize more the recurrent patterns of life, than others; e.g., arming-scenes, sacrifices, or the passage in ι (432 ff.) describing the arrival of the ship in Chryse, on which Russo comments in this volume, pp. 228 f.

flow of the narrative. Once he is introduced in 230–1, 232 is not compelled, and again 232 could stand without 233. But the whole scene would have been less what it is if any of these lines were not there. On the other hand, it would surely not have been improved, quite the reverse, if the theme of Idomeneus had been further developed. A complex and delicate reference would have become a digression.

Another self-revelation in the midst of Helen's description is line 180, again uncompelled by grammar or sense, after her identification of Agamemnon:

$$\delta a \grave{\eta} \rho \ a \mathring{v} \tau' \ \grave{\epsilon} \mu \grave{o} s \ \check{\epsilon} \sigma \kappa \epsilon \ \kappa v v \acute{\omega} \pi \iota \delta o s, \ \epsilon \mathring{i} \ \pi o \tau' \ \check{\epsilon} \eta v \ \gamma \epsilon.$$

The poignancy of the last phrase needs no comment; but it is revealing to consider that almost every reader of Homer has been struck by it, whereas few who were not thumbing the pages of the text or of Schmidt's Parallel-Homer will recall the other occasions the identical formula is used in the identical part of the line, and to express similar regret (*Il.* xxiv.426, *Od.* 19.315, 24.289). Its peculiar effectiveness here comes about partly from the context, because we have already caught Helen's character and mood, so that we know exactly how to intone the formula. But it also helps to create the context, deriving much of its emotion from the juxtaposition with κυνώπιδος. This formulary word occurs always in this grammatical case, always in this position in the line. Sometimes it joins the preceding group of words, sometimes the following. The closest parallel here is xviii.396 ff., Hephaestus to Thetis, who has come to ask him to forge new armor for her son:

$$\mu \eta \tau \rho \grave{o} s \ \grave{\epsilon} \mu \hat{\eta} s \ \iota \acute{o} \tau \eta \tau \iota \ \kappa v v \acute{\omega} \pi \iota \delta o s, \ \mathring{\eta} \ \mu' \ \grave{\epsilon} \theta \acute{\epsilon} \lambda \eta \sigma \epsilon$$
$$\kappa \rho \acute{v} \psi a \iota \ \chi \omega \lambda \grave{o} v \ \grave{\epsilon} \acute{o} v \tau a \ . \ . \ . \ .$$

Hephaestus is a character with whom our emotions are little involved. The complaint about his mother is scarcely more than amusing. The juxtaposition of formulae, in accordance with the simple and uncharged tone of the speech, is straightforward: "Hera is a *bitch because she wanted* to hide me and my lameness away." But the juxtaposition in the τειχοσκοπία has, even apart from its context, far more edge. The remoteness of the past expressed by εἴ ποτ᾽ ἔην γε does not follow in any simple way from the self-castigation of κυνώπιδος. The thought is "If I were not a bitch, then I should not have to say that Agamemnon *was* my brother-in-law; I would not have failed to appreciate so great a family, and all this would not seem so beautiful and so far away." It can be observed that the juxtapositions of εἴ ποτ᾽ ἔην γε, in the other instances where this formula occurs in its fixed position after the bucolic diaeresis, are likewise less delicate and complexly significant than here in III.180.[45]

This analysis of what creates in the τειχοσκοπία the qualities a good reader can recognize in it could be extended. But the fundamental point is, I believe, already clear: its particular qualities depend on an exact economy of the formulae within it. Change the order of statements, add a bit here, subtract a bit there, develop the thoughts in some other manner, and we no longer have the great scene we know. But the *Iliad* is made up of

45. The student of M. Parry may object that it is not easy to find a formula filling the last two feet of III.180 and beginning with a vowel which will at the same time complete the sense in any satisfactory manner. (ὀλβιοδαίμων, as in 182, only in the nominative, jars, and ἄλγε᾽ ἐχούσης [cf. *Odyssey* 17.142] seems odd too. Such expressions are obviously flat; we do not even know whether they are possible at all. ὀκρυοέσσης, cf. VI.344, is of course not possible, because it almost certainly is a MS. distortion of κρυοέσσης—see Chantraine, I.45.) Was not this particular juxtaposition arrived at by an intuitive process of elimination?

Such an observation has force, and one should never ignore it in assessing the style of the *Iliad*. It is in fact very difficult, I believe not possible at all, to find in our texts a formula which could replace εἴ ποτ᾽ ἔην γε and give an adequate sense. But just though the observation is, it does not constitute an objection. We know what the sense of the line is, because we have it in our text. Any different development—say a new sentence beginning with something like ἀλλά με δαίμων—brings us to the realm of the completely conjectural. If anything plausible could be constructed, it would give us a different sense. We must define the sense of what we have and measure its exact relevance to the effect of the passage. No one could seriously argue that the self-revelation of Helen as we have it in book III is an automatic creation of the formulary system.

a succession of such scenes, arranged in a fairly exact order. Some of course are more moving, or more highly charged, than others. But they must all be such as to create the impressions they now create, or we shall not have our *Iliad*. We should at best have a poem with discernible similarities to our own. And to be such as to create the impressions we receive now, they can endure very little change. The margin of flexibility of language and structure in our version of the *Iliad* is, I submit, rather small, certainly much smaller than one would have to assume in order to sustain the theory of an orally transmitted *Iliad*. For the minimum of change that we can calculate from the only evidence we possess, the observed tradition of Yugoslav poetry (as opposed to the inferred tradition of ancient Greek heroic poetry), will imply changes that would destroy the exact texture and therewith the essence of our poem.

It follows that the name "Homer," if by this we mean the author of our poem, must be reserved for the poet who composed the *Iliad* at the time when it was put into writing. The poets who preceded him, even if we imagine them as singing poems the length of the *Iliad* and dealing with the same theme or group of themes, cannot have been responsible for the essential quality of what we possess. We must conclude that Kirk's belief that "There is no compelling reason from the point of view of transmission why the *Iliad* and the *Odyssey*, once they gained wide repute, as they presumably did in the lifetime of their monumental composers, should not have been handed down from singer to singer with comparatively minor deviations" is, as he says of Lord's theory of the necessity of dictation, "fallacious and must be absolutely rejected as it stands." It is hard to imagine why or under what conditions singers would hand down to each other a poem of that length; more important, if they did so, it would not be the *Iliad*.

Having argued (incorrectly, I think) that Yugoslav poetry itself reveals the possibility of sufficiently accurate oral reproduction, Kirk (*Poetry*, pp. 277 ff.) argues in favor of such reproduction which insist on the difference between Slavic and Homeric poetry. (*a*) The "powers of memory of the Greek *aoidos* can have been no less than those of his modern Yugoslav equivalent." No doubt; but memory in our sense is not in question here, since bards in general do not memorize. (*b*) "But his formulary equipment and his dramatic and imaginative capacities must have been far superior." Certainly, given the superiority of the *Iliad* and the *Odyssey* to anything which has appeared in the Yugoslav tradition. But do greater poetic resources make for closer imitation, or the reverse? Kirk's "monumental composer" was presumably very far from an imitator. (*c*) The formulary structure of the *Iliad* and the *Odyssey* is more "rigid." The Homeric line is evidently more formulary than the Yugoslav. The style as such was more developed, and the Homeric poet dealt more in blocks of words, so that there is in Homer less play of individual words. It does seem true, as Kirk well sums up the matter, "that the traditional language of the Greek oral poets was much more highly organized, as it was much richer, than that of any modern oral poet of whom we know." In other words, Yugoslav heroic poetry, though it is far more formulary than any literary poetry could well be, still cannot be analyzed into the same systems of formulae as M. Parry was able to analyze in the *Iliad* and the *Odyssey*. All this is true; but it does not follow that Homer and his successors were better verbatim transmitters than the singers of modern Yugoslavia. Homer himself, by Kirk's own account, was presumably not. But there is no reason why his immediate successors at least should have been, either. A rich and complex tradition imposes restrictions and at the same time provides greater possibilities of expression. We have seen that in the τειχοσκοπία the exact tradition of heroic diction made possible juxtapositions of formulae which we meet nowhere else in the *Iliad* and the *Odyssey*, and which create a unique texture of meaning for this scene. Other scenes can be shown to possess the same creative individuality within the clear framework of the tradition. Parry was the first (as far as I know) to adduce the analogy of rhyme in modern poetry as an element directing the thought of the poet.[46] Of the rich stock of formulary language in Homer, it could be said, as Proust remarks of modern poetry: "comme les bons poètes que la tyrannie de la rime force à trouver leurs plus grandes beautés." The *tyrannie de la formule* can be observed in Homer. But neither its purpose nor its effect, when the tradition was in its vigor, would have been to make of the ἀοιδός an accurate imitator.

Kirk's final point (*d*) to show that Homer's contemporaries and successors would have copied a poem in performance more accurately than their modern Yugoslav counterparts relates not to the diction of the poems, but to their thematic material. "As for thematic changes...it may be conjectured that there too the Greek oral tradition, at any rate by the time of Homer, was more highly organized than any modern equivalent." By "more highly organized," Kirk seems to refer to a narrower variation in choice of theme on any single subject than was allowed in Greek heroic poetry. This is very doubtful. The number of epic themes alluded to in the *Iliad* and the *Odyssey* themselves[47] is an impressive indication of how careful and particular a selection the author or authors of these poems made from the thematic material available to them.[48] Some of these themes are so close to those of the *Iliad* in particular that a number of theories of the old Analytic school have been formed to show that the poet or poets of the *Iliad* drew their material directly from them.[49] If we add the other epic tales we know from the Cyclic Epics, and then consider how many themes will be simply unknown to us, it becomes questionable whether the plots of the *Iliad* and the *Odyssey* were fixed in comparison with the Yugoslav material, as Kirk appears to suggest.

An argument of a different sort, one which is not so much concerned with the question of transmission as with our evaluation of the Yugoslav analogy in general, is Kirk's theory of *creative* and *reproductive* stages in traditions of epic poetry. This

46. *L'Épithète*, pp. 166 ff.
48. So Aristotle, *Poetics*, 1451 a 16 ff.
47. *Lesky*, pp. 37 ff.
49. *Lesky*, p. 38.

theory is obviously related to his theory of transmission. A reproductive phase, if such existed, would help make accurate oral transmission possible. We shall only note here that arguments (*a*) to (*d*) can all be used at least as well to show that the Homeric poet was more creative than his Yugoslav counterpart, as to show that he was a better reproducer. Kirk's implied argument appears to be that the Greek poet was simply better, therefore better at whatever he put his hand (or voice) to, whether creation or reproduction.

The argument of distinct stages in the tradition of unlettered heroic song has, however, its own interest. It is set forth most clearly in *The Songs of Homer*, pp. 95 ff., where the author imaginatively describes the "life cycle of an oral tradition." There are four stages: *originative, creative, reproductive,* and *degenerate.* The first represents the origins of narrative poetry. In the case of Homer it might have begun with Mycenaean poetry, perhaps slightly later.[50] No one would want to question the existence of this phase, though some might describe it differently from others. The second phase is that of Homer. He would be a special type within this category: the *monumental* creative singer. By *creative*, Kirk means possessing the qualities which Parry and Lord ascribed to unlettered singers in general: the ability to absorb the formulary and thematic tradition and turn it to account by improvising new and distinct versions within the received framework. As long as no clear demarcation is set between these first two stages (for creativity must have existed as soon as poetry did), few would want to dispute the value of these first two categories.

It is with the third stage that Kirk's theory becomes controversial. The *reproductive* singer is still a bard.[51] He still works within the formulary tradition. But he cannot really do anything new. At most he *varies* or *contaminates* (see *Poetry*, p. 279). He uses the tradition for "memorization and to facilitate the

50. See Kirk, *Dark Age and Oral Poet, passim.*
51. Though *Dark Age and Oral Poet* states otherwise. Kirk later abandoned this view, which would make the Yugoslav bards into rhapsodes.

transposition, often though not always unintentional, of language or minor episodes from one acquired song to another" (*Songs*, p. 97). This is the stage in which we find all the bards of modern Yugoslavia. But it existed in Greece too. "Such reproductive singers must have existed for a time in Greece—particularly, one would conjecture, in the mid-seventh century B.C.; but we have no direct knowledge of them" (*ibid.*).

Economy of hypothesis is perhaps the point of view from which we should regard this proposed third stage of development. We know that there was something that could well be called a *creative* stage: for we have the *Iliad* and the *Odyssey*. We know also that there was a rhapsodic period when the *Iliad* and the *Odyssey*, known as such and ascribed to Homer, were recited by professional reciters, like Plato's Ion, who carried a staff and were called *rhapsodes*. This is Kirk's fourth or *degenerate* stage.[52] Exactly how and when this change took place is impossible to say. But the introduction of an intermediate stage about which nothing can be known hardly brings us closer to a solution. Nor does this conjectural stage help to explain the transmission of the *Iliad* and the *Odyssey* on Kirk's hypothesis. For, in the first place, the inferior poetic capacities of Kirk's reproducing

---

52. When the rhapsodic stage begins, to what extent it spelled the end of improvising song, and how much it coincided with the replacement of the lyre by the ῥάβδος, are questions not easily answered. The extremes are given us by the descriptions in the *Odyssey* of Phemius and Demodocus on the one hand, and by Plato's Ion on the other. Between these two points it is very difficult to trace the development. Schadewaldt argues that Homer is already *archaisierend*, and that though he describes singers accompanying themselves on the lyre, he himself sang (or *spoke*, for Schadewaldt denies any clear demarcation here) with the staff. Wade-Gery too wants Homer to be a rhapsode in this sense. Webster holds the now more conventional view that the shift from the lyre to the staff was the shift from creative improvisation to recitation from written texts. Stressing the fact that Hesiod portrays himself as receiving a ῥάβδος from the Muses, he sees the crucial change as taking place between Homer and Hesiod. Notopoulos and others argue that Hesiod is as much oral poetry as Homer, which would confirm Schadewaldt's point that the staff did not necessarily mean the replacement of creative singing by the virtuoso recitation of an Ion.

bards would not seem necessarily to be an advantage in the
matter of accurate reproduction. And even if we agree with
Kirk that they were somehow such an advantage, still by his
own account such inferior improvising bards existed "particularly...in the mid-seventh century B.C." We still have to get
from a monumental composer whose acme was at the latest
725 B.C. to our reproducers of the mid-seventh century whose
feebleness of poetic gift could guarantee that we have the song
that was originally sung. If, however, he were to revise this
conjecture, so that the reproductive stage begins immediately
after Homer (as he seems to say, *Poetry*, p. 278: "the Homeric
poems came at the end of the true oral tradition"), then we shall
still have to assume, as I argue above, that these reproducers
approached medieval scribes in accuracy, which is against all
evidence, and we shall moreover have the difficulty of explaining
why the most creative of all singers in the Greek heroic tradition was straightway followed by the least creative and most
reproductive.[53]

The conjectural third stage of reproductive bards does not,
when you follow out its implications, help Kirk's hypothesis of
transmission. It will be of still less help to those who are dis-
inclined to adopt the hypothesis in the first place. Moreover it
is, by the definition of its creator, a stage about which virtually
nothing can be known. Surely those inferior, contaminating,

---

53. Actually, the complete sentence in Kirk's article, of which the
beginning is quoted above, is yet more confusing: "The third factor [in
accurate word-of-mouth transmission] is that the Homeric poems came at
the end of the true oral tradition, so that their oral transmission depended
for much of its course not on singers but on reciters or rhapsodes." The
statement here is hedged; but it suggests that the creative singer *par excellence,*
Homer, was almost immediately followed, not by inferior ἀοιδοί of the
reproductive phase (whom Kirk himself cannot seem to fit in here) but
by rhapsodes of the degenerate stage, men noted for their clumsy additions to the text (*Songs*, p. 97) (though there are also "non-decadent
aoidic expansions," p. 322), but still responsible for keeping the delicate
unwritten text in its essential shape from generation to generation over the
centuries.

pointlessly varying, mechanically reproducing bards should be forthwith put out of their misery by the rapid demolition of the stage of development invented to house them.

Two further arguments for the "reproductive stage," not directly connected with the problem of transmission, have their own interest. The first is that such a stage would help to explain some of the difficulties of our texts.

Kirk distinguishes (*Songs,* pp. 316 ff.) three main kinds of difficulties. The first consists of structural anomalies (*Songs,* pp. 211 ff.). As he is aware, no reader or scholar will precisely agree with another on what is a structural anomaly, or on exactly how they should be explained once they are recognized as such. But most scholars (Page is the notable exception) will now be ready to agree with Kirk's main judgment that such anomalies are fewer and less anomalous than they appeared to old-line Analysts, and that in any case they are an inevitable aspect of the conditions of traditional improvising song.

The second and third kinds of difficulties defined by Kirk consist of places where the usually clear flow of Homeric narrative gives way to expressions that appear to us awkward or obscure or both (pp. 316 ff.).

One of these two kinds of difficulty involves really bizarre expressions such as ἠέ ποθι πτολέμοιο μέγα στόμα πευκεδανοῖο (x.8: p. 205). These Kirk would assign to his *degenerate* stage. Since they do not therefore involve the "reproductive stage," we shall only point out here that mere reproducers (whether bards or rhapsodes) are unlikely candidates, on the face of it, for the authorship of such bold, though puzzling, expressions as this. Would a reciter be likely to invent, or introduce, the powerful *hapax legomenon* πευκεδανοῖο?

The other kind of difficulty Kirk can assign to his reproductive stage. It seems to consist (pp. 320 ff.) of passages in the *Iliad* which sound like (the judgment here is inevitably subjective) passages from the *Odyssey*, such as the scene between Priam and Hermes in xxiv; and passages which remind us of Hesiod,

like xii.20–2, the list of Trojan rivers. In Kirk's view, such
passages are too good to be the work of the thoroughly degenerate rhapsodes, but at the same time jar too much with the
tenor of the *Iliad* (passages from the *Odyssey* do not seem to
come into play here) to be the original work of the monumental
composer. They are in between. So there is a stage in between.

It helps us to be aware of such passages in the *Iliad*—though,
as I said, and Kirk is admirably willing to concede, not all will
agree what they are: the whole of the apocalyptic beginning of
xii, as it stands, for example, strikes me as one of the most
powerful passages of the *Iliad*. But to assign them to a stage later
than Homer, even more to assign them to a particular stage
for which there is no clear evidence, requires a knowledge of the
exact state of the tradition when Homer sang the *Iliad* such as
we can never possess. There is no sure sign that the *Odyssey* is
much later than the *Iliad*. If so, we cannot say that "Odyssean"
passages—what one has in mind in reference to the Hermes–
Priam scene is mostly its rambling tone—were not known to
Homer, or that he had not sung such himself, or that he did
not choose to introduce such a scene in book xxiv.

Or again, the *Theogony* is the great catalogue poem of all
time. The *Iliad* and the *Odyssey* do not obviously depend much
on the catalogue technique.[54] Therefore scholars tend to regard
catalogues, when they do appear in Homer, as "Hesiodic." The
"Boeotian School" theory owes its origin to such general considerations. But there is, after all, no reason to believe that lists
of names were not a common element of poetry when Homer
sang. There is indeed reason to believe that they were, because
the catalogues in Homer reveal a strict adherence to the
formulary structure defined by M. Parry.[55] Homer used them
when they seemed to him useful and effective, and there is

54. The (unpublished) Harvard dissertation of C. R. Beye (1958) and
the (unpublished) University of California (Berkeley) dissertation of
J. H. N. Austin (1965) both argue the importance of the catalogue style as
an informing principle in the *Iliad* and the *Odyssey*.

55. Parry, *Formules et métrique*, esp. pp. 23 ff.

nothing specifically "Hesiodic" or "Boeotian" or "late" or "reproductive" about them at all.[56]

Such passages are the first of Kirk's two illuminating, though inadequate, reasons for the proposition of a "reproductive stage." The second is yet more interesting, and brings us back to the heart of the question. Kirk is, as we have seen, in general reluctant to accept the analogy so confidently drawn by Lord between the Homeric poems and the modern Yugoslav tradition. Yet he must concede that both Homer and the Yugoslav poetry are unmistakably the products of a true oral tradition of heroic song. But the difference in quality, admitted by Lord but otherwise passed over by him, seems to Kirk crucial. So he invents a stage where poetry is still clearly the product of the old tradition, but by definition vastly inferior to the poetry of an earlier, Homeric stage, or to that of one equivalent in value.

If we take Kirk's biological (almost Spenglerian) metaphor of a "life-cycle" literally, it would seem to follow that at some point in the Yugoslav tradition poems were being sung that were not much inferior to the *Iliad* and *Odyssey*, or at least were far closer to them in value than anything we now find in that tradition. "The creative stage in Yugoslavia," he says, "ended at some time in the past: probably quite recently, in the last century" (*Songs*, p. 96). This is his concession to the notion implicit in Lord, and to some extent in Parry, that the difference between an unlettered and a literary tradition of poetry is so much more important than any difference between one unlettered tradition and another, that the latter can be for practical purposes ignored. Ćor Huso, then, coming at the end of the true creative period, may well have had qualities comparable to those of Homer, though his work perhaps never equaled the "monumental" compositions of the *Iliad* and the

---

56. This does not mean, of course, that we *know* that, e.g., the κατάλογος was composed by the probably single composer of the *Iliad*. It bears signs of earliness (see Page, *History*, with Parry and Samuel's comments, *CJ*, 56 (1960), 85). But we do not finally know if it is Homeric in this sense or not.

Odyssey. But it is certain that the quality of the recorded Yugo-slav material is mediocre by Homeric standards. Therefore it must represent a declining stage in the tradition.

Now Kirk's judgment here may be fundamentally correct. The solution he proposes to the problem, however, may be quite unnecessary. For there is a simpler solution, which Kirk's respect for the convictions of Parry and Lord may have kept from him. This is that the Yugoslav tradition, so far as we can know anything about it, was never more than immeasurably inferior to the Homeric. It may once have been more flourishing than it is now; doubtless it was more widespread. But there is no reason to assume biological stages to explain its present lack of greatness, and then to import these stages into the Greek tradition for symmetry.

Artistic traditions can never be wholly explained in positivistic terms. No definition of the economic conditions and intellectual history of Florence in the thirteenth century would explain the *Divine Comedy*, though now that we have it, we can see much of Dante's debt to his contemporaries and predecessors. He is a fairly isolated figure, in a rich tradition, to be sure, but one which never produced anything to equal his work; and possibly Homer was that. But similarly nothing in the economic condi-tions and intellectual history of nineteenth-century Russia could have guaranteed the existence of the tradition of the Russian novel, represented by at least four major figures. Perhaps Homer was one in such a constellation. We need not grow mystical about the emergence of the great artist to see that while he works in a tradition, the quality of his work cannot be either predicted or explained; and we need not be mystical about art in general to see that while we can trace the development of traditions, their height and intensity can be neither predicted nor explained.

These and like considerations can remind us not to hope to explain Homer by the historical and cultural conditions in which he lived. But at the same time the existence of a rich tradition can make the emergence of a great artist easier, or at least easier for us to understand. And we can consider with profit some of the conditions which favor or discourage the growth of a great poetic tradition.

M. Parry's work was at first designed to describe the *tradition* of Greek heroic song. His original antithesis was not between the oral and the lettered poet, but between the poet of a *traditional*, and the poet of an *individual*, style. So much was he concerned to establish the tradition, and Homer's participation in it, that he consistently underplayed the uniqueness of the creator (or creators) of the *Iliad* and the *Odyssey*. The tradition had never been understood; it was Parry's purpose to make it understood, and few scholars have realized their aims so well. He is not to be blamed for not having stressed, or only in rare moments, the distinctiveness of Homer.[57] To do so, he clearly felt, would have run the danger of confusing Homer with the other kind of poet, the poet of individual style. But this feeling should not lead us, his successors, to confuse Homer with the splendid tradition which he represented. Such a confusion of Homer and the tradition is possibly an error from which Homeric studies are only now beginning to emerge.

In Parry's later work, the traditional–individual antithesis was replaced by the antithesis of the oral and the literary poet. The occasion for this change in terminology was Parry's

---

57. E.g., the conclusion to his first long article in *HSCP*, 41 (1930), 147, where he comments on the "wondrously forceful" line

xvi.776 = 24.40   κεῖτο μέγας μεγαλωστὶ λελασμένος ἱπποσυνάων

and shows how it "is made up of verse-parts found in other parts of the poems." Even here, of course, his discussion leaves entirely open the possibility that the whole line might have been traditional—or the two lines, because the previous line in both cases is virtually the same. One might go on to observe that the line is indeed "wondrously forceful" in xvi, where it forms a handsome conclusion to a paragraph of agitated description of battle, beginning with a violent simile; but that it is not especially effective, let alone "wondrously forceful," in 24.40. What has Achilles' horsemanship to do with this scene? The distinctiveness of Homer, I suggest, is what makes the line, traditional or not, so masterful a stroke in xvi.

discovery of the analogy between Serbian and Greek heroic poetry. This analogy too, I believe, is only now beginning to be understood. For the tendency has been, on the part of some, to dismiss it altogether, and on the part of others, Parry's followers, to accept it to the point of making another error: the assumption that different traditions of unlettered song are similar in value and complexity. Here again, Parry himself led the way. In his desire to show that Yugoslav poetry has more light, in many ways, to shed on the *Iliad* and the *Odyssey* than does Vergil or Milton, he underplayed the evident difference between the Yugoslav and the Greek traditions themselves. Because the style of Homer was an oral style, and part of an oral tradition, and because in Yugoslavia Parry found and heard bards singing songs in an oral style which was part of an oral tradition, the difference between those traditions seemed to him of far less account than the immensely exciting similarity.

Again, it is up to us, Parry's successors, not to stop where he stopped. Kirk is one of the severest and subtlest critics of the Yugoslav analogy, but even he, as we have seen, seems at moments to assume that one oral tradition must be much like another, and his stages of development seem partly occasioned by this assumption. And yet he is fully aware that the tradition of Greek heroic poetry, in the beauty and complexity of its process of expression, was something far beyond any other tradition of heroic poetry we know, Norse poetry being possibly the nearest thing to an exception. Parry and his direct successors, Lord and Notopoulos, are of course also aware of this, but their awareness rarely becomes operative in their criticism.

An external difference in the traditions of ancient Greek and Yugoslav poetry has been oddly overlooked. It is that unlettered culture in Yugoslavia has been a rural, one might almost say, backwoods phenomenon, existing alongside a literary urban culture. This means, first, that much of the best poetic talent would be lost to it; and, second, that there was an entirely different relation between literacy and the power of unlettered song from any that could have existed in Ancient Greece at the end of the eighth century. One of the few scholars to have seen this clearly is T. B. L. Webster, who says in his review of Kirk's book: "Unlike the Greek poems, the Yugoslav poems were not continually brought up to date, perhaps because the social status of the audience (unlike the Greek) continually declined; literacy killed the Yugoslav poets because it brought them into touch with a higher culture; there is no reason why it should have had the same effect on Greek oral poets, and the transition may have been much more gradual."[58]

When a Yugoslav poet learns how to write, a whole literary culture, the culture of the cities of his own country and of what we call the civilized world, becomes accessible to him. It is a culture of books and newspapers. If he abandons the traditional formulae which have enabled him to improvise his heroic narratives, this is not necessarily, or even probably, because he is corrupted by a new technique. It is because he has become part of a different world, a world with new values and new habits of thought.

An example in Lord's article on dictation shows, I believe, the disadvantage of overlooking this point. He says: "There are in Yugoslavia a number of oral poets who can write. Their first attempts at writing were mere recordings of the songs which they knew. When they go beyond this and begin to break the formula patterns in which they have thought poetically all their lives, the results are not felicitous. They abandon such imaginative introductions as 'Once in the days of old, when Sulejman held empire,' for prosaic beginnings like, 'In the bloody year of 1914, on the sixth day of the month of August, Austria and all Germany were greatly worried.' They become wordy and stilted to the point of being unconsciously mock heroic. The natural dignity of the traditional expressions is lost and what remains is a caricature."[59] Lord speaks as if the process of writing itself had created the "prosaic beginning" which he

58. *JHS*, 83 (1963), 157.
59. *TAPA*, 84 (1953), 129.

cited. But the poet who sang that was obviously trying to copy
the style of the newspaper, or possibly the school textbook. The
implication that if Homer or a contemporary learned to write,
this is what would have happened to them, is wrong.

We do not know exactly how the advent of writing affected
the Ionian singer of the end of the eighth century B.C. No
modern analogy will take us far, because the conditions of that
time have no modern analogue. We know from Homer princi-
pally, and in the second place from archaeology, that there was
in Greece a civilization highly developed both economically
and artistically. We know that, before the introduction of the
Phoenician alphabet, this civilization was innocent of the art of
writing,[60] and that it had developed without any pervasive
influence from surrounding cultures which did know writing.
One could in short be an extremely civilized person, living in
the heart of an advanced culture, without having any notion of
what writing is. That is not possible today, nor was it in the
1930s, or long before that.

When a man of that society learned writing, after the introduction of the Phoenician characters, he was thereby initiated into
no organized literary culture. There is to my knowledge virtually
no evidence for Phoenician influence on Greek society apart
from the alphabet. When an Ionian of 725 B.C., singer or other,
learned to write, he learned only that: how to put down marks
which would afterwards remind him of something said or sung.
These marks entailed no new style of saying or singing whatever.

These conditions cannot be found in the modern world. We
can find societies where the idea of writing is unknown, like
parts of New Guinea. Some of these societies have perhaps some
song, but writing can be introduced to them only by persons of
vastly superior, or at any rate vastly more organized, culture.
Or we can find societies, like that of Yugoslavia, where unlettered
song, of a fairly high order, has existed for centuries in country

60. Need I say that the use of Linear B centuries earlier (probably, in my
opinion, by Minoan scribes with a limited knowledge of Greek: so Kirk,
Songs, pp. 26f.) does not constitute an exception?

districts but where much of the business of life is carried on in cities where life depends on literacy. In both cases, the introduction of writing involves the introduction of new ways of thought.

In the absence of any valid analogy, we are driven back to conjecture. It seems to me a reasonable guess that the Ionian singer of 725 B.C., trained in the use of a formulary technique far more subtle and elaborate than any other we know, would, if he had learned how to manipulate the magical σήματα which had come to him from the Phoenicians, not be inclined to change his thoughts or modes of expression at all. Why should he? The epic style, such as we know it from the Homeric poems, would at first have remained unchanged. Only in later generations, when the use of writing had made possible the growth of new indigenous ways of thought, would the style of heroic poetry decline and give way to new forms of expression.

All this is conjecture, of course, but some conjecture is more reasonable than other. What we can conclude with some certainty is that the analogy which Lord assumes between conditions in twentieth-century Yugoslavia and eighth-century B.C. Ionia is very shaky, and that his statements about the effect of writing on improvising poets cannot be applied in any simple way to the composer of the *Iliad*. The corollary to this is that the notion explored by Lesky, Whitman, Wade-Gery, and Bowra,[61] that Homer himself knew the art of writing, is in fact

61. (1) Bowra, *Heroic Poetry* (London 1952), pp. 240–1. Bowra in his later Andrew Lang lecture (*Forerunners*), pp. 9 ff., written after Lord's proposition of the dictation argument, 1953, came out more for dictation than for knowledge of writing on the part of the poet himself. (2) Wade-Gery, in his *Poet of the Iliad* (Cambridge 1952), argues not only that the poet could write, but also that the alphabet was adopted for the recording of hexameter poetry. (3) Whitman, like Bowra, leans more to the dictating than to the writing poet, and argues that the availability of writing was partly responsible for the creation of the large epic: "the monumental purpose of the large epic is profoundly served by anything which bestows fixity of form." Rather than Whitman's abstract notion of "permanence" as the value of writing in composition, I would suggest the usefulness of writing in enabling the poet to compose a long but coherent work without immediate dependence on the vagaries of his audience.

not ruled out by modern research into the processes of oral poetry, as Lord and Dow would have it.

The two principles which Lord has articulated concerning composition and transmission of poetry in the improvising style are, we remember, that (1) an orally composed poem cannot be handed on by the tradition of oral song without fundamental change and (2) "the [oral] poet's powers are destroyed if he learns to read and write." Kirk has rightly felt that it is all too easy for such principles, supported by the dubious analogy of Yugoslav and ancient Greek poetry, to become standard belief. But Kirk's attack on the first principle has not been successful. The second principle, which Kirk accepts, seems in fact the weak point of Lord's argument, for it rests on the weakest part of the Yugoslav–Homeric analogy.

If Lord's first principle is correct, as I believe it is, the *Iliad* will somehow have been put into writing at the time of its composition. Lord has insisted on dictation as the only way this could have been done because of his (as I believe) mistaken notion of the impossibility of a bard who can write. If the man who, on this hypothesis, put the poems into writing was more an amanuensis than a recording scholar in the manner of Parry and Lord, then perhaps the difference between this sort of dictation and actually writing by hand would not be enormous.

In either case, we have the striking conicidence that in the *Iliad* and the *Odyssey* we have poems far longer than improvised heroic poems are likely to be, longer than the usual conditions of improvised singing (as we learn from the *Iliad* and the *Odyssey* as well as from comparative studies) would suggest or allow; and that in this very same period, the use of writing becomes available. It seems difficult not to see in the use of writing both the means and the occasion for the composition, in the improvising style, of poems which must have transcended their own tradition in profundity as well as length, just as that tradition itself surpassed all subsequent traditions of heroic song.

The Structural Formula in Homeric Verse

JOSEPH A. RUSSO

The Structural Formula in
Homeric Verse

I

Now that the classical world has, rather belatedly, caught up with the work of Milman Parry,[1] and scholars in many places may be heard talking about a "Homeric formula," we must face the fact that very little has been done to define with real precision or detail exactly what should be considered "formulaic" in the language of the hexameter. Recent Homeric criticism often refers to the presence of formulas, drawing some of its critical insights from the use and the recurrence of formulas and from the unique poetic value inherent in the very language of formula.[2] It therefore becomes imperative that the formula be more clearly defined and its mode of functioning documented in greater detail, lest our interpretations begin to outstrip our information.

The kind of precise definition and documentation that is called for seems to have been put off by the assumption (stated at the outset by Parry, but with varying degrees of certainty,[3]

1. I refer primarily to *L'Épithète traditionnelle dans Homère* (Paris 1928); *Les Formules et la Métrique d'Homère* (Paris 1928); and "Studies in the Epic Technique of Oral Verse-Making: I. Homer and Homeric Style. II. The Homeric Language as the Language of an Oral Poetry," *HSCP*, 41 (1930), 73–147 and *HSCP*, 43 (1932), 1–50.

2. See, for example, E. A. Havelock, *Preface to Plato* (Cambridge, Mass. 1963), Part 1 *passim*, and especially chs. IV and IX; C. H. Whitman, *Homer and the Heroic Tradition* (Cambridge, Mass. 1958), chs. VI and VII *passim*.

3. See *L'Épithète traditionnelle*, pp. 99, 103, 125 ff.; and *Formules*, pp. 7f., 22f. These citations are taken from Whitman, *op. cit.* p. 334 n. 16, who notes (p. 11) Parry's awareness that absolute certainty could not be reached on this point. Parry regularly uses phrases like "le caractère complètement ou presque complètement formulaire de la diction d'Homère."

and usually followed by present-day critics[4]) that everything in
Homer is oral, traditional, and formulaic. While the assumption may be difficult to disprove, it really tells us very little; and
the tendency to use the terms "oral," "traditional," and
"formulaic" to define one another does nothing to advance our
understanding of the matter. More clearly stated, the assumption generally shared today is that the Homeric poems are put
together wholly, or at least largely, from a traditional language
of formulas, formulas which must be very flexible and varied
and which must admit many possibilities for analogous formation and minor adjustments so as to fit new circumstances of
meter and meaning. This description is more helpful; but it
hardly represents any advance beyond what was known to
Parry. Parry saw quite clearly thirty-five years ago that it must
be the extensive use of analogy that gives the formula-systems
their great flexibility and range.[5] The problem is that no one
has as yet traced out this process in any detail. It is true that
A. B. Lord has given us an excellent appreciation of the working
of analogy in his third chapter ("The Formula") of *The Singer
of Tales* (Cambridge, Mass. 1960), but his discussion and
illustrations are all from Yugoslav epic. We still stand in great
need of a thorough study of the formulaic system in Homeric
Greek.

It is already evident from the writings of Parry and Lord that
if we wish to trace the wide range of formulaic systems in
Homeric verse, and ultimately to understand in what way this
verse is composed along formular lines, we must look beyond
the literal repetition of words and consider the repetition of
phrasing based upon certain favored grammatical and metrical
patterns. Following Parry's suggestion of the similarity of
pattern between τεῦχε κύνεσσιν and δῶκεν ἑταίρῳ,[6] and leaning

4. See, for example, Whitman, *op. cit.* p. 7, "practically every phrase in
Homer is formulaic"; p. 111, "It is more than likely, therefore, that
essentially everything in Homer is formulaic."

5. *L'Épithète traditionnelle*, pp. 85–92, 218–38; *HSCP*, 41 (1930), 145–7.

6. *HSCP*, 41 (1930), 133.

strongly on the work of O'Neill and Porter (in *YCS* 8 (1942) and 12 (1951) respectively) on the structure of the hexameter, I recently analyzed some Homeric lines in order to show how they are based upon the use of certain parts of speech of prescribed metrical form at certain favored positions.[7] I singled out several patterns found in the opening lines of the *Iliad*, and should like now to present a fuller list of structural patterns most commonly relied on in the traditional diction of the Homeric poems. Such a list will be in the form of an appendix to the present study. The study itself will be an analysis of three passages in book i of the *Iliad* which are especially interesting in their use of formulaic structural patterns.

II

Before proceeding to my analysis, I should like to anticipate and clarify the major problem underlying such a study— namely, the definition of "formula"—by reviewing an important recent contribution to the literature on the subject. J. B. Hainsworth, in an article[8] which focuses sharply on some key problems in present-day discussion of the formula and contains serious strictures against the methodology of earlier studies, objects to the view that formulaic usage is easily described in terms of repeated phrasal or structural patterns, and warns that the term "formula" has been overextended and meaninglessly diluted. He fears that J. A. Notopoulos has taken

7. "A Closer Look at Homeric Formulas," *TAPA*, 94 (1963), 235–47. I would show position in the verse by using numbers from 1 to 12 to locate word-endings, according to the following scheme:

$$
\begin{array}{c|c|c|c|c}
\text{A}^2\ \text{A}^1 & \text{B}^2\ \text{B}^1 & & \text{C}^1\ \text{C}^2 & \\
1\ 1\tfrac{1}{2}\ 2\ |\ 3\ |\ 3\tfrac{1}{2}\ 4\ |\ 5\ |\ 5\tfrac{1}{2}\ |\ 6 & 7\ 7\tfrac{1}{2}\ 8 & 9 & 9\tfrac{1}{2}\ 10\ 11\ 12
\end{array}
$$

$$- \cup \cup\ |\ -\ \cup \cup\ -\ |\ \cup\ |\ \cup\ -\ \cup \cup\ |\ -\ |\ \cup \cup\ -\ \cup$$

Parts of speech are noted by N = noun, V = verb, p = preposition, a = adjective, av = adverb, pcp = participle. Thus the common end-line formula seen in ἄλγε' ἔθηκεν, ἄλγε' ἔδωκεν, μῦθον ἔειπεν, ἀνδρὶ μάχεσθαι, κ.τ.λ. is represented as $\overset{\text{N}}{-\ \cup}\ |\ \overset{\text{V}\ \ 12}{\cup\ -\ \underset{\smile}{\cup}}$.

8. "Structure and Content in Epic Formulae: The Question of the Unique Expression," *CQ*, NS 14 (1964), 155–64.

too bold a step in invoking analogies of word-type, rhythm, and position in the verse as formulaic criteria; and he thinks Parry was going too far when he suggested that the end-line phrase τεῦχε κύνεσσιν was much like δῶκεν ἑταίρῳ, a repetition of structure rather than of content, or that two verses could share a significant similarity in structure or sentence-pattern, while *not* having any specific words or content in common.[9] Parry, however, Hainsworth claims, did not take the bold step of "counting τεῦχε κύνεσσιν as formulaic on this ground," or of "forcing any conclusions out of the structural similarity" of νοῦσον ἀνὰ στρατὸν ὦρσε κακήν (*Il.* 1.10) to παῖδα δ᾽ ἐμοὶ λύσαιτε φίλην (1.20). "Parry's instinct," he says, "soundly chose the point at which to halt the extension of the term 'formula.'"[10] What this point is, Hainsworth has already indicated by citing with approval Parry's original criterion for the formulaic phrase, that it keep one constant repeated term among the words it uses.

Hainsworth goes on to state that some of our present difficulties in discussing formulaic language stem from the assumption that there is a simple and necessary connection between repetition of structural patterns and oral, formulaic style. He would call attention to the suppressed premise involved here: that when the frequency of pattern repetition reaches a certain point it becomes explicable *only* in terms of an oral style. The trouble with this premise, he says, is that no one can know just where that point lies. Repetition of patterns of phrasing is found outside oral epic, in Roman oratory, for example; and so even the existence of very frequent repetition of such patterns in Homer would in itself merely set the epics off as "different only in degree."[11]

In my opinion Hainsworth has gone much too far in his desire to minimize the role played by the formula of structure or pattern in the creation of epic hexameters. First of all, let it be

9. Hainsworth, pp. 156f. For the passage in Notopoulos, see *AJP*, 83 (1962), 356f. For Parry, see *HSCP*, 41 (1930), 133.

10. Hainsworth, pp. 156f.   11. *Ibid.* p. 158.

noted that Parry did go significantly further than Hainsworth claims, and did suggest that structural patterns are formulaic. Reading the passage in Parry closely, we find that the examples of structural similarities of phrase and verse quoted by Hainsworth are taken from a list that Parry uses *specifically for the purpose of illustrating the principle of the more general type of formula.* He introduces the examples with the words:

> In the two passages analyzed above I marked with a broken line only those formulas which are like others in rhythm, in parts of speech, and in one important word; *but* [italics mine] there are more general types of formulas, and one could make no greater mistake than to limit the formulaic element to what is underlined.[12]

Thereupon follows an enumeration of similarities, chiefly of structure, *not* noted in Parry's commentary on the underlined phrases in the passages he analyzed. Hainsworth, then, has mistaken Parry's intention.

My chief argument against Hainsworth is that the structural patterns of the Homeric hexameter at times reach a frequency of repetition so surprisingly high, and so clearly exceed in importance the repetitions found in any other literary style, that it is pointless to deny that these repetitions have to do with the formulaic style itself; and we already know this style is of oral formulaic composition. The repetitions are necessary to oral recitation because they provide pre-established verbal configurations with which the poet is comfortable and through the use of which he is spared much of the mental effort that a non-oral poet would invest in deciding where best to place his verb, his object, his adjective or qualifying participle or adverb, and so on.[13] For example, the habit by which Homer so frequently

12. *HSCP*, 41 (1930), 133.

13. In fairness to Hainsworth it should be made clear that there is of course no reason for *always* equating the terms "formulaic" and "oral." My point is that in the case of the Homeric poems we *must* make such an equation. When we come to the hexameters of Apollonius and Callimachus, however, we find that they too exhibit some of the same patterns for

keeps a verb of the length $\cup - \underset{\cup}{-}$ for the end of his verse (and often its subject or object $- \cup$ will immediately precede it)[14] contributes toward the easy creation and repetition of hexameters. An examination of any page of Homer will show that the bard could not do without this pattern of language, although in theory there is nothing to prevent him from using another pattern to express whatever idea is expressed by this formula, with either word placed somewhere else in the verse. Similarly we may note that the use of the verb types $\cup - \cup$, $\cup\cup - \cup$, or $- \cup$ at position $5\frac{1}{2}$ (or, less frequently, $\cup\cup -$ or $\cup -$ at position 5; for this positional notation see n. 7 on p. 221), is so common that we may consider it the kernel of several formulaic patterns, or even as a formulaic usage in and of itself.[15]

organizing words within the hexameter framework. But we know that they follow a traditional hexameter diction derived from Homer, and so we would not begin to conceive of their formularity as arising from the exigencies of oral composition. We are admittedly at a loss when we confront poetry like the Homeric Hymns. They are no doubt late enough for literacy to have played a role in their composition, yet so close to the traditional Homeric diction that it is impossible to say whether their formularity is due to oral composition or to the imitation in writing of oral style. Some of the hymns may well fall under the first category, and some under the second (cf. pp. 164ff.).

14. Comparative statistics for this usage in Homer and Apollonius are interesting. Although the literate imitator makes considerable use of the verb $\cup - \overset{12}{\underset{\cup}{-}}$ and the combination $\overset{N}{-} \cup \mid \overset{V}{\cup} \overset{12}{-} \underset{\cup}{-}$, his dependence on such a regularly recurring pattern is not nearly so great as that of the oral poet, who needs this pattern to complete the expression of an idea as he comes to the end of a verse. (The composer of literary epic, as M. Parry noted (see above, n. 22), is much more given to running over his thought from one verse to the next.) In the first 1000 lines of the *Iliad* we find 177 instances of $\cup \overset{V}{-} \overset{12}{\underset{\cup}{-}}$, of which about 41% are in the combination $\overset{N}{-} \cup \mid \overset{V}{\cup} \overset{12}{-} \underset{\cup}{-}$. In the *Argonautica* I.1–1000 we find 150 instances, of which only about 27% are in that combination. These figures exclude participles, which are ambiguous, but more frequent in Apollonius (53 to 31), where they tend to be adjectival and often serve to carry the thought over to the next line.

15. Parry called attention to one of these patterns when he noted the system αὐτὰρ ἐπεί (ῥ') $\cup\cup \overset{V}{-} \overset{5\frac{1}{2}}{\underset{\cup}{-}}$, or, for shorter verbs, αὐτὰρ ἐπειδὴ $\overset{V}{-} \overset{5\frac{1}{2}}{\cup}$ (*HSCP*, 41 (1930), 85).

If we pause here to ask *why* these verb-types became fixed in certain positions in the first place, we raise a difficult question. My argument is that once they are so fixed, they help the oral poet greatly in remembering and recreating his verses, and as such they are part of the formulaic style. This argument derives support from the analysis of certain Homeric passages where the importance of structural or pattern repetitions is beyond question. It may, however, be argued (and Hainsworth would no doubt so argue) that such fixing of word-types, and the consequent structural similarities and repetitions, are automatically imposed on the language by the hexameter form itself.[16] If this were completely true, the significance of structural patterns would be considerably diminished. But rhythmical rules and inhibitions cannot be so easily invoked as a first principle here, as if they preceded the use of language itself. To some extent they must grow out of the use of rhythmical language for poetic ends, and it is quite likely that at an early stage certain word combinations, fashioned under the influence of such factors as word-availability, word-order, grammatical forms, rhetorical effectiveness, and so on, once they began to be established as regular and formular, would have had considerable influence in determining what were to be the rhythmical norms and inhibitions for the construction of new phrases. On the other hand, some rudimentary sense of rhythmical correctness must have existed to dictate the shaping of the earliest attempts at hexameter composition. There is no point in forcing ourselves to make a chicken-or-egg choice over what happened at some dim period in early Greek history. Such a posing of alternatives is much too simple to correspond meaningfully with the realities we are trying to describe. It is probable that each of these factors, rhythm and natural word patterns, has had some effect in shaping the other; that each has sought out and reinforced tendencies it found congenial in the other, as they evolved between them the finished form and diction of the Homeric hexameter as we know it.

16. See A. M. Dale, *Lustrum*, 2 (1957), 34; also G. S. Kirk in this volume, e.g. p. 104.

III

If we are, then, to accept the repetition of the localized word-type as a phenomenon of formulaic style, we must face, with Hainsworth, the problem of achieving a more exact and meaningful definition of the formula than any offered to date. Hainsworth wants no extension of the term unless it is protected by adequate conditions. The difficulty of his position is that when he comes to discuss these conditions, he asks that they be no less than the measurement of the structural patterns against the same rigorous standards of extension and economy that Parry used in his classic treatment of the traditional epithets.[17] Surely this is an unreasonable demand. The patterns of structure are more complex, less conspicuous, and maintain many more possibilities for different variations and combinations, than the formulas of literal repetition. Hence their extent and economy would be extremely difficult to measure,[18] and are not likely to be comparable to those observed for the traditional-epithet formulas.[19] Once we move from the noun–epithet formula to other patterns that are "formulaic" precise measurement seems less and less attainable. We do not want the term to lose all meaning through indiscriminate extension. Yet I must agree with Parry and Lord that "more general types of formulas" do exist, and may reasonably be called "formulas."

Part of our problem here is semantic, and a clarification of terms may take us part way toward a solution. The language of Homer appears to be built upon the following elements: (1) The formula of exact repetition, in which one or more of the

17. Hainsworth, p. 158.

18. Hainsworth, pp. 158f., goes through the preliminary motions of such an examination and, not surprisingly, finds very little economy. But he himself admits that economy is not important or needed where the bard has considerable freedom and flexibility in the content of his language.

19. Parry singled out the noun–epithet system for analysis because, he says, it was one of the few systems where length and thrift were so striking as to afford sure proof of its traditional origins. He notes the difficulty in measuring other less striking formulaic systems (*HSCP*, 41 (1930), 86f.).

important words remain constant. These are the formulas to which Parry, and most later critics, have given their primary attention, and the designation "formula." (2) The formulaic pattern or structure, in which the same grammatical and metrical word-types are repeated, but with no constant words, all the terms being variables. In its briefest form this structure would be reduced to the single formulaic word-type, where a single usage, such as *οὐλομένην*, representing the pattern $-\overset{\text{pcp}}{\cup\cup}\overset{3}{-}$, or *ἵκοντο*, representing $\overset{\text{V } 5\frac{1}{2}}{\cup\cup - \cup}$, appears to be in itself formulaic, because it plays such a frequent part in the poet's style. (3) The originally created phrase, where the poet has not relied primarily upon the imitation involved in (1) and (2). It is at once apparent that, while the presence and extent of (1) is susceptible of close measurement, the usages included in (2) may easily be either underestimated or overestimated, and may not always be distinguishable from those of category (3). The patterns of (2) may be so used as to achieve highly original and creative expression, or the newly-created phrase may use as its point of departure a simple formulaic word. It becomes most important, therefore, that we free ourselves from the presupposition that the unique or original expression and the formulaic expression are antithetical or mutually exclusive. I suspect that Hainsworth inclines toward such an assumption. Since his ultimate concern is to identify the unique or original expression in Homer,[20] he would like to keep the concept of the formulaic limited to that which is easily perceived as an overt repetition.

IV

The problem before us, then, is to devise an acceptable method for studying structural or pattern formulas. This can best be done by the close examination of Homeric passages in which the use of structural or pattern formulas is especially obvious because of their frequent repetition. Let us look at three

20. See his discussion, *op. cit.* pp. 161–4.

brief descriptions taken from the larger context of 1.432–87, which describes the Achaeans' return of Chryseis by ship to her father, the prayer and sacrifices that follow, and the return of the ship. The mooring and disembarkation, and later the return journey, are described as follows:

οἱ δ' ὅτε δὴ λιμένος πολυβενθέος ἐντὸς ἵκοντο,
ἱστία μὲν στείλαντο, θέσαν δ' ἐν νηὶ μελαίνῃ,
ἱστὸν δ' ἱστοδόκῃ πέλασαν προτόνοισιν ὑφέντες
435   καρπαλίμως, τὴν δ' εἰς ὅρμον προέρυσσαν ἐρετμοῖς.
ἐκ δ' εὐνὰς ἔβαλον, κατὰ δὲ πρυμνήσι' ἔδησαν·
ἐκ δὲ καὶ αὐτοὶ βαῖνον ἐπὶ ῥηγμῖνι θαλάσσης,
ἐκ δ' ἑκατόμβην βῆσαν ἑκηβόλῳ Ἀπόλλωνι·
ἐκ δὲ Χρυσηὶς νηὸς βῆ ποντοπόροιο.
440   τὴν μὲν ἔπειτ' ἐπὶ βωμὸν ἄγων πολύμητις Ὀδυσσεὺς
πατρὶ φίλῳ ἐν χερσὶ τίθει, καί μιν προσέειπεν.

480   οἱ δ' ἱστὸν στήσαντ' ἀνά θ' ἱστία λευκὰ πέτασσαν·
ἐν δ' ἄνεμος πρῆσεν μέσον ἱστίον, ἀμφὶ δὲ κῦμα
στείρῃ πορφύρεον μεγάλ' ἴαχε νηὸς ἰούσης.
ἡ δ' ἔθεεν κατὰ κῦμα διαπρήσσουσα κέλευθον.
αὐτὰρ ἐπεί ῥ' ἵκοντο κατὰ στρατὸν εὐρὺν Ἀχαιῶν,
485   νῆα μὲν οἵ γε μέλαιναν ἐπ' ἠπείροιο ἔρυσσαν
ὑψοῦ ἐπὶ ψαμάθοις, ὑπὸ δ' ἔρματα μακρὰ τάνυσσαν,
αὐτοὶ δὲ σκίδναντο κατὰ κλισίας τε νέας τε.

We sense immediately in these verses a tightly organized and almost rigid diction.[21] The language is heavily schematized, and moves in clearly perceived blocks or units. The effect is stately,

21. It should be noted that Havelock, *op. cit.* pp. 83f., has called attention to these two passages as examples of the way that oral epic, serving as a "tribal encyclopedia," stores and transmits technical knowledge in a generalized or typical form. He is aware of what he calls a "nursery-rhyme" style, and that it is achieved through "verbal and rhythmic mechanisms," such as the assonance of the words for "sail" and "mast" in the first passage and the repetitive use of prepositional clauses in the second. While he appreciates the patterned quality of the language, he refrains from more detailed analysis of the devices used to achieve this quality.

predictable, and often heavy, quite devoid of unusual twists or surprises. Enjambment is kept to a minimum and in only one place is it "necessary" enjambment (481–2).[22] Such qualities of language are especially appropriate to the representation of familiar, traditional activities; what is achieved is an almost ritualistic air.

How exactly are these effects produced? The chief means is repetition. But repetition of what? There is much more going on here than the simple and highly effective repetition of ἐκ δέ to begin four consecutive verses (436–9), or the frequent use of the words ἱστόν, ἱστίον, ἱστία in consecutive verses. These lines are dependent to an extraordinary degree on clearly established structural patterns, and the same patterns are repeated with amazing frequency within a very short space. A reader will not at once be conscious of all the individual repetitions involved here. They are peculiar to an oral style, worked out by the ear and meant to be heard, and some of their effects are primarily acoustic, leaning heavily on echoes of rhythm and on assonance. The frequency and the proximity of these echoes leads me to suggest that we have in these verses a phenomenon that may be termed "local influence," in which a recited verse exerts an influence upon the structure and the sound of a forthcoming verse.

Let me attempt to describe precisely what is being repeated and echoed. Verses 432, 434 and 436 all use the common end-line verb ∪ – ∪, and 434 and 436 use the object ∪∪ – ∪ immediately before—objects which sound somewhat alike, προτόνοισιν and πρυμνῇσι'. The verse that separates these two concludes with a phrase that reverses the verb and noun, προέρυσσαν ἐρετμοῖς, but interestingly keeps both the assonance (προτόνοισιν–προέρυσσαν–πρυμνῇσι') and the closing rhythm, ∪∪ – ∪ | ∪ – ∪. Looking before and after these verses, we see that this rhythm has been carried from 433, ἐν-νηὶ μελαίνῃ, to

___

22. For the distinction between "unperiodic" and "necessary" enjambment see M. Parry, "The Distinctive Character of Enjambement in Homeric Verse," *TAPA*, 60 (1929), 206 f. and 216 f.; summarized on pp. 106 f. above.

437, ῥηγμῖνι θαλάσσης. The recurrence of this common rhythmic division is not in itself unusual in Homeric verse, but I am suggesting that one verse organized on such a rhythm often tends to call forth another.[23] The bard composes by a stream of aural associations. On a simple level, mere rhythmic echo clearly plays some part in this.

Returning to verses 433 and 434, we find the verbs ⏑ $\overset{7}{-}$ and ⏑⏑ $\overset{7}{-}$, θέσαν and πέλασαν, used after their respective B caesuras; and in 436, 437 and 438, the action modified by the series ἐκ δ᾽, ἐκ δέ, ἐκ δ᾽ is described in the three verbs ἔβαλον, βαῖνον, βῆσαν, each placed just before the B caesura, representing the standard usages ⏑⏑ $\overset{V\ 5}{-}$ and $\overset{V\ 5\frac{1}{2}}{-\ ⏑}$. There is moreover a strong echo in ἐκ δὲ καὶ αὐτοὶ βαῖνον and ἐκ δ᾽ ἑκατόμβην βῆσαν.

Finally, in 440–1, the pattern of ἐπὶ βωμὸν ἄγων is immediately repeated in ἐν χερσὶ τίθει. We have here an extremely common structural pattern, the association of a preposition ⏑⏑ $\overset{4}{}$ with the immediately following noun $\overset{5\frac{1}{2}}{-\ ⏑}$, seen in such frequent phrases as σὺν νηί, ἐπὶ νῆα, παρὰ νηυσί, κατὰ λαόν, κατὰ κῦμα, κατὰ θυμόν, κατὰ φῦλα, ἐν χειρί, ἐνὶ οἴκῳ, ἐπὶ δεῖπνον, παρὰ θῖνα, πρὸς δῶμα, κ.τ.λ. These prepositional phrases are most often preceded by the verb that governs them, but in the two lines under discussion we have an alternative structure where the verb form is used *after* the prepositional phrase, and has the form ⏑ $\overset{7}{-}$. While ⏑ $\overset{7}{-}$ represents the most common localization for verbs of this metrical type,[24] the combination $\overset{p}{⏑⏑}$ | $\overset{N}{-}$ ⏑ | $\overset{V\ 7}{⏑\ -}$, though easy to make, is not an especially common one[25]—a fact which suggests

23. See G. S. Kirk, in this volume, p. 133, for other examples of this phenomenon.

24. Of the 107 uses of verbs of shape ⏑ – in the first 1000 lines of the *Iliad*, for example, slightly more than half occur in this position.

25. In the whole of book I of the *Iliad* there are 29 instances of the combination $\overset{p}{⏑⏑}$ | $\overset{N\ 5\frac{1}{2}}{-\ ⏑}$, of which eight continue with a verb form ⏑ $\overset{7}{-}$. Of these eight, the two instances of the idiomatic ἐπὶ ἦρα φέρων (φέρειν) (572, 578) and the phrases ἐν δ᾽ ἀρχὸς ἔβη (311) and κατὰ μῆρε κάη (464) are similar

all the more that a real imitative force is at work here. It should be added that not only is ἐν χερσὶ τίθει of 441 repeated five verses later in 446, but also the phrase πατρὶ φίλῳ, which begins verse 441, is echoed in παῖδα φίλην, which begins verse 447, contributing still another echo to this sequence.

In the first excerpt quoted above, then, every verse from 434 to 439 repeats one or more words, phrase-patterns, or sound-patterns from the verse preceding it. The texture of structural repetitions has been woven rather thickly. It is quickly dissipated in verses 440–1, which offer a sudden change from the slow and solemn tone used to narrate the traditional movements of docking and disembarkation. This tone has reached its climax in the heavily spondaic verse 439 with the appearance of Chryseis. It is suddenly broken off with the lively rhythms of 440, which has no spondaic substitutions at all and a totally different movement, continued in 441. The mid-line (B) caesuras are bridged not literally but semantically by the tightly connected phrases ἐπὶ βωμὸν ἄγων, ἐν χερσὶ τίθει, whose similarity has already been noted. Instead of having the even balance of the preceding verses, organized in natural phrase-groups of two or four around a semantically marked central caesura, verses 440–1 fall, as one hears them, into a tripartite rhythmic division:

$$- \cup \cup - \mid \underset{\smile}{\cup\cup} - \cup \cup - \mid \underset{\smile}{\cup\cup} - \cup \cup - \underline{\cup}.$$

Local influence is especially prominent again in 480 ff. The actions opening 480 and 481 are described by the parallel use

in form only, since $\overset{4}{\cup\cup}$ here qualifies the following verb instead of serving as a preposition governing the noun $- \overset{5\frac{1}{2}}{\cup}$. They should probably be counted as the same phrase-pattern, however, since they represent the similar handling of similar words. It may be likewise possible to claim local influence in the sequence δὲ παρ' αὐτὸν ἔχον (πεμπώβολα χερσίν) (463) and κατὰ μῆρε κάη (464), again a repetition purely of form. The remaining four examples are ἐν χερσὶ (χειρὶ) τίθει (441, 446, 585), and ἐπὶ βωμὸν ἄγων (440), where $\overset{4}{\cup\cup}$ is more truly prepositional.

of στήσαντ' and πρῆσεν, verbs of type $\smallsmile\smallsmile\overset{5}{-}$, and the symmetry is reinforced by the idea and sound of ἀνά θ' ἱστία and μέσον ἱστίον following the caesura, as well as by the nouns ἱστόν and ἄνεμος—the mast which is set up, the wind which fills it, the two most important ideas in these lines—nouns of the same length placed in the same position ($\smallsmile\smallsmile\overset{3}{-}$). The two verses are closely related in content and strikingly similar in rhythm, so much so that the words used to form each line have exactly the same metrical length except for the final πέτασσαν of 480 and δὲ κῦμα of 481. Verse 483 has no echo of the verses right before it, but it may be noted that the pattern $\overset{p}{\smallsmile\smallsmile} \mid \overset{N\ 5\frac{1}{2}}{-\ \smallsmile}$ used earlier in ἐπὶ βωμόν, ἐν χερσί (440, 441), is repeated here with κατὰ κῦμα. The next verse, 484, is a close repetition of 478, which in turn has echoed in part verse 476:

476   δὴ τότε κοιμήσαντο παρὰ πρυμνήσια νηός

478   καὶ τότ' ἔπειτ' ἀνάγοντο μετὰ στρατὸν εὐρὺν 'Αχαιῶν

484   αὐτὰρ ἐπεί ῥ' ἵκοντο κατὰ στρατὸν εὐρὺν 'Αχαιῶν.

The common structure here is the verb $(-)\ \smallsmile\smallsmile - \overset{5\frac{1}{2}}{\smallsmile}$ plus the preposition $\smallsmile\overset{7}{-}$, plus an object of varying length, used after a temporal expression that opens the verse.

Verses 484–7 are all organized similarly around a prepositional phrase introduced immediately after the B caesura to describe the consecutive movements of the Achaeans as they return to their army, beach the ship, secure it, and go their several ways to their tents and ships. Different requirements of meter and phrasing allow the poet to use three different prepositional types after the B caesura in the four lines: $\overset{6}{\smallsmile}$, $\overset{6}{\smallsmile\smallsmile}$, and $\smallsmile\overset{7}{-}$. The verses form a neat quatrain, held together by content and structure. Close examination shows it to rest on a balanced ABBA sequence of structural patterns. Verses 484 and 487 are based on the action of ἵκοντο and σκίδναντο, the standard $\smallsmile\smallsmile - \overset{V\ 5\frac{1}{2}}{\smallsmile}$, followed by κατά introducing the direction and destina-

tion of the action; while 485 and 486 are based on the equally
standard verb form $\cup - \overset{12}{\cup}$, the prepositional phrase preceding.
The two middle verses are further bound together by the neat
enjambment of ἔρυσσαν | ὑψοῦ ἐπὶ ψαμάθοις. Finally, ὑπὸ δ'
ἔρματα μακρὰ τάνυσσαν of 486 reveals a structural pattern identical
to that used in 480 for ἀνά θ' ἱστία λευκὰ πέτασσαν,

$$\overset{P}{\cup}\cup \mid \overset{N}{-}\cup\cup \mid \overset{a}{-}\cup \mid \cup \overset{V\ 12}{-}\cup.$$

So exact a repetition of a purely structural phrase-pattern
within six lines of verse, in a context where so much other
repetition, structural and literal, is used, should make clear to
us that oral formulaic style may depend—and at certain points
very heavily—on structural repetitions as well as on literal ones.
There would be little point, then, in refusing to admit both
types to the category of the formulaic.

Structural formulaic patterns do not always come to the fore
so noticeably. There are visible high points and low points of
the poet's dependence on established pattern, and one may
fairly assume that this reflects either his moving in a highly
traditional comfortable context, or his striking out into relatively new realms of description and phrasing. In the latter
cases, having failed to get his words into the better-established
patterns, he may be successful at composing his own patterns,
as long as they follow the proper general rhythmic outlines.
Thus in the long passage *Il.* 1.432–87 we find the repetitions
clustered most thickly about the points of the least unusual, or
most traditional, descriptions: the launching of a ship, mooring
and disembarkation, the performance of sacrifice. In Chryses'
prayer to Apollo, the first two verses (451–2) conclude with ὃς
Χρύσην ἀμφιβέβηκας and Τενέδοιό τε ἶφι ἀνάσσεις: the place name
followed by the verbal idea $- \cup \cup - \cup$. In the next two verses,

453   ἠμὲν δή ποτ' ἐμεῦ πάρος ἔκλυες εὐξαμένοιο,
         τίμησας μὲν ἐμέ, μέγα δ' ἴψαο λαὸν 'Αχαιῶν,

ἐμεῦ is repeated in ἐμέ, while πάρος ἔκλυες ($\overset{av}{\cup}\cup \mid \overset{V}{-}\cup \overset{8}{\cup}$) is
structurally repeated in μέγα δ' ἴψαο. The ἔκλυες of 453 is

repeated in 457, in the same position. A few lines later, in the description of the ritual sacrifice to Apollo, the frequency of pattern repetition again increases (458–71). Especially conspicuous is the tendency to describe the action performed by the third person verb form – ‿‿ – opening the verse. Thus ἀνέρυσαν of 459 is repeated, as a structural type, in μίστυλλον, 465, ὤπτησαν, 466, and νώμησαν, 471. Further, μίστυλλον is followed by τ' ἄρα τἆλλα, and νώμησαν by δ' ἄρα πᾶσιν, where the poet found it convenient to proceed in each case a little further along the same track. Other striking echoes in this passage include ἐρύσαντό τε πάντα (466) and τετύκοντό τε δαῖτα (467), and καῖε and λεῖβε beginning the consecutive verses 462–3.

We have seen, then, that in certain Homeric passages structural formulas are not only obvious, but also exert a local influence upon subsequent verses, so that the structures, or patterns, are the more easily recognized by virtue of their close recurrence. In other passages the structural patterns used may be "repetitions" only in the broader sense that they are used again somewhere in the Homeric corpus. Both types of pattern repetition should be considered formulaic, since they are natural expressions of the schematization of language that makes possible a traditional, orally-evolved style.

I have found it convenient to use Hainsworth's skeptical view of the formulaic qualities of structural patterns as a position against which to direct my argument. But it should be noted that by the conclusion of his article his initial reluctance to give formulaic status to phrase-patterns has yielded to an acknowledgment that they must, at least in their more conspicuous aspects, be the products of the formulaic, oral diction. He says (p. 164),

> In short, it is certain that there are regularities at all levels in Homer, in theme, structure of narrative and phrase, and diction. At favourable points we can show that these regularities are different in kind from regularities seen in other writers and that a special hypothesis is needed to

explain them. The rest yield ambiguous testimony in themselves, but are set in order by the clarification of unequivocal material.

My argument, then, may be taken as calling attention to one of the "favourable points," where these regularities can be shown to be so different from those of other literary styles[26] that the hypothesis of an oral style is needed to account for them.

26. See n. 14 above for a precise example.

[Appendix follows]

Appendix of Common Structural Formulas

It is the purpose of this appendix to call attention to some of the formulas of phrase-pattern and word-type most frequently used in the Homeric epics. It in no way seeks to be exhaustive, either in its listing of formulas or its illustration of them.

Although I describe the phrases as localized, it is true that some of them may be used with ease at one, and occasionally two, alternative positions in the line. Such positions are indicated by a numeral in parentheses. The system of numerals and abbreviations has been given above in note 7.

I. *Patterns used in the first half of the verse*

A. Single long words used before the A or B caesura

       pcp 3 (5)
1. – ⏑ ⏑ –   οὐλομένην, χωομένῳ, ἑστάμεναι, τειρομένους, σπεί-
σαντες, ἐσβάντες, εἰσορόων, καγχαλόων, κ.τ.λ.[27]

       av 3 (5)
2. – ⏑⏑ –   καρπαλίμως, ἀσπασίως, ῥηιδίως, νωλεμέως, σμερ-
δαλέον, ἀντίβιον (-ίην), κ.τ.λ.

       a 3 (5)
3. – ⏑⏑ –   ἀντίθεος, ὠμοφάγοι, ἀμφοτέρω, ἐννύχιοι, παννύχιοι,
ἡδυεπής, ὠκύποδες, κήδιστοι, ἔχθιστος, κ.τ.λ.

       V 3
4. – ⏑⏑ –   δούπησεν, ὤπτησαν, βέβληται, βεβλήκει, πέπτανται,
ἐκφερέμεν, κ.τ.λ.

B. Verb forms used before the B caesura

       V 5½ (12)
1. ⏑ – ⏑   νόησε, νοῆσαι, ἔτερπεν, ἔχεσκε, ἔρυτο, ὄφελλεν, κ.τ.λ.

       V 5½ (1½)
2. – ⏑   ἐστί, ἦρχε, ὦσε, ἷζε, ἵκεν, δαῖεν, βῆσαν, βαῖνον, κ.τ.λ.

27. It is apparent that an ample supply of words of the shape – ⏑⏑ – is available in the middle–passive participle and the uncontracted active participle, in the compound adjective, in the adverb terminating in -ίως and -έως, and in many finite verb forms whose structural features supply the necessary long syllables. Such participles, adjectives, adverbs, are good examples of the freely added descriptive word often used in what Parry called "unperiodic enjambement." The use of such a word to provide an easy and natural opening for a new verse is one of the hallmarks of the oral style.

3. ⏑⏑ – ⏑ ὥρμαινε, ἵκοντο, ἐπέοικε, καλέουσι, δώσουσι, ἐθέλῃσι, κ.τ.λ.

4. ⏑⏑ – πρῆσεν, στήσαντ᾽, ἔβαλον, ἐθέλω(-ει), ἀγέμεν, κρατέειν, προίει, κ.τ.λ.

C. Noun-combinations lasting to the B caesura

1. – ⏑ | ⏑ – ἀνδρὶ φίλῳ, πατρὶ φίλῳ, μητρὶ φίλη, μητέρ᾽ ἐμήν, πατρίδ᾽ ἐμήν, ἔγχος ἐμόν, τέκνον ἐμόν, χεῖρα ἑήν, χεῖρας ἐμάς, κ.τ.λ.

2. – ⏑:⏑ ⫶ – ⏑⏑– Ἰλίου αἰπεινῆς, πέτραι τ᾽ ἠλίβατοι, ἤχῃ θεσπεσίῃ, νῆας ἐϋσσέλμους, ἀνέρε κυδαλίμω, ἰὸς χαλκοβαρής, Τρῳαὶ ἐϋπλόκαμοι, ἔγχεϊ χαλκείῳ, κ.τ.λ.

3. – ⏑ | ⏑ – | ⏑⏑ – (⏑) νηυσὶν ἔπι γλαφυρῇσι, νῆας ἔπι (ἀνὰ) γλαφυράς, ὤμῳ ἔνι στιβαρῷ, χειρὸς ἀπὸ στιβαρῆς, εὐνῇ ἔνι μαλακῇ, ποσσὶ δ᾽ ὑπὸ λιπαροῖσι, δώρῳ ἔπι μεγάλῳ, σκήπτρου ὑπὸ χρυσέου, κ.τ.λ.

4. – ⏑ | ⏑ | – ⏑⏑ – (⏑) πέτρῃ ὑφ᾽ ὑψηλῇ, χώρῳ ἐν οἰοπόλῳ, φάτνῃ ἐφ᾽ ἱππείῃ, χῶρον ἀν᾽ ὑλήεντα, νύκτα δι᾽ ἀμβροσίην (ὀρφναίην), χερσὶν ὑφ᾽ ἡμετέρῃσιν, κ.τ.λ.

5. – ⏑⏑ | – | ⏑⏑ – (⏑) Περγάμῳ εἰν ἱερῇ, οὐρανὸν ἐς πολύχαλκον, Ἴλιον εἰς εὔπωλον, κ.τ.λ.

6. – ⏑⏑ | – | ⏑⏑ – (⏑) δηΐῳ ἐν πολέμῳ, νείατον ἐς κενεῶνα, ποικίλου ἐκ δίφροιο, κ.τ.λ.

7. – ⏑⏑ – | ⏑⏑ | – ⏑⏑ ἡμετέρῳ ἔνι οἴκῳ, ἀμβροσίου διὰ πέπλου, δεξιτερὸν κατὰ μαζόν, δεξιτερὸν δ᾽ ὑπὲρ ὦμον, Νεστορέῃ παρὰ νηί, κ.τ.λ.

8. – ⏑⏑ – | ⏑⏑ – (⏑) ἐκπάγλοις ἐπέεσσιν, χρυσείοις ἥλοισι, ὀξείης ὀδύνῃσιν, παντοίων ἀνέμων, σκηπτοῦχοι βασιλῆες, ἴφθιμον Μελάνιππον, κ.τ.λ.

9. ⏑⏑ | – ⏑ παρὰ νηυσί, σὺν νηυσί (νηί), παρὰ θῖνα, ἐν χερσί, κατὰ κῦμα, κατὰ θυμόν, κατὰ ἄστυ, διὰ νύκτα, πρὸς δῶμα, ἀνὰ θυμόν, πρὸς τεῖχος, κ.τ.λ.

C 3, 4, and 5 represent what may be considered essentially the same formula, N–p–a filling the first half-line, with small variation in the length of the individual words that make up the phrase. Formulas 6 and 7 form a similar grouping. 5 and 6 are the least commonly found in each group, probably because of a low availability of vocabulary.

D. Participial phrases lasting to the B caesura

1. $\overset{N}{-} \cup \mid \cup \overset{pcp}{-} \underset{\smile\smile}{} \overset{5}{-} (\cup)$ ἱστὸν ἐποιχομένην, μῦθον ἀγασσάμενοι, θηρὸς ἀκούσαντες, λαοῦ ἀποτμήξαντε, νύκτα φυλασσόμενοι, ῥυσί' ἐλαυνόμενος, κ.τ.λ.

2. $\overset{av}{-} \vdots \cup \vdots \cup \overset{pcp\ (V)}{-} \underset{\smile\smile}{} \overset{5}{-} (\cup)$ ἔνθα καθεζόμενοι, ἐνθάδ' ἐλεύσεσθαι, αἰὲν ἀποκτείνων, αἰὲν ἀριστεύειν, δεῦρο μαχησόμενος, λαβρὸν ἐπαιγίζοντα, ἂψ ἀπονοστήσειν, ἂψ ἀναχωρήσουσι, κ.τ.λ.

II. *Phrase-patterns commonly used toward the end of the verse*

A. Noun–verb combinations after the C¹ caesura

1. $\overset{N}{-} \cup \mid \cup - \overset{V}{\smile} \overset{12\ (5\frac{1}{2})}{}$ ἄλγε' ἔθηκε (ἔδωκεν, ἔχοντα, ἔχουσιν, κ.τ.λ.), κῦδος ἔθηκε (ὄπαζεν, ὀρέξαι, ἀρέσθαι, ἄροιο, κ.τ.λ.), χεῖρας ἀνασχών (ἀνέσχον, ἐφείω, ἀείραι, κ.τ.λ.), δώματ' ἔχοντες, μῦθον ἔειπε (ἄκουσε, ἄκουον, ἐνίσπω, κ.τ.λ.)

1a. $\underset{\smile\smile}{\overset{p}{}} \mid \overset{N}{-} \cup \mid \cup - \overset{V}{\smile} \overset{12}{}$ ἐπὶ χεῖρας ἔχευον, ἐκ θυμὸν ἕληται, ὑπὸ τεῖχος ἰόντας, μετὰ δ' ἰὸν ἕηκε, ἐπὶ μῦθον ἔτελλεν, ὑπὸ κῆρας ἀλύξας, κ.τ.λ.

2. $\overset{}{-} \cup \cup \mid \overset{V}{-} \overset{12}{\smile}$ ἄλγεα τεύχει (δοῖεν, πάσχει, πάσχων, κ.τ.λ.), ἱερὰ ῥέξας (ῥέζον, ῥέζων), νείκεα βάλλει (λύσω, λύει), ἀσπίδα θέσθω (νύσσων), κ.τ.λ.

B. Patterns using a long final word, often of participial formation.

1. $- \overset{pcp}{\smile\smile} - \overset{12}{\smile}$ αἰθομένοιο, χωομένοιο, ὀρνυμένοιο, τειρομένοιο, δερκομένοιο, εὐξαμένοιο, μαρναμένοιιν, ἐρχομενάων, βοσκομενάων, ἐμβεβαῶτα, ἀμφιέποντες, κ.τ.λ.

2. (–) $\underset{\cup\cup}{\overset{N}{}}$ | $\overset{a\ (pcp)}{- \underset{\cup\cup}{}} - \underset{\cup}{\overset{12}{}}$ οὐρανοῦ ἀστερόεντος, αἰγίδα θυσσανό-
εσσαν, ἡνία σιγαλόεντα, ἀσπίδες (-ος) ὀμφαλόεσσαι (-ης), ἔντεα
μαρμαίροντα, Ἴλιον ἠνεμόεσσαν, Ἴμβρου παιπαλοέσσης, Πλάκῳ
ὑληέσσῃ, ἵππων ὠκειάων, κόνιν αἰθαλόεσσαν, πυρὸς αἰθομένοιο,
Πύλου ἠμαθόεντος, χθονὶ πουλυβοτείρῃ, κ.τ.λ.

C. Noun combinations after the C¹ caesura

1. $\overset{N}{- \cup \cup}$ | $\overset{a\ 12\ (9\frac{1}{2},\ 5\frac{1}{2})}{- \underset{\cup}{}}$ ὅρκια πιστά, κτήματα πάντα, ἤματα πάντα,
τεύχεα καλά, σήματα (ἔχθεα, κήδεα) λυγρά, κύματα (τείχεα,
δούρατα, δένδρεα) μακρά, ἔγχεϊ μακρῷ, κ.τ.λ.

2. $\overset{V}{- \cup \cup}$ | $\overset{N\ 12}{- \underset{\cup}{}}$ ὤλεσε (ἔνθεο, ἔλλαβε, ἵκετο) θυμόν, ὤλεσα
(ὤπασε) λαόν, ἔκπεσε (ἔκφυγε, ἔκβαλε) χειρός, ἔκπεσε δίφρου,
κ.τ.λ.

3. $\overset{a}{- \cup \cup}$ | $\overset{N\ 12\ (9\frac{1}{2})}{- \underset{\cup}{}}$ οἴνοπα πόντον, εὐρέες ὦμοι, δεξιὸν ὦμον,
ἀγλαὸν (ἄλκιμον, νήπιον) υἱόν, φαίδιμος (ἄλκιμος, ἀγλαὸς) υἱός,
νήπια (ἀγλαὰ) τέκνα, δήιον (ἄγριον) ἄνδρα, χάλκεον (ὄβριμον,
μείλινον) ἔγχος, αἴθοπι (ὀξέϊ, νηλέϊ, νώροπι) χαλκῷ, πίονα (καρτερὰ,
σχέτλια, θέσκελα) ἔργα, κ.τ.λ.

D. (∪) $\cup - \cup \cup$ $\overset{V\quad 8\ (10)}{}$ ἐπιδεύομαι, ἐπιμέμφεται, μαχήσομαι, παρελεύ-
σεαι, παρέσσεται, ἀγορήσατο, ἀνεχάζετο, προσεβήσατο, ἐχώσατο,
καλέσσατο, παρίστατο, ἐπείγετο, ἀνεδύσετο, ἐπιτέλλεο, ἀποτίσομεν,
κελεύομεν, πεπληγέμεν, ἐπέπλεον, ἐπέδραμε, κατέκτανεν, προσεφώνεε,
ἐπέκλυε, μετέπρεπον, παρέδραμον, κ.τ.λ.

III. *Phrase-patterns commonly extending over the B caesura*

A. (∪) $\overset{p}{-}$ | $\underset{\cup\cup}{} - \cup$ | $\overset{N\quad B^1\ pcp\ \overset{(V)}{7}}{\cup -}$ ἐν χείρεσσιν ἔχων (ἔχοντ', λαβών, βάλω,
ἄγῃ), ἐν κονίῃσι πεσών (μακών), ἐνὶ στήθεσσι βαλών (ἔχων, τίθει,
θέτο), ὑπὲρ μαζοῖο βαλών, σὺν νήεσσιν ἄγων, ἐν νήεσσι πέσον, πὰρ
νήεσσι μένειν, κ.τ.λ.

B. $\overset{N}{-} \cup \mid \cup - \vdots \underline{\cup\cup} \vdots \overset{V}{-} \cup \mid \overset{B^1 a}{\cup} \overset{7}{-}$ παῖδα δ᾽ ἐμοὶ λύσαιτε φίλην
                                           νοῦσον ἀνὰ στρατὸν ὦρσε κακήν
                                           νύκτα φυλασσομένοισι κακήν

And cf.   τάων ἤν κ᾽ $\begin{cases} \dot{\epsilon}\theta\dot{\epsilon}\lambda\eta\sigma\iota \\ \dot{\epsilon}\theta\dot{\epsilon}\lambda\omega\mu\iota \\ \dot{\epsilon}\theta\dot{\epsilon}\lambda\eta\sigma\theta\alpha \end{cases}$ φίλην

                                           αἰεί τοι τὰ κάκ᾽ ἐστὶ φίλα
                                           αἰεὶ γάρ τοι ἔρις τε φίλη

Note that all the patterns in this category III depend on the word $\cup \overset{7}{-}$, an adjective, participle, or other verb form needed to complete the phrase.